LIVING LARGE

*Transformative Work
at the Intersection of
Ethics and Spirituality*

JOHN GREENFELDER SULLIVAN

Tai Sophia Institute
for the **Healing Arts**

7750 Montpelier Road
Laurel, Maryland 20723

Printed in the United States of America
Book and cover design: John C. Wilson
Editors: Guy Hollyday, Mary Ellen Zorbaugh

Grateful acknowledgment is given for permission to reprint from the following sources:

HOW CAN I HELP by Ram Dass and Paul Gorman, copyright © 1985 by Ram Dass and Paul Gorman. Used by permission of Alfred A. Knopf, a division of Random House, Inc.

THE ESSENTIAL RUMI, translations by Coleman Barks with John Moyne (San Francisco: HarperSanFrancisco, 1995). Used by permission of Coleman Barks.

Library of Congress Control Number: 2004098878

ISBN-13: 978-0-912381-06-X
ISBN-10: 0-912381-06-X

Living Large

Dedicated to
Gregg Winn Sullivan

Contents

CONTINUED

PART THREE

THE EXISTENTIAL STEPS: UNITING ETHICS AND SPIRITUALITY THROUGH A SET OF CONCRETE PRACTICES

CONTINUED

CONTINUED

Introduction

To find our calling is to find the intersection
between our own deep gladness and
the world's deep hunger.[1]

"Living large" — shorthand for living in large mind-and-heart. Living a wider and deeper life. Engaging in transformative work at the intersection between our own deep gladness and the world's deep hunger.

Why is such transformative work needed? Let me answer with a story: One of my students was given an inheritance by her grandmother — money for college and beyond. Her mother, an alcoholic, spent her own money and then found a way to access and spend her daughter's inheritance. The daughter, feeling betrayed, had to drop out of school and work a full-time job to gain enough money to return to college.

This mother was in a trance of sorts, focused entirely on herself as separate and unconnected to wider realities, as separate from her relationships, her family. She was *constricted in space,* not realizing that she belonged to units larger than herself. In her trance, this mother focused on the "fleeting now" of instant gratification. She was *constricted in time,* not thinking in terms of generations.

Each of us is this mother, not realizing we belong to units

larger than ourselves, forgetting we belong to the universe, forgetting we are the earth.

Each of us is this mother, forgetting we stand between the ancestors and the children, forgetting we are the children.

Each of us is this mother, squandering the inheritance of the children — the human ones and the other creatures on the planet.

We must find another way, a way of transformation. This book offers a beginning — modest steps to live a larger and deeper life. These perspectives and practices have proven successful with adult learners and university students over more than 15 years.[2] Urgently needed, these perspectives and practices lie at the intersection of a renewed ethics and an expanded spirituality.

Ethics revisioned is, at its core, an invitation to live a larger life, to live consciously and responsibly in contexts larger than oneself. I see ethics as transformative, involving commitment and character-building, new perceptions and new actions for the sake of all our kin. I propose this mission for a revitalized ethics:

> *To come to life more fully*
> *so as to act more wisely and more effectively,*
> *to reduce unnecessary suffering, and*
> *to promote creative possibilities for our common life.*[3]

This sense of ethics is

positive — coming to life more fully.

action-oriented — suggesting ways to act more wisely and effectively.

anchored in practical criteria — reducing unnecessary suffering and promoting creative possibility.

directed to our common life — seeking what is good for the whole and fair to each participant part, whether the whole be a friendship, a corporation, a nation or the planet itself.

Ethics, so constructed, can be thought of as a *horizontal dimension* where we take time and steps to seek a full life for all.

Spirituality revisioned is, at its core, an invitation to live a larger life, to live intentionally and gratefully from a depth dimension that is ever-present right here and right now. I envision spirituality as also transformative, providing practical ways to know we are already home, already at one, already reflecting all-that-is and its mysterious source.

This is a spirituality that

adds tones and overtones to life.

offers a set of practices that aid us to come from oneness, reawaken wonder, move toward wisdom, and increase compassion and loving-kindness for all beings.

puts us in touch with myths and rituals, symbols and stories, poetry and prose.

invokes contemplative deepening and prophetic calls to justice and care from the great wisdom traditions, East and West.

Spirituality, so construed, can be thought of as a *vertical dimension* where the timeless intersects time, and where the deep worth of the whole and all of its participants shines forth.

Standing at the intersection of the horizontal and vertical, the intersection of time and the timeless, we begin to sense what I call the Great Paradox Chant:

Everything *is* / quite all right, our worth secure and true,
and
Everything's *not* / quite all right, we've worthy work to do.

Spirituality reminds us that on the vertical dimension of contact with the source, all is well; our deep worth is secure; nothing is needed — there is full abundance. Ethics reminds us that on the horizontal dimension of time unfolding, there is worthy work to do. At the opening of a new century, the destructiveness is so great and the stakes so high that a full shift of worldview is required. Happily, that change is already underway.

This book is an invitation to reverse a trend, to *reverse a worldview* that is so widely shared as to be called the "real world"! To *reverse habits of living*— of thinking and acting — that are so ingrained we are scarcely aware of them. All this involves unlearning and relearning. So let's begin with our current state of education, its discontents and dysfunctions.

Our current schooling promotes a kind of education from the neck up: education as information, with different information coming from the "barrels" of the different disciplines; "jug and mug" education, where the teacher as "jug" pours information into the student as "mug," where the teacher is seen as the "doer" and the student as the "done to." The student hopes to retain enough information to pour it back at final exam and get a reasonable grade. Then the mug is empty; or, to say it differently, the short-term memory files are erased. Suppose summer vacation has begun. It is July and a group of college students is relaxing on a warm beach. Suddenly, as if beamed down from a spaceship, a samurai warrior materializes on the beach. He says, "Tell me what you learned last semester or you die!" The beach would be awash in blood!

What is amiss? To fathom the depth of discontent, we must shift from the domain of institutions to the domain of worldview. We must examine how our current paradigm of meaning, value, and purpose shows itself in our notions of schooling.

1. We are starting from a paradigm of *separate substances.* Teacher and student are seen as what Alan Watts would call "skin-encapsulated egos."[4] In focusing on separate substances, we neglect to see how deeply interrelated we are, how, as Robert Kegan says, each person is an individual *and* an "embeddual."[5]

2. We are starting from a paradigm of *scarcity,* living in a world of measurement where grades are seen as scarce resources.[6] In focusing on scarcity, we tend to promote zero-sum games: someone wins at the expense of another losing. We neglect to understand what it means to start with sufficiency — the sense, as Gandhi put it, that we have enough for our need but not for our greed.

3. We are starting from a paradigm of *seen only*. We neglect meaning, value, and purpose — those qualitative features of life that are not easily reducible to the quantitative and tangible. Hence, for many students their learning has a disconnected quality, seemingly removed from lived experience with its qualities of heart as well as mind, emotional engagement as well as detached observation.

4. We are starting from a paradigm stressing the *short term*: information learned for a test and then forgotten — education by inoculation. "I've had such and such a course, so I never have to look at that material again." We neglect the cumulative, embodied, practiced habits. We do not see the possibility of shifting from a short-term, ego-involved sense of time to a sense of time involving generations — including ancestors, contemporaries, and children yet to be. In a discussion with a college student, I asked what he had taken last semester. "History," he replied. "What kind of history?" I rejoined. "Was it European or American or Asian history?" "Well," he responded, "I think it was a green book."

5. We are starting from a paradigm of power seen as *superiority over* or *control over*. We neglect to see the possibility of exchanging "power over" for "partnership with."[7] And we neglect to see that a sense of human superiority over other humans and over nature itself lies at the root of our disconnected and destructive living.

Surely, there is a deeper way to learn, a larger way to live. This book offers an alternative. What would it be like to reverse the trend and recover a more excellent way to learn and live our lives? To stress *commitment* and *character* (as ethics does)? To think of education not as information, but as *transformation*? What would it mean to *cultivate what connects us*? To begin with a *prior oneness,* with *interconnection* and *relationship*? To exchange *"power over"* for *"partnership with," including our partnership with the earth in its unfolding*? What would it be like to integrate into learning the *heart* with its values and dreams? The *seen and unseen* aspects of life? What would it be like to offer an *embodied learning*, one that transformed body, mind, emotions, and spirit? What would it mean to go beyond the short-term, personal time to live in *longer-term generational time*? The Navajo, it is said, offer this advice: "Before you make any decision, ask two questions: Will this honor the ancestors — your parents and their parents and their parents? Will this serve the children — your children and their children and their children?"

All these features, here illustrated in terms of education, are part of a much larger shift. The modern worldview crystallized around 1500 CE and still dominates. However, a new trans-modern, ecological worldview is emerging. This emerging ecological view is implicit in how I re-envision ethics and spirituality. Those who prefer to see the large picture earlier in the journey may wish to turn to appendix xvi or glance at chapter 15 before continuing.

Whether the largest horizon is explicit or implicit, transformational work involves the following: commitment and character, integrity and an integral approach, practice and performance, transformation into a deeper knowing and deeper caring and loving. Living large means following a "path with a heart." Living large means bringing stillness and service to all the domains of life.

THE CALL TO CHANGE OUR WAYS OF LIVING IN THREE, NESTED DOMAINS

Rilke writes:

> *I live my life in growing orbits,*
> *which move out over the things of the world.*
> *Perhaps I can never achieve the last,*
> *but that will be my attempt.*
>
> *I am circling around God, around the ancient tower,*
> *and I have been circling for a thousand years,*
> *and I still don't know if I am a falcon, or a storm,*
> *or a great song.*[8]

Rilke offers the picture of life circling around a center — call it the Great Mystery or God or the ancient tower. Around the center are the things of the world. The growing orbits are perhaps an attempt to live and love more widely and deeply, an ongoing, never-ending circle dance. In the circling we seek to understand ourselves, our place, our calling. Sometimes we seem to be a bird of prey, and sometimes a storm of anger and confusion, and sometimes a great song.

Suppose we think of the things of the world as circles within circles. We might simplify by speaking of three domains, all existing between the center and circumference of Great Mystery:

The *planetary domain* (nested in cosmic unfolding) — the web of all life on the planet, together with the conversations that give our planetary life meaning and value and purpose.

The *institutional (corporate) domain* — our organizations, together with our corporate conversations that give our organizational life meaning and value and purpose.

The *interpersonal (one-on-one) domain* — our one-to-one relational fields, together with our conversations that give our interpersonal life meaning and value and purpose.

We expand and contract in these nested domains. We can relate to each domain in smaller and larger ways. The Sufis, the mystics of Islam, have a saying: "When the pickpocket meets the saint, all the pickpocket sees is pockets." Difficult pockets, easy pockets, full pockets, empty pockets. The pickpocket dwells in a "pickpocket conversation," a conversation too small for the saint to show up — in the other and in himself.

All of us dwell in conversations. Some are small-minded conversations — too small to live in; others are larger-minded conversations — large enough for possibilities to flourish. In each of the domains, we can live in smaller and in larger ways. Positive change begins when we realize and act on these possibilities.

The circling describes a spiral path, a pilgrimage of the heart, the work of the heart in pilgrimage. The heart in pilgrimage is re-turning — turning again, as a person might turn from living in an unbalanced way to living in a more harmonious way; as learning and living might seek to recover its heart and reclaim its spirit and soul.

The breeze at dawn has secrets to tell you.
Don't go back to sleep.
You must ask for what you really want.
Don't go back to sleep.
People are going back and forth across the threshold
where the two worlds touch.
The door is round and open.
Don't go back to sleep.[9]

In this poem, the Sufi poet Rumi pleads for wakefulness. The breeze at dawn has secrets, just as do the things of the world. Listening is primary. Listening is joined to speaking: "You must ask for what you really want." The poem points to intersections, mysterious thresholds where the two worlds touch. For the moment, we might think of these two worlds as small-minded and large-minded worlds. We move back and forth across the threshold of these worlds many times a day. Yet the door to possibility remains open. Don't go back to sleep.

One doorway is the *intersection of our deep gladness and the world's deep hunger.* Here, two poles meet: awareness and a world, with different levels of awareness revealing different worlds of possibility — *deepening awareness* on the side of the seeker, and a *deeper sense of oneness or interconnection* on the side of the world that enfolds the seeker.

The late Jesuit retreat master, Anthony De Mello, characterizes spirituality as "waking up."[10] He tells the story of a disciple who went to the master asking for a word of wisdom. The master, who was engaged in a day of silence, wrote on a pad one word, "Awareness." But the disciple wished for more, and asked the master to expand. The master wrote, "Awareness, Awareness, Awareness." That is the key on the side of the seeker. On the side of the deepening world, we could say, "Oneness, Oneness, Oneness," or "Interconnection, Interconnection, Interconnection." Our deepening occurs between those two poles.

Another way to describe the doorway is to speak of the *intersection where the ethical and the spiritual meet.*[11] A renewed ethics reminds us of the horizontal dimension of time, and measures our efforts at betterment by the criteria of "reducing surplus suffering and promoting creative possibility for our common life." A renewed spirituality reminds us of the vertical dimension that touches the timeless, where we experience the source and know we are already and always whole, already and always home.[12]

This is the meeting point between our own deep gladness and the world's deep hunger, between spiritual deepening for the sake of ethical acting, and ethical acting for the sake of spiritual deepening. Here, we sow seeds of transformation for all the levels of life — personal, political, planetary — a vast context for the heart's journey.

OVERVIEW OF THE BOOK

Think of this book as mapping three stages on a spiral path and providing practices to turn embodied learning into a sustainable path. The arc of the book:

Part One
The Ethical Steps: Opening the Heart

Part Two
The Ecological/Spiritual Steps: A Cosmic Context

Part Three
The Existential Steps: Uniting Ethics and Spirituality through a Set of Concrete Practices

Part Four
Living Large As a Way

By way of overview:
- The *Ethical Steps* offer new possibilities for an ethics of mind-and-heart in service of all domains.
- The *Ecological/Spiritual Steps* offer new possibilities for an inclusive spirituality.
- The *Existential Steps* offer a set of practices and a particular field of application that integrates the ethical and the spiritual. The field of application is the smallest unit larger than the separate self — one-to-one

relationships — a friendship or family relationship or a work relationship. The existential steps provide (i) a new way to think about such relationships, and (ii) a model rooted in nature and the seasons to organize the practices and aid us to embody them.

- *Living Large as a Way* shows how the path may be sustained and expanded to apply to larger units — the institutional and the planetary contexts. More significantly, wherever applied, this path draws from the intersection of the ethical and spiritual, and offers a way that harmonizes service (the ethical) and stillness (the spiritual) in an ever-deepening and ever-expanding spiral.

Returning to the Heart

The contexts are both vast and simple — as vast as "all that is," as simple as one-to-one relationships with friends and within families and the workplace. Our work is cultivating the heart — awakening first, then moving from prior interconnection to conscious partnership. Finally, we have the task of "keeping the music going," of sustaining the process of wakeful living. The ethical traditions as well as the spiritual traditions offer aid on the journey. Indeed, doing the work of transformation at the intersection of the ethical and the spiritual provides us with a paradox. We strive for something — awakening, interconnection, partnership, love — and yet we already have (in seed) the very things we seek.

To make this paradoxical pilgrimage is to know the power of coming from the one, to know the depth of taking the relationship as the primary unit, to practice healing by tending the relational garden and what is in the garden — in a surprising courtship of the heart. An exciting prospect.

This journey of the heart holds deep implications for learning and living, for our own formation and the formation of those given to our care. On this journey we move from separateness to interconnection, from controlling to collaboration, from "power over" to "partnership with," from a lesser to a greater love.

So why wait? Let us begin.

References

1. This is the form of the Buechner remark as I first heard it and have come to cherish it. So far as I can tell, the original version occurs in Frederick Buechner's *Wishful Thinking: A Seeker's ABC* (San Francisco: HarperSanFrancisco, 1993), p. 119. There he speaks of vocation as "the place where your deep gladness meets the world's deep need." I shall continue to use the variation, with all due respect.

2. The perspectives and practices presented here have been tested in a variety of settings, including Elon University in Elon, North Carolina, where I am Powell Professor of Philosophy, and the Tai Sophia Institute for the Healing Arts in Laurel, Maryland, where I am a faculty member.

   At Elon, I teach a wide range of courses and since 1992 have offered a mentorship for select juniors and seniors called "Quest for Wholeness." This two-semester course is a practicum in direct, daily practice — transformative work in living large.

   At Tai Sophia Institute (formerly the Traditional Acupuncture Institute in Columbia, Maryland), I cofounded in 1987 the Institute's SOPHIA project (School of Philosophy and Healing in Action), a program for adult learners that applies to everyday life the principles and practices underlying Eastern healing arts. I taught in that program until recently, and since January of 2002 have taught in Tai Sophia's innovative Master of Arts in Applied Healing Arts program, which I also co-designed.

3. This is a mission statement I use in teaching classes in ethical practice. It is a variant of a mission I designed for the adult learning programs connected with Tai Sophia Institute for the Healing Arts in Laurel, Maryland. That mission invites us "To come to life more fully so as to serve life more wisely and more nobly. Sagely stillness within; sovereign service without." The Chinese saying states, "Sheng, nei; wang, wai" — literally, the sage within and the king without. I sought to render this phrase in a more gender-inclusive way, and spoke of "sagely stillness within; sovereign service without."

4. Philosopher Alan Watts sounds the theme, if not the exact words, in *The Way of Zen* (New York: Random House Vintage Books, 1989, first published by Pantheon Books in 1957) and in *Psychotherapy East and West* (New York: Pantheon Books, 1961). The phrase "skin-contained ego" appears in Watts's *The Book: On the Taboo Against Knowing Who You Are* (New York: Pantheon, 1966).

5. See Robert Kegan, *The Evolving Self* (Cambridge, MA: Harvard University Press, 1982), p. 116.

6. See Rosamund Stone Zander and Benjamin Zander, *The Art of Possibility* (Boston: Harvard Business School Press, 2000) on the world of measurement vs. the universe of possibility.

7. I owe this formulation to Rianne Eisler. See Rianne Eisler, *The Chalice and the Blade: Our History, Our Future* (San Francisco: Harper & Row, 1987); and Riane Eisler and David Loye, *The Partnership Way* (San Francisco:

HarperSanFrancisco,1990). I offer a different grounding for life as partnership in the final section of this book.

8. This translation by Robert Bly appears in Robert Bly, James Hillman, and Michael Meade, editors, *The Rag and Bone Shop of the Heart* (San Francisco: Harper Perennial Division of Harper Collins, 1993).

9. See Coleman Barks, et al., trans., *The Essential Rumi* (San Francisco: HarperSanFrancisco, 1995), p. 36.

10. For this characterization of spirituality as "waking up," see Anthony De Mello, *Awareness: The Perils and Opportunities of Reality* (New York: Doubleday, 1992), p. 11.

11. In my view, the ethical without the spiritual tends to a minimal rule-following, often with absolutism and self-righteousness thrown in. The spiritual without the ethical can lack resources for self-criticism, and hence either become a retreat from the world, or result in actions where sentimentality overshadows mature service.

12. Roger Walsh uses the term "spirituality" as referring to "direct experience of the sacred...that which is most central and essential to our lives." See Roger Walsh, *Essential Spirituality* (New York: John Wiley & Sons, Inc., 1999), p. 3. Philosopher Robert C. Solomon even offers a spirituality for the skeptic, seeing spirituality as "the thoughtful love of life." For him, the essence of spirituality lies in love, reverence, and trust. See Robert C. Solomon, *Spirituality for the Skeptic: The Thoughtful Love of Life* (New York: Oxford Press, 2002). For the three passions he takes as the essence of spirituality, see p. 29.

PART ONE

The Ethical Steps

Opening the Heart

CHAPTER ONE

The Call to Large Mind-and-Heart

We begin with a story...

Once, long ago in a kingdom far away, there was a very unusual custom. In most kingdoms when the ruler dies, his son or daughter succeeds to the throne after him. But in this kingdom when a king died, a special bird called the "bird of good fortune" was released. This bird flew around in the air above the subjects in the land, and the person upon whose head it finally landed became the next king. A strange custom, indeed.

In this kingdom, there was a slave who worked in the king's palace. He was a musician who entertained the king and his family and guests by dressing in funny clothing — a cap made of chicken feathers and a raggedy belt — and by playing music on a drum. The slave was not happy about his lot. He felt that it was degrading, and prayed to be a free man.

It came to pass that the king died, and the "bird of good fortune" was released. It circled the sky while the people of the kingdom watched in anticipation. Finally it came to rest on the head of the slave, nesting itself in his hat of chicken feathers. Immediately, and to his great surprise, he was declared king of the entire empire. In an instant, the slave was transformed into a powerful sovereign.

The new king moved into the palace, donned his royal attire, and sat upon his throne. As his first royal decree, he had a tiny hut built next to the palace. The only furnishing in this little shack was a large mirror. Early every morning the new king entered this little shack, disappearing behind the door for a short time. Then he would emerge, lock the door behind him, and return to the palace. His ministers and advisors thought that this was very peculiar behavior but, after all, he was the king now, and who would question the king?

As the years went by, the king passed many laws aimed at reducing, and finally eliminating, all slavery and suffering. The changes were made so gradually that no one noticed them. The king was known to all for his kindness, his justice, and his compassion, as well as his strange habit of visiting the odd little hut early every morning.

One day, his closest advisor asked, "Your Majesty, what is it that you keep in that hut of yours?"

The king led the advisor into the hut and showed him a burlap sack containing the chicken feather hat, the ragged belt, and the drum.

"These," he said, "are my most treasured possessions."

"But these are reminders of slavery!" the advisor replied in disgust. "These are not the possessions of a king, Your Majesty!"

"Ah, but they are," replied the king. "You see, once I was a slave and now I am free. When you made me your king, I promised myself and God that I would never forget that I was once a slave. I feared I would grow arrogant and haughty, and treat people as I once was treated. Every morning, I come here and dress as I once was forced to dress — as a slave. I stare at myself in the mirror until tears come to my eyes, and only then am I prepared to leave this hut and rule as a good king should. It is this memory that makes me the king I am. These are my most treasured possessions."[1]

This wonderful story comes from Iraqi Jews. For them, it was a Passover tale, reminding them of the time that their ancestors "passed over" from slavery to freedom.

In this story, the musician-jester makes two transitions in the flick of an eye. First, he goes from being a slave to being free. Second, he goes from being free to becoming king, or perhaps better, becoming "one who has the care of the community."[2] For now, let us focus on the first transition — slave to free.

What must we do each day in order to be free? The former jester instituted a daily practice: to go into his hut, to put on the dress of slavery, to take it to heart, to feel the experience until tears came to his eyes. Then he could care for the community — fairly, humanely, and compassionately.

One key teaching is this: *If you want to be free, you need to have a daily practice.* Put differently, the "passing over" is not just something that happened once long ago. Every day we are called to pass over from slavery to freedom. Every day we are invited to become free.

How are we enslaved?

• By old habits of mind and heart: resentments, prejudice, addictions.

• By living in imitation of others, fearing their blame and desiring their praise.

• By thinking we are free when we are not, when we are still victims of outer and inner forces — victims of our society's unsorted values and our own inner whims and compulsions.

The degree of our enslavement is hidden from us. The ancients would say we are doubly ignorant: first, ignorant of who we are and what is real; second, ignorant of being ignorant. We think we know when we don't. Similarly, we are doubly enslaved. We are enslaved but think we are free. The first constriction is covered over by a second, as if the jester thought he was free because he was well cared for. What "hut of practice" can we build that will reveal our chains and set us free? What sort of mirror do we need in order to see ourselves as we are?

FOUR BEGINNINGS

Here is one "mirror." I call it the Four Beginnings:

We are partial;	we seek to be whole.
We are asleep;	we seek to be awake.
We are enslaved;	we seek to be free.
We are reactive;	we seek to be "response-able"
	(able to choose our response)[3]

Every day we move back and forth between these two columns, between what we are (at least at the surface) and what we seek to be (or *already are* — at our depth). Of course, it is not so cut and dried. There are degrees of "unfreedom" and freedom, degrees of wakefulness and forgetfulness, and so on.

Confucius (Master K'ung) would say that we have a *small-minded person-in-us* and a noble or *large-minded person-in-us* — both possibilities existing at any moment.[4] He would encourage us to remember our nobility and to live in large mind. He would remind us that this takes daily practice.

What is "practice" in this model? It is *to recognize when we are in small mind and to shift to large mind*. Look back at the Four Beginnings. The first column partly defines small mind and the second column partly defines large mind.

In small mind, we tend to be partial in the double sense of being biased and of seeing less than the whole. In small mind, we are asleep in our life, on automatic pilot, "going through the motions" according to cultural scripts. In small mind, we are enslaved in the ways discussed. In small mind, we are reactive in the sense that someone or something triggers us and we react immediately — with no space and no time between the incoming stimulus and the automatic response.

In large mind, we see more of the whole and live in a larger world. In large mind, we are more mindful, more wakeful, opening the senses and opening the heart. In large mind, we are freer, acting from a place beneath surface disturbance. In large mind, we are response-able — able to choose our response in a way that benefits the whole.

RECOGNIZING TWO LEVELS[5]

Practice begins with recognizing when we are in small mind. To do this, we must distinguish two levels — a WHAT and a HOW. Call this the fundamental distinction for all inner work: the distinction between (a) *what is going on* and (b) *how I am relating to what is going on*.

(b) How I am relating to
and   ⅄
(a) What is going on   (What is going on)

Always there are two levels. Yet often we merge the two. "How we are relating" disappears from our awareness, as if how we are relating to the situation is the only possible way we could relate.

Victor Frankl was an Austrian psychiatrist and a Jew. During the time of the Holocaust, the Nazis sent him to the camps. While he was a prisoner under unimaginable conditions, Frankl discovered this fundamental distinction. His way of phrasing it was to distinguish "liberty" (on the first level) and "freedom" (on the second level). In the camps, Frankl had no liberty — he could not go and come as he wished. Yet Frankl discovered that he did have a bit of freedom — the freedom to choose how he would relate to his situation. This he came to call "the last human freedom." It was something his Nazi captors could not take from him.[6]

Consider liberty and freedom in our own lives. We may or may not have the power to change what is occurring. Hurricanes and floods, sicknesses and accidents may restrict our liberty. Yet we still have an important freedom — the capacity to recognize, and possibly alter, how we relate to what is occurring in our life.

Leadership consultant Stephen Covey uses the Frankl example to emphasize the first of his seven habits of highly effective people.[7] "Be proactive," Covey says. "Develop the capacity to choose your response."

Covey speaks not of small and large mind, but of reactivity and proactivity. The stimulus happens — someone makes a cutting remark. The response follows immediately — an angry retort. *Reactivity.* No freedom, no ability to choose your response. *Proactivity,* on the contrary, is another name for "response-ability." Proactivity is the ability to choose one's response. Being proactive is often confused with being nice. This misses the key distinction. At times, hard truths must be faced. Proactivity, in this instance, is the ability to choose what you will say, and when, and how. It may or may not be "nice."

Several years ago, my wife, Gregg, discovered she had breast cancer. At that moment, she had no choice about having cancer. Cancer was already present. But she did have a second-level choice: how to relate to the cancer. First, she could choose her treatment. Second, during and after treatment, she could choose how she would live with this illness. She chose not to let cancer be her identity (not to be "Miss Cancer of the Year," she would say). And she chose not to die before she died. By cultivating *awareness,* she realized that she was at least *free to choose* **how** she would understand and respond to this event in her life.

I have been using the phrase "ways of relating" as shorthand. Sometimes it is useful to expand this phrase to my Way of Understanding and Responding To [what is happening].[8]

Notice that the phrase "Way of Understanding and Responding To [what is happening]" calls attention to two features: a meaning aspect (the "U" of understanding) and a value aspect (the "R" of responding).

- The meaning aspect can best be observed in noticing the *language* I am using.
- The value aspect can best be observed by noticing the *emotional charge* I am experiencing — my moving toward or away, my "liking-wanting-clinging," or my "disliking-hating-condemning."

Meaning and value are linked. I like or dislike, favor or disfavor, depending on how I interpret the situation, how I understand its meaning.[9] All this may happen instantly. "Who is that woman across the room?" "Oh," my friend says, "that's Alice." Immediately, I dislike her. All I understand of her is the name "Alice." Instant label. Instant emotion. Perhaps when I was five years old, I encountered a girl named Alice who made my life miserable. Just the name "Alice" is enough to trigger dislike.

We humans are meaning-creating, value-generating beings. The odd thing is that generally we forget that *we* are labeling situations. We forget that *we* are generating the emotions we feel. It's as if we are wearing glasses and forgetting we are wearing them. We "see through" our stories and emotions. We do not see that the stories and emotions are produced by us.

Without awareness, I take my interpretation as the truth of the matter. I define it as such. I am unaware that I have any choice about the story I am telling. I think, "That is just the way it is!"

Without awareness, I fail to see that, in the wake of the story, I am the one putting an emotional charge on the situation. It is as if situations arrived already wrapped in language and already charged with strong emotion. I simply think: "That's the way it is." Aren't I justified to be angry about it?

When the stakes are high or emotions are high, reactivity increases. Yet, even in these situations, with awareness, I can notice the key distinction: what is happening is one thing; how I interpret and respond is another. Victor Frankl could distinguish liberty and freedom even under horrendous conditions. My wife could distinguish between having cancer (no liberty here) and how she would relate to having cancer (some freedom here). To notice this fundamental distinction does not come easily. We need practice.

A WAY TO LOOK AT PRACTICE, STEP-BY-STEP

Step 1. Recognize the fundamental distinction —
the distinction between events and ways of relating.

This distinction between events and ways of relating to those events lies at the threshold to all inner work. Some people speak of it in terms of phenomena and the stories we tell about the phenomena, or as phenomena and our conclusions about the phenomena. When we return home, for example, do we see our wife or husband or child or friend as phenomena, able to surprise us anew? Or have we already concluded that we know exactly how they are?

When we are awake and alert, we can recognize and untangle the two levels. Think of step one as prologue: There are the events of a life and my ways of relating. Once I see both aspects, I am in a position to proceed. The further steps can be represented as a Wisdom Chant:

> *There are, at least, TWO ways to relate to anything:*
> *a small-minded way and a large-minded way.*
> *Choose large mind.*

Step 2. There are at least TWO ways of relating to anything.

Always, there are at least two ways — and usually a number of ways — to interpret and respond to the events of our life.

Two colleagues of mine, Dianne and Julia, were working in the same building. They met in the hall. Dianne was coming one way — head down, muttering to herself. Her friend, Julia, passed her going in the other direction. All Julia said was, "Well, Dianne, that's one way to look at it." Dianne stopped as if stunned, then laughed heartily. A reminder: There are at least TWO ways of relating to anything. Usually more. As one saying has it: "If you have one choice, you have no choice. If you have two choices, you are caught on the horns of a dilemma. Only when you have three or more choices do you begin to be free."[10]

Step 3. Recognize that some ways of relating are larger than others.

When we realize that there is more than one way to relate to a situation, a new possibility arises — a value possibility. Will we choose a way that opens or closes life? Will we choose a small-minded or a large-minded way? In reality, there are a number of small-minded ways, a number of large-minded ways to relate to what is going on. For simplicity, picture the options in this way:

When we are awake and alert,
WE CAN CHOOSE…

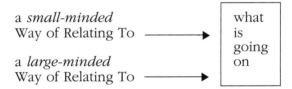

a *small-minded*
Way of Relating To   ⟶   what is going on

a *large-minded*
Way of Relating To   ⟶

Remember again: We are the users of language. We are the producers of emotion. Remember that in small mind we are partial, asleep, enslaved, and reactive. In large mind we are more whole, more wakeful, freer, and more able to choose our response.

I want now to add an explicitly ethical criterion. I see the aim of ethics as:

To come to life more fully so as
to act more wisely and more effectively
to reduce suffering and
to promote possibility
for our common life.[11]

For our purposes, the key lies in *reducing suffering* and *promoting possibility* for our common life.

Some suffering may come with life itself — there are storms and accidents, we age and we die. This may be "necessary" suffering in the sense that it comes with the human condition. All we can do is to bear it together. However, in addition, there is much unnecessary or surplus suffering—needless suffering we inflict on ourselves and others. So better to say, "to reduce *surplus* suffering for our common life." In like manner, some possibilities are constructive and some destructive. Hence better to say, "to promote *constructive* possibility for our common life."

In small mind, we increase surplus suffering and decrease constructive possibility for our common life. In larger mind, we reduce surplus suffering and promote constructive possibility for our common life.

When we see that there are always several ways of interpreting and responding, we can begin to notice that some are small-minded ways and some are larger-minded ways.

Step 4. Choose Large Mind.

"Choose large mind" — advice that Confucius, Victor Frankl, and my wife would approve! Here is a Zen story to make the point:

Once upon a time, a towering samurai warrior approached Hakuin, a small Zen monk. "Teach me about heaven and hell!" the samurai growled.

"Teach you?" the monk responded. "You are a dirty, smelly, unkempt poor excuse for a samurai. Even your sword is rusty!"

The samurai, stung to the quick, flushed with anger and, in an instant, drew his sword, raising it high so as to cleave the insolent monk in two. A split second before the sword began its downward arc, the monk pointed and said, "That's Hell!"

A flash of insight washed over the samurai. This little monk, he thought, had gone to the brink of death to teach him. The samurai's body relaxed, and a sense of gratitude welled up in him as he sheathed his sword. At that very moment, the monk said, "That's Heaven!"

So moment by moment we create heaven and hell — creating hell when we are reactive, asleep, enslaved by our patterns; creating heaven when we are awake, free, and choose our responses for the sake of less suffering and more possibility.

I have noted that "practice" on this model is to recognize small mind and shift to larger mind. To recognize small mind requires that we cultivate what some wisdom traditions call the "Observing Self."[12]

With an observer present, I recognize the distinction between the two levels, between what's happening and how I relate to that. I notice that I have already wrapped the happening in language. I notice my likes and dislikes arising.

With an observer present, I realize that my meaning-making and value-generating are providing only one of several ways to structure life. There are other options.

With an observer present, I can ask myself: Is my current way of speaking and responding large enough? Does it open life or diminish life? Does it reduce or increase surplus suffering? Does it expand or constrict constructive possibility? Then I can choose a large-minded way of relating. Then I can consciously seek to reduce surplus suffering and promote creative possibilities for our common life.

Aiding oneself and others to move from smaller to larger mind-and-heart is what deep training in leadership and spiritual growth is all about.

In the opening story of this chapter, the slave went directly from being a slave to being a king. Actually, we saw two transitions: from slave to free person, and from free person to "one who takes on the care of the community." The "community" can be as universal as the Great Pattern or as particular as a one-to-one relationship. The first step is to become aware.

Taking a cue from Confucius, I associated being partial, asleep, enslaved, and reactive with being in small mind-and-heart. I associated becoming more whole, awake, free, and responsible with being in large mind-and-heart. This gave us a first sketch of "practice": *to recognize when we are in small mind and to shift to large mind.*

The slave who became king instituted a daily practice of going to his hut, dressing in his jester's clothes, looking at himself in the mirror until he realized what it was to be a slave all over again. Each day the sovereign put off the clothes of a king to become as a slave again. Taking a clue from this story, we recognized the need for daily practice. We realized that we needed a mirror.

The story tells us that the king continued his practice for many years and that the kingdom was better for it. I imagine that along the way, the king learned many things. Suppose we stand in the place of the king. Suppose we move into that large-minded, noble place in ourselves. How can the king's practice give us a hint of what we too will discover?

Like the king, we may learn that we have within us both a slave and a sovereign. We may see ourselves as both slave and ruler, inhabiting two points of view.

Like the king, we may notice that there are at least two ways of understanding and responding to the first-level fact of "being a slave." There are small-minded ways to be with slavery (and other situations where one has no liberty) and larger-minded ways. Some people see no options and "double" their victimhood. Others, like Victor Frankl in the camps and Nelson Mandela in prison, choose to live in large mind and preserve their inner dignity and worth.

Like the king, we may realize that there are at least two ways of understanding and responding to the first-level fact of "being a leader." There are small-minded ways of being a leader — for example, when we think of power as a way to inflate our own egos. And there are large-minded ways of being a leader — for example, when we exercise a form of "servant leadership," and prize working in partnership with others for the common good.[13]

Like the king, we may recognize that large mind has space enough to recognize small mind and more.

Like the king, we may come to see how, in small mind, we create "hell on earth." We may also see that in large mind we can create something of "heaven on earth."

Above all, we shall see both the need for daily practice and the good effect that such practice has on all the relationships of our life.

As the years went by, the king passed many laws aimed at reducing, and finally eliminating, all slavery and suffering. The changes were made so gradually that no one noticed them. The king was known to all for his kindness, his justice, and his compassion, as well as his strange habit of visiting the odd little hut early every morning.

References

1. A Passover tale told by Iraqi Jews. I heard the story from my friend, Arthur Z. Steinberg, Rabbi of Temple Sinai in Portsmouth, Virginia, who used the story at a congregational seder in April 1997. He claims that the source is lost from memory, so I am crediting him for preserving the story in oral tradition.

2. I take the phrase from St. Thomas Aquinas in his definition of law.

3. These insights which I call "Four Beginnings" come from many sources. For earlier discussions of partialness, see my earlier book: John Greenfelder Sullivan, *To Come to Life More Fully: An East West Journey* (Columbia, MD: Traditional Acupuncture Institute, 1990), pp. 54, 94, 212. The notion of being asleep and awakening is, of course, Buddhist. My thoughts on inner slavery owe much to Robert S. deRopp who, drawing on the Gurdjieff teachings, has a version of my "Beginnings" on page 86 of his book *Self Completion* (Nevada City, CA: Gateways/IDHHB, Inc., 1991). The last notion stems from Stephen Covey's discussion of reactivity and proactivity. The title "Four Beginnings" I take from the ancient Chinese, who use this term in a different though related way.

4. I am rendering the Confucian term "hsiao jen" as the small-minded person-in-us. I am rendering the Confucian term "chün-tzu" as the noble or large-minded person-in-us. This distinction can be seen in the Image section of the commentary on each hexagram in the *I Ching,* where Wilhelm translates the terms as "the superior man" and "the inferior man." See *I Ching or Book of Changes,* trans. Richard Wilhelm, 3rd ed. (Princeton, NJ: Princeton University Press, 1967). It is also a key distinction used by Confucius in the Analects. See Confucius, *The Analects* (Lun Yu), trans. D.C. Lau (New York: Viking Penguin, 1979), where the distinction appears more than 50 times.

5. A first draft of the material in this chapter appeared as "Small Mind, Big Mind" in the journal *Meridians,* Vol. 3, No. 2, Spring 1996. I thank the publishers of *Meridians* for allowing the work to appear here.

6. See Victor Frankl, *Man's Search for Meaning,* 3rd ed. (New York: Simon & Schuster, 1984).

7. See Stephen Covey, *The Seven Habits of Highly Effective People* (New York: Simon & Schuster Fireside Book, 1990), pp. 66-93. Covey acknowledges that the first habit must be joined to the second — "Begin with the End in View" — and, in fact, that all the habits interlock.

8. For certain purposes, I find it helpful to abbreviate one's Way of Understanding and Responding To [what is happening] as a WURT. Thus, we can say there is a WHAT and a WURT. Without an observer, this distinction collapses, as if we were writing WHAT and WURT over each other — writing them over and over until we could not see them as separable. Another way to say this is: "What is happening" comes to us already interpreted through language and already wrapped in an emotional

(like/dislike) charge. "That's just the way it is," we say. We do not see that we are the makers of meaning and the generators of value; and hence we also do not see that we can change our way of relating, change our WURT. I will often return to this shorthand in the endnotes.

9. My colleagues in the Tai Sophia Institute's SOPHIA program often use a distinction between "phenomena" and "conclusions" (grounded and ungrounded). Again, in my language, I would say that what we think of as *the situation* ("the way it is") is a combination of WURT + a Situation (a WHAT), although, without practice, we will be unconscious of our WURT, of the meaning and valuing we bring to the situation. Because the WURT is invisible to us, we are operating with a "concluded phenomenon." Sorting out conclusion from phenomena is like becoming conscious of WURT as well as situation. Becoming conscious of both *what is happening* and *how I am relating to it* "moves over," so to speak, the initial WURT to the side of the object observation. Then, as in meditation, we are observing a wider field — we are aware of both inner and outer weather. For this notion of "moving over" what was subject to object of awareness, see Robert Kegan, *The Evolving Self* (Cambridge, MA: Harvard University Press, 1982). For widening the field of awareness in meditation and group work, see John Heider, *The Tao of Leadership* (New York: Bantam, 1986).

10. I quote this saying from memory. I heard it in a workshop on Neuro-Linguistic Programming many years ago in Winston-Salem, NC. The presenter was Leslie Cameron-Bandler. For a taste of her work, see Leslie Cameron-Bandler, David Gordin, and Michael Lebeau, *Know How* (San Rafael, CA: Future Pace, 1985).

11. As noted earlier, I formulated this mission statement for my undergraduate ethics classes. The first half of the mission statement accents the positive and takes a "virtue approach" to ethics. The second half of the statement looks to reducing suffering and draws on the project of the Buddha.

12. From the Sufi tradition, for example, see Arthur J. Deikman, *The Observing Self: Mysticism and Psychotherapy* (Boston: Beacon Press, 1982).

13. See, for example, Robert K. Greenleaf, *Servant Leadership* (Mahwah, NJ: Paulist Press, 1977).

CHAPTER TWO

From Being Asleep to Being Awake

The breeze at dawn has secrets to tell you.
Don't go back to sleep.
You must ask for what you really want.
Don't go back to sleep.
People are going back and forth across the doorsill
where the two worlds touch.
The door is round and open.
Don't go back to sleep.[1]

— RUMI

Rich imagery — "being asleep" and "being awake." We are asleep when we are forgetful of what really matters; we awaken when we remember who we are at our core and act from our center.

The last lines of Rumi's poem speak of people "going back and forth across the doorsill where the two worlds touch." The "two worlds" can be understood as this world and the next. However, in the spirit of last chapter's story of the monk and the samurai, I prefer to think of the "two worlds" as *two modes of consciousness in this life*. On this interpretation, we are constantly moving back and forth between a small-minded world (enslaved, reactive, and ego-centered) and a large-minded world (free, responsible, and partnership-centered).

"The door is round and open. Don't go back to sleep."

Imagine you are driving along a highway. Suddenly, you realize you have driven past your exit. Who was driving? You were, and, in a sense, you were not. You were operating on automatic pilot and not paying attention. Where were you? Perhaps in the past, replaying a previous episode. Perhaps in the future, rehearsing a possible future event.[2] This is an example of being asleep in your life: going through the motions; acting on autopilot; running a soap opera of your mind; daydreaming, with thoughts and images arriving from all over (what some Buddhists call "mind weeds").[3]

Suppose that while you are driving, a child suddenly darts out into the road. Suddenly you awaken, take control, swerve, and miss the child. For awhile you stay alert and awake, realizing what is important — being present to your life. Then, little by little, you go back to sleep, perhaps with one more story to add to the soap opera.

In this case, the observing self broke out of the soap opera to attend to what was real in the moment. At other times, the observing self — the wakeful self-in-us — notices how we are labeling our situation and observes the emotions coming up within us.

In a restaurant near my home, a jukebox plays dozens upon dozens of songs. We are like a jukebox — stocked with tapes rather than CDs. Over the course of life, we have recorded a multitude of tapes about parents and family, teachers and schools, sex and relationships, jobs and bosses, taxes and political figures, religion, drugs and violence, and on and on. Often, our conversations consist of "playing our tapes."

Suppose I am to meet some friends for lunch. I arrive a bit late, make excuses, sit down and ask, "What are you talking about?"

"The people at work."

"Oh, good," I think. "I have some good tapes about work — tapes 11 and 23. I wish you would stop talking so I could play my tapes."

Perhaps my friends shift the conversation to another category, to sex and relationships. "Even better," I think. "I have great tapes on that topic — tapes 9, 17, 24, and 58! I'll start playing them as soon as someone pauses."

Jukeboxes are designed with a "play" button, but without a "record" button. Likewise, many conversations have little to do with listening, even less to do with learning, and hardly anything to do with revising our views. We are simply playing tapes. Do we really believe those things we've been saying for years? We don't ask. They are good tapes, we assume — people like them.

Of course, telling our stories may be benign, a form of entertainment. Storytelling has a long history among humans. Good storytellers are performers who are very much awake and attuned to their audience. The best stories are "teaching stories" that subvert our defenses and go straight to the heart.[4]

However, not all of our storytelling is beneficent or even benign; some is downright harmful. Think of conversations of complaint — not the conversations that begin in complaint and then seek to improve a situation, but conversations that are "complaint fests" through and through. Here, we lack an observer: We realize only dimly what we are doing and the harm we are spreading. We dwell in the stories, and so do not see that they are only stories, only one way to interpret and respond to situations. Furthermore, we forget that we are the tellers and elaborators of these tales. We are the ones inflaming emotions, blaming others, and feeling victimized. Such conversations are toxic. We come away from them diminished. If this is the habitual conversation a family dwells within, if this is the habitual conversation colleagues dwell within, observe how unhealthy it is. Notice what infectious diseases are being spread! Notice how the family or the workplace is being poisoned.

In teaching, I often draw a small figure on the chalkboard that looks a bit like a spy in a trench coat, a hat covering his face. I call this figure JUD A.B.C. He is a reminder of how we make ourselves sick by the unmindful ways we think and speak, of the recipe for poisonous conversations — Justify. Defend. Attack. Blame. Complain. In shorthand, JUD A.B.C. When we are telling or dwelling in such stories, we are causing unnecessary suffering to others, to ourselves, and to the "relational space" we share. We have no observer present to notice how we are labeling situations and the emotions we are stirring up. We undermine morale and sabotage hope.

TEACHING STORY 1: FIGHT OR KEY?

When my daughter Heather was very little, she thought that I existed solely to play with her. So in order to get my work done, I decide on a Sunday afternoon to go over to my office in the Carlton

Building on the Elon campus. When I arrive, I find that the locks have been changed and I cannot get to my office. Immediately the soap opera of my mind scoops up the whole situation and I launch into high drama: "That's just the way THEY are." (THEY being the nasty, unfeeling administration, and WE being the hardworking, noble faculty). "Just the way they are — never thinking of faculty, acting without any consultation, so insensitive as to not even bother telling us!"

I start to fume and get into a state. I try to call campus security, with no results. Anger mounts. Finally, I spy the Vice President for Academic Affairs coming out of a campus luncheon. I jump him like a hungry lion. He produces a key, and I get into the building.

Yet the soap opera of oppression continues to pop up when I'm working, when I'm driving home, when I'm lying in bed. And of course, I tell the tale on Monday. This, I now am ashamed to say, continues for several days.

Finally, after days pass, I become conscious of a small voice that cuts through the tattered tale of imagined abuse. The voice says, "John, do you want a fight or do you want a key?"

Now, part of me wants a fight. After all, I am Irish. I share the heritage of the Irish man who saw a fight and inquired, "Is this a private fight or can anyone join in?" So a part of me wants a fight. Yet the better part of me answers, "Well (long pause), I guess I really want a key." I dial Physical Plant and ask, "May I have a key to the Carlton Building?" "Sure," comes the reply, "it'll be ready in an hour."

I had been in small mind, echoing a time when I was what? — three or four years old? Like the bratty child within, or Cookie Monster on Sesame Street, I was, in effect, chanting, "Me! Me want! Me want it! ME want it NOW! Me want it NOW — regardless."[5] I was acting in a me-centered way — wanting everything to serve me, wanting everything now, wanting everything regardless of the agendas of others. Immediately, anger welled up. Frustration at not getting my way. Then blaming others. Creating opposition: Us vs. Them, Right vs. Wrong, and on and on.

Eventually, a larger view emerged, a view with a place for partnership: "May I have a key?" "Yes, of course." In large mind, we can again see one another as persons collaborating in a common task — in this case, all the varied work of running a college. The Sufis might say I moved from a me-centered form of love (a narrow *eros*) to a wider sense of love, capable of sharing (a kind of *philia*).[6]

When I was in a fit, my context in time and space was small: My time frame was small (this moment!), and my world revolved around me. In full reactivity, my context did not include others as existing in their own right; others were there simply to serve me. Moving to larger mind expands the space to include others; it expands the time so I may look at consequences of actions as they ripple out in the world.

Moving to larger mind is a process. To review: First, I become aware of both *what* is going on plus *how* I am relating to it. Next, I notice that there is more than one way to relate to anything. Finally, I notice that some ways of relating are better than others. I see that my small-minded ways of "seeing-and-being" cause unnecessary suffering. I notice that my larger ways of "seeing-and-being" do the opposite: They reduce needless suffering and promote creative possibility. These insights move me from a *small-minded, me-centered way of relating* to a *large-minded, partnership-centered way of relating.*

Only when I let go of my small mind can I truly see other people in their own right. Only when I put myself at the service of a reality larger than my little self can I experience a love capable of sharing. Whenever I move to larger mind, the "little me" grows up a bit. Or, to put it differently, I become clearer that the "little me" is not all I am.

Meaning and value. Language and emotional charge. Recall how I understood — how I made sense of, interpreted, labeled the situation I encountered when I went to my office on that Sunday afternoon. Notice how the emotional/evaluative aspect — the response — arose almost immediately. Meaning and value are linked. I like or dislike, favor or disfavor, depending on how I interpret the situation, how I understand its meaning.

My emotions would have been very different that Sunday if the meaning I attached to my frustration had been different. Suppose, for instance, I had thought, "Oh, they've changed the locks. The locksmiths must have worked overtime to do it when the fewest people would be around to be inconvenienced — too bad I'm one of the few!" From that understanding my response might have been a hearty laugh — and then I could have sought a key in a completely different spirit. Or I could have worked under a tree. Or I could have taken the whole event as a sign from the gods to go home and take a nap, or take my family for a picnic. Any such response flowing from a larger understanding would have caused a good deal less suffering, both for me and for other people. My ranting was far from harmless!

That's not what I did, though. In the grip of my small-minded self, my understanding was small, and my language followed. On the basis of my quick judgment, my response was anger, resentment, and condemnation. And I locked onto those feelings; I froze together my interpretation and valuation by saying, in effect, "that's just the way it is!"

"That's just the way it is" or "that's just the way I am" is a hallmark of a small mind. Labels, emotions, stereotypes — these are part of the dynamic. Also, in small, ego-centered mind, I move very quickly to EITHER-OR (dualistic understanding and response — us vs. them; right vs. wrong; win vs. lose). In such a mindspace, true partnership cannot be thought or spoken, let alone achieved. Alternatively, by remembering the large-minded-person-in-me, I lay the groundwork for partnership, for community.

TEACHING STORY 2: HARRIET'S CHILDHOOD

Some years ago, I participated in a group that included a woman in her mid-sixties whom I'll call Harriet. She told the group this story:

"When I was a little girl, I lived in Texas with my mother. I never knew who my father was. My mother would be in and out of work. Whenever she was 'laid off' she would send me to my grandmother, who would care for me. Then back I went to my mother, and the cycle started again."

On the basis of what she perceived was going on, Harriet installed a "story" about her mother. The story centered on Harriet's mother sending her away. Harriet came to believe that her mother did not want her, never loved her. Harriet's evidence? The fact that her mother kept sending her away — to stay with her grandmother. When did Harriet install this story? At age four or five, perhaps. At any rate, quite early on.

Suppose that you were Harriet, the little girl, and you interpreted the situation as a sign that your mother never loved you. What thoughts and emotions might arise? Perhaps confusion, anger, resentment — all directed outward. Perhaps feelings of being unworthy, worthless, alone, unloved — all directed inward.

The interpretation and consequent emotional charge arose early and lasted long. Harriet and her mother were estranged for all of her mother's life. Even after her mother's death, Harriet's alienation continued.

In the group, people listened to Harriet, hearing the pain and suffering this story had caused and was causing still. Then the group members began to explore what life must have been like for Harriet's mother, a "single mother" before there was such a term. How was it in Texas at that time for a young woman with a young child — a woman poorly educated and without many skills, a woman who had to pick up what work she could, a woman working in situations where she was easily laid off? Yes, the mother did send Harriet away. And she also asked for her back. Again and again and again. Was Harriet's interpretation the only way of understanding the situation? Would an alternative interpretation open up alternative emotional responses? We who have an observer present within us can see how Harriet "languaged her life." We who have an observer present can understand the emotional charge that followed her interpretation. Harriet had no observer for this story. For her, it was the truth of the matter — that was exactly how it was!

Through the group work we were doing, Harriet awoke to notice that this was not the only way to interpret and respond to the events. The events were in the past, "frozen in amber" as it were.[7] Harriet had no liberty to change the past but, with awareness, she did have the freedom to observe her story and the emotions arising with the story. She did, with awareness, have the freedom to shift her story. This she did. She came to see that perhaps her mother did love her after all, that her mother did the best she could for Harriet under difficult circumstances.

Tears, grieving, and then regret. "Why did I not see this possibility while my mother was still alive?" Harriet asked. And finally, came closure. She was able to tell her mother certain things — even now, and even though she did not quite have the words.

Harriet experienced forgiveness — for herself and for her mother, for the human condition we all share.

How easy it is to see such possibilities for healing in others, to see a different way to tell a "story" and respond to life's events. And how difficult to see these possibilities in our own lives! Being asleep in our lives can cause great unnecessary suffering. Waking up can bring the capacity for compassion, forgiveness, and renewed hope.

THE OBSERVING SELF REVISITED

The observing self is that part of us that notices what is happening and, as well, notices how we are labeling our situation and generating emotions. The observing self might just as truly be called the listening self — listening to the words we are using to name what we are doing and what is being done to us. Or call it the feeling heart, since what we observe is not only language but also what arises in our bodes as we dwell within a world thus described. This feeling heart, observing and listening self — this awakened mind-and-heart — neither praises nor condemns. "How interesting" is its first comment.

In awakened mind-and-heart, we are able to look with compassionate eyes at what we are doing; hear with compassionate ears how we are speaking; feel with compassionate heart how the currents of fear and desire, of dislike and attachments are stirring the waters. Physically, we live in air. Mentally, we live in language, live in story. Emotionally, we respond according to the interpretation we live within.

BRINGING AN AWAKENED MIND-AND-HEART TO READING THIS BOOK

In the next chapter, I point out that we dwell within both personal and cultural conversations. My Wisdom Chant holds for both:

> There are at least TWO ways to relate to anything —
> a small-minded way and a large-minded way.
> Choose large mind!

In this book, I invite us to notice what happens when we dwell in the assumption that we are separate. I suggest that beginning from interconnection offers a larger way to live. But how will we be able to see or to hear in this larger way without an observing, listening, compassionate heart?

At the end of his poem that thanks God "for most this amazing day," e.e.cummings writes,

> *now the ears of my ears awake and*
> *now the eyes of my eyes are opened*

A wonderful image: being asleep and waking up. What is more wonderful is this: We have the capacity to be awake and present here and now — we can go beyond the surface level where fear and desire create a second (half-true) reality, and move to the deeper level of mindfulness where the ears of our ears awake and the eyes of our eyes are opened. We need not strive to bring into existence something we lack. We only need to let go of the veils that hide from us our abilities to see and hear. Then we shall see and hear all things as interconnected and as suggestive of beauty and value far beyond our ability to say. Let Rumi have the first and last word:

> *The breeze at dawn has secrets to tell you.*
> *Don't go back to sleep.*
> *You must ask for what you really want.*
> *Don't go back to sleep.*
> *People are going back and forth across the doorsill*
> *where the two worlds touch.*
> *The door is round and open.*
> *Don't go back to sleep.*[1]

References

1. See *The Essential Rumi*, translated by Coleman Barks with John Moyne, A. J. Arberry and Reynold Nicholson (San Francisco: Harper SanFrancisco, 1995), p. 36.

2. Freud once noticed that much "thinking is rehearsing." Much of our thinking is also replaying. "Rehearsing" and "replaying" are two ways we can avoid the present and, in fact, avoid a deeper kind of thinking.

3. See Shunryu Suzuki, *Zen Mind, Beginner's Mind* (Trumbull, CT: Weatherhill, Inc., 1972).

4. On teaching stories, especially as used in the Sufi tradition, see Arthur J. Deikman, *The Observing Self* (Boston: Beacon Press, 1982).

5. I call this the Ego Chant. You can act it out by pounding your hands in the air and saying, "Me! Me want! "Me want it! Me want it NOW! Me want it NOW regardless," and then stamping your feet as if in a temper tantrum. Suddenly the bratty child that dwells in each of us shows up and an angry energy fills the room.

6. See Kabir Edmund Helminski, *Living Presence* (New York: Jeremy Tarcher/Perigee Books, 1992), p. 52 and p. 144.

7. The phrase is from Kurt Vonnegut.

CHAPTER THREE

Large Mind and Interconnection

The mind is an ocean...and so many worlds
Are rolling there, mysterious, dimly seen![1]

– RUMI

We live at the threshold of time and the timeless. This chapter explores both.

For our practice to be effective in the world of *time,* we must see ourselves as individuals, yes, but also as embedded in ever-expanding contexts — for example, from interpersonal through institutional to planetary contexts. The first part of this chapter sets the scene for understanding larger units in terms of a notion of "conversations."

For practice to touch the *timeless,* we must reclaim ancient teachings concerning levels of consciousness. The second part of this chapter expands the notion of awareness from small-minded consciousness through larger-minded awareness to awareness of the deep unity at the source — what one writer calls "the ever-present origin."[2]

LIVING WITHIN LANGUAGE

We live within conversations. Often we forget that we are the makers of meaning and the shapers of value. We forget that we are the speakers who can enhance or diminish life. When forgetful, we quickly come to "freeze in" our value-soaked interpretations and say, "That's just the way we are," or "That's just the way it is."

However, with an observer present, we can remember what we have forgotten. We can remember the Wisdom Chant: "There are always — at least — *two* ways of relating to anything, a small-minded way and a large-minded way. Choose large mind."

With an observer present, we can begin to notice (a) our mindset, (b) our speaking with its emotional charge, and (c) the conversations we create. The basic conversations in which we dwell define our "world." In whatever context, the question is, "Are these conversations large enough to live in?"

SMALL-MINDED CONVERSATIONS AND LARGE-MINDED CONVERSATIONS

Recall the Sufi adage: "When the pickpocket sees the saint, the pickpocket sees only pockets." The pickpocket, we might say, lives in a "pickpocket conversation," lives in a world of nothing but pockets — full pockets, empty pockets, difficult pockets, easy pockets, and so on. Small mind, small conversation, small world.

What is required for the pickpocket (the pickpocket in us) to see the saint (the saint in ourselves and others)? We need a larger mindset — a more expansive way of making meaning and shaping value, a bigger conversation, a larger world of meaning and value.

Small-minded conversations tend to be ego-centered and quickly go oppositional. Furthermore, they bewitch us to think that these stories are "the real world." We forget that our story represents only one of many possible stories, and that we and others like us are the authors of the story. Think of my conversation in the story of the fight or key. Think of Harriet's conversation about being sent away. Larger-minded conversations move to become partnership-centered, collaboration-centered, and seek to express the harmony that already joins us. In larger-minded conversations we are mindful that we are the author and teller of the story, that we are the generator of the emotional charge. Think of my coming into harmony with my college. Think of Harriet's coming into partnership with her mother.

The Wisdom Chant asserted that there are always several Ways of Understanding and Responding To [what is happening].[3] The chant further specified that some ways are larger and some are smaller. The small ones promote needless suffering and reduce possibility for all. The larger ones reduce suffering and promote possibility for all.

Here I invite you to a slight shift of focus. Different understandings and responses, different meanings and values are expressed in words, becoming different *conversations*. We dwell in conversations. Some are small-minded and others are larger-minded.

The conversations that matter to us are not emotionally neutral. We are committed to them as they express our beliefs; we are passionate about them as they reflect who we are. Such conversations or basic stories are shared and repeated by many. The fundamental meanings and values they express define who we are individually and collectively. These fundamental meanings and values, expressed through language, become "worlds" — that is, shared spaces of what is meaningful and valuable.[4]

As ways of making meaning and generating values can be smaller-minded or larger-minded, so the worlds of what we take as meaningful and valuable can be larger-minded or smaller-minded. This opens up a powerful tool for finding our way.

What kind of conversations are we living in — in our interpersonal relationships? What kind of conversations are we living in — in our institutions? What kind of conversations are we living in about the planet and all who inhabit it? About our collective fate?

Are we aware that in each of these circles or domains we live within conversations?

Are we aware that we — individually and collectively — generate those conversations?

Are we aware that the conversations we generate — the "meaning and value worlds" we live in — can be larger-minded or smaller-minded?

RECOGNIZING AND SHIFTING CONVERSATION

For me, being in practice points to (a) recognizing when we are in small mind, (b) realizing we have a choice, and (c) shifting to larger mind-and-heart. Or, we can say: being in practice points to (a) recognizing when we are in a small-minded conversation, (b) realizing that we have a choice, and (c) shifting (plus inviting others to shift) to a larger-minded conversation.

Stephen Covey gives examples of reactive language and how to shift to more proactive language.[5] Consider a person or group of persons who live in a conversation about all that they "have to" do. Such a conversation is toxic. It promotes surplus suffering and reduces possibility. Consider shifting from "I have to..." to "I choose to..." We now can see that such a shift, if practiced over and over, can move us from living in a conversation of duty-bordering-on-victimhood to living in a conversation of empowerment.

Consider a person or persons who live in a conversation of "if only": If only I had more money or more time. If only I were smarter or thinner or more popular. If only I grew up in another family or worked with different people.

Let us call this a conversation of lack. Such a conversation is toxic. It promotes surplus suffering and reduces possibility. Consider shifting from "If only I had or were..." to "I have all that I need in myself and my relationships to live a worthy life, and I can take steps to gain or be..." Here we shift from a conversation of lack to a conversation of abundance. We begin in abundance and move to make the changes desired. This can make all the difference. The shape of our typical conversations defines the shape of our world. Some worlds are too small to live in. Some worlds give us space to be a larger self and to live a larger life for ourselves and others.

In small mind, we fail to notice the conversations in which we live. No observing self present. In small mind, we fail to realize that we co-conspire in generating the meanings and values under which we live. No observing self to invoke the Wisdom Chant. We fail to observe that this is only one story, not the only story to be told. In small mind, no observing self is present to ask: Is this story big enough to live in?

How odd! We generate meanings and values and then forget that we did so. The stories we dwell in become part of our "world."[6] We forget that we authored or adopted the story. We forget that it is only a story, one story. There are others. We forget that some stories are large-minded and some are smaller-minded. We are deluded into thinking that the stories are imposed on us from outside and that they are "just the way it is" or "just the way we are."

We do the same thing with the emotional aspect. We generate our emotions and then forget we have done so. We say, "He or she makes me mad or glad." Again the language of victim. And notice, in this conversation, we are still under the unexamined influence of another — whether we say the other makes us mad or makes us happy. Perhaps we might practice saying, "In the presence of such and such a person or event or story, I notice that I am generating such and such emotions." I am generating them, and with practice I can stop generating them, or notice what I am doing until the emotional charge diminishes.[7]

Notice how we now have a variation of our Wisdom Chant, centering on conversations. There are at least two ways to tell stories and to generate emotions regarding anything — a small-minded way (one of forgetfulness and "that's just the way it is"), and a large-minded way (one of mindfulness and awareness which, when we are awake and alert, allows us to choose our stories). Choose Large Mind. Choose to speak and respond in ways that create more possibility and less suffering for all concerned.

SPHERES OF CONVERSATIONS

Thus far, I have written about conversations that are fairly local in scope: my encounter with the changed locks in my college building, Harriet's encounter with her mother. Suppose we take another step. Suppose we consider a *culture* as a *widely-shared conversation about basic issues.* Suppose we see a culture or worldview as a collective way of making meaning and ascribing value, a conversation in which many people participate and dwell. Cultural ways of relating become cultural conversations. When we think of culture as a conversation, we usually are thinking of our widest worldview or paradigm — sometimes the culture/conversation/worldview of a nation or, wider still, the culture/conversation/worldview of an epoch, e.g., the worldview of modernity.

Next step: Notice that *cultural conversations can be small-minded or large-minded.*

Being a practitioner to a partnership means, in part, to notice when interpersonal conversations are too small and then to offer larger possibilities. Similarly, being a practitioner to a culture means, in part, to notice when cultural conversations are too small and then to offer larger-minded conversations to replace them.

Such cultural conversations generate meaning and value and purpose which define our common way of life. Although we often are unaware of these deep cultural assumptions, they mark our thinking and speaking, our valuing and responding at every level.

The turn to conversatons is a powerful tool. I'm thinking of shared conversations about basic matters as "cultures." Conversely, I'm thinking about cultures as shared conversations about what is deeply meaningful and valuable to a group. Such basic shared conversations — basic shared cultures — have differences in scope. Consider how widely shared a conversation is. Think of a marriage as having a conversational or cultural dimension. What fundamental ways of understanding and ways of responding mark the marriage? What are the deepest conversations — the deepest shared meanings and values and purposes — which give shape to the marriage? And if we think of basic conversations as cultures, we can ask, what is the marital culture? Is the basic conversation/culture small-minded or large-minded? Is it healthy or unhealthy? Does it increase creative possibility and reduce needless suffering for all concerned — or the opposite?

We can think of one dimension of a family as an ongoing conversation about what it means to be that family and what values that family exhibits or desires to exhibit.

When we come to institutions — a corporation or a college, for example — we are on more familiar ground. We can speak more easily of a corporate culture and of a corporation having the dimension of an ongoing conversation about meaning, value, and purpose.

When we expand the scope to nation-states, the notion of culture or collective ways of understanding and responding is already in place. We speak of worldviews and the values that flow from them.

Expand the scope still further to think of the planet itself situated in the universe. What sort of basic conversation or cultural story or basic paradigm are we living in at the present time? How do we think in the most basic way about the planet and all the beings who share it, all beings that co-create the conditions for life on the planet? Are we living at a time that is between stories, between basic paradigms, concerning how to dwell in sustainable ways on the planet?

More of this later. For now, I wish to introduce a simplified form of what I elsewhere have called domains.[8] Think of the interpersonal domain and the institutional domain and the planetary domain. Think of each as not only an organized group of beings but also a fundamental conversation. Then we can point out the following:

the **planetary domain** (nested in cosmic unfolding) — with
our collective conversation (worldview) by which we give our
planetary life meaning, value, and purpose.
Some worldviews are small-minded and destructive;
others are larger-minded and constructive.

the **institutional (corporate) domain** — with
our corporate conversations (corporate cultures), which give our
organizational life meaning, value, and purpose.
Some corporate conversations are small-minded and destructive;
others are larger-minded and constructive.

the **interpersonal (one-on-one) domain** — with
our conversations (interpersonal culture), which give our
relational life meaning, value, and purpose.
Some interpersonal conversations are small-minded and destructive;
others are larger-minded and constructive.

I claim that when we are awake and alert we have a choice, a choice relative to each domain: first, to recognize where our planetary or corporate or interpersonal stories are too small to live in; then to shift to larger-minded conversations which bring less surplus suffering and more possibility for our common life.

Later in the book, I will argue that our widest planetary paradigm is more and more being revealed as unsustainable. The conversation we and much of the world dwell in is too small to be viable. In other words, we are between paradigms, moving from a modern, basically industrial way of understanding and responding, toward a more ecological way of understanding and responding. Our widest meaning and value system colors corporate culture and interpersonal culture. Hence, in each domain or context, we do well to become aware of what stories we are generating and reinforcing, and to what extent they truly serve our common life.

All this will become clearer as we proceed. Here we are working with the notions of small-minded and larger-minded conversations. As a preview of the next chapter, I want to mention that *large-minded conversations center on what is good for the whole and fair to the participant parts*. Thus, large-minded conversations center on what joins us together. They open the way for recovering oneness in all our relational contexts. This is the point I wish to consider next: how large mind reveals interconnection.

When we recognize small mind and shift to larger mind, we *move from one state of consciousness to another*. This is what poet Robert Bly calls "vertical thinking."[9] The spiritual traditions speak of a path from delusion to reality, from separation to oneness. My way of speaking of this vertical dimension is with a Lake Analogy.[10] Small mind and larger mind are only a start. The spiritual traditions enumerate more states of consciousness than these two. The Lake Analogy gives a glimpse of what lies ahead.

LIVING BEYOND LANGUAGE: THE ANALOGY OF THE LAKE

Imagine a lake with three levels — surface, mid-level, and the deepest level. Let these three levels symbolize three ways of understanding and responding: a surface way; a deeper, more observing way; and the deepest level of seeing and being.[11] Let us imagine a process of deepening, and think of this process as a story in three stages.

1. At the Surface of the Lake — A Conventional Way of Grasping What is Meaningful and Valuable

Imagine that you are a center of awareness coming from the great unknown. As in a dream, you float down from great heights until you hover above a lake in the midst of a primal forest. The day is bright, the sun warm, the surface sparkles in the sunlight. In an instant, the center-of-consciousness-that-you-are becomes a ripple on the lake's surface.

Forgetful of all that went before, you identify yourself as a ripple, thinking ripple thoughts, feeling ripple emotions, engaging in ripple conversations with yourself and with others. Your ripple conversations, in large part, *focus on you* — on what you want now, on what you fear, here and now. Your ripple conversations, in large part, *focus on how you compare with others.* As a ripple, you think: "How am I doing compared to others — to her and to him and to them?" You find yourself thinking how much better off you are than these other ripples over on your left. Or you find yourself thinking how inadequate you feel compared to those other ripples over on your right. Your ripple world is filled with desire for what you like, and fear of what you dislike. Furthermore, you identify with the ripple conversations; you dwell within these conversations of comparison, of likes and dislikes. So identified, you do not notice what you are thinking and saying; you do not realize how your fears and desires shape you and your world. You are asleep in your life, on automatic pilot. You have no space for choice between stimulus and response.

This surface way of understanding and responding to life is a *literal* mode of comprehension. (Material things seem most real, and life is about gaining such things, thereby winning esteem and power.) It is a very *me-centered* way of relating. (How will I be affected? Will I be rewarded or punished, praised or blamed?) It is *highly moralistic.* (Certain things are good and to be done. Certain things are bad and not to be done. People who do as we try to do are good people, and people who act otherwise are bad.) It tends to *dualistic and oppositional* thinking. (Either-Or, Black vs. White, Us vs. Them, Right vs. Wrong, Justified vs. Blamed). It is *unaware* of its own part in generating the stories and generating the emotions; meanings and values appear to be independent of me and imposed on me.

When we dwell in surface thinking we are doubly ignorant: ignorant of what is deeply true and good and beautiful, and ignorant of being ignorant. We think that we are awake and realistic and in control of our world, yet we are mistaken. The place to begin our journey of awakening, the great traditions tell us, is to recognize what is happening on the surface.

2. Halfway Down in the Lake — The Awakening of Our Observing Self

Imagine that even while we continue our "labeling and valuing" at the surface, another part of us descends further into the waters of the lake. Very safely and easily, without fear, this part of us moves about halfway down under the surface. We are under water, and yet, as if by magic, we can breathe easily and comfortably. We can turn in the water like astronauts in weightlessness, and look up through the clear blue waters at the surface illuminated by the sun. As we do, we can observe that other, suffering part of ourselves — our ripple selves on the surface, speaking in ripple ways, reacting in ripple ways, desiring ripple success and fearing ripple failure. We hear our chatter clearly, yet with a compassionate heart. We love *the little us* that twists and turns on the ripple stage, performing for self and others according to the ripple rules. Poor ripple, there we go again, telling that story, worrying about how others see us, trying so hard to be liked.

Who is this part of us that watches without judgment, that observes from a compassionate heart? We have called it the large-minded person-in-us.[12] We have called it the Observing or Witness Self. The awakening of this large mind and compassionate heart is the first step in any spiritual path. From this mode of consciousness, we can see that we are partial, asleep, enslaved, and reactive. With this awareness, we can become more whole, more wakeful, freer, and more able to choose our responses.

3. At the Depth of the Lake — A Glimpse of Oneness

At the midpoint we begin to feel an attraction to the depth, the All. Let us suppose that a part of us descends farther down, into the deepest regions of the lake.

Initially it is dark. We are guided not by our sight, but by hearing and bodily senses. We hear and sense a deeper dimension — as if the lake is connected to the great ocean, as if the longer rhythms of the tides provide a sense of timeless time. Listening deepens to touch the silence before sound. As we grow acclimated to this new way of living, we realize that all of the water is one — ripples and depth — and *we are that.* We are the surface conversations; we are the observing, listening, compassionate heart; and we are everything else. In fact, the "all that we are" and "the All that is" are resonating together. "Not one, not two," as the Buddhists say. At this moment, at the deepest level of understanding, all is loving-kindness and joy and gratitude and immense compassion. Here we experience what mystics call unitive consciousness.

As the Sufis might say, when we polish the mirror of the heart, we begin to feel an attraction to the depth, to the All. Here we move beyond language, a place where Lover and Love and the Beloved are mysteriously dancing and there is only the dance. We experience the grace of Oneness Itself arising in and through and around us. Yet, paradoxically, we are never more ourselves than in the Oneness, uniquely mirroring *all that is* from our unique place in the whole.

4. The Way Down and the Way Up

In all the great traditions, the issue is not mystical experience for its own sake. The aim is to live a life of increasing gratefulness, increasing "presence" wherein love can blossom into service. No matter how deeply we descend, we must return to the community, to the partnerships of our lives, with more wisdom and compassion.

In this story we descend to contact the Oneness, and then we return with a fuller observer to the level of the everyday. In the Zen tradition we return to the marketplace with a different awareness. We bestow blessings simply by remembering the oneness in all beings and in all we do. The commentary accompanying the tenth of the famous Zen Ox Herding pictures describes how such persons look and act after realizing the oneness. "Even the wise cannot find [such persons].... They go their way, making no attempt to follow the steps of earlier sages. Carrying a gourd, they stroll into the market; leaning on a staff, they return home. They lead innkeepers and fishmongers in the Way...."[13]

In Part Two of this book, we shall explore further how to bring the oneness into everyday life. Yet already, we have begun to remember oneness and practice partnership. The Lake Analogy widens the picture considerably, showing us that large mind is connected to the oneness itself. The Lake Analogy shows us that large mind-and-heart, the observing self, exists between the surface and the depth.

In Taoist and sometimes Zen traditions, all that we see or

touch or sense is given the name "the ten thousand things." One of the Zen Masters, Seng-Ts'an, reminds us how to relate to the ten thousand things. He says:

> *When the ten thousand things*
> *are viewed in their oneness,*
> *we return to the Origin*
> *and remain where we have always been.*[14]

May it be so for us, who are both travelers and already home. We dwell at the threshold of time and the timeless.

References

1. Rumi, "The Jar with the Dry Rim," trans. Coleman Barks in Robert Bly (ed.), *The Soul Is Here for Its Own Joy* (Hopewell, NJ: The Ecco Press, 1995), p. 236.

2. The phrase is that of Jean Gebser. See his *The Ever-Present Origin,* trans. Noel Barstad with Algis Mickunas (Athens, Ohio: Ohio University Press, rev. ed. 1991).

3. In my shorthand, we can say that there are many WURTS for every WHAT.

4. In my shorthand, we can say that WURTs are expressed in WORDS and establish WORLDS. The "U" of understanding points to the aspect of meaning. The "R" of response points to the emotions — liking or disliking, valuing or disvaluing. WORLDS are defined as what we take to be meaningful and valuable —again, the same two aspects.

5. See Stephen R. Covey, *The Seven Habits of Highly Effective People* (New York: Simon & Schuster, 1989), p. 78. For adapting these insights into my framework, see appendix I.

6. Again, WURTs expressed in WORDS become WORLDS — especially when widely shared.

7. For excellent insights on this process, especially as it occurs in institutions, see Peter L. Berger and Thomas Luckmann, *The Social Construction of Reality: A Treatise in the Sociology of Knowledge* (Garden City, NY: Doubleday & Co. Anchor Book, 1967).

8. For more on the domains, see my *To Come to Life More Fully* (Columbia, MD: Traditional Acupuncture Institute, 1990). There, I distinguish seven domains — the personal, the interpersonal, the familial, the institutional, the cultural (basic epochal paradigm), the planetary, and the sphere of mystery. Here, I both simplify the number of domains and emphasize that each domain has a meaning and value dimension — or, in light of the discussion in this chapter, a conversational/cultural dimension.

9. See Robert Bly, *The Sibling Society* (New York: Addison-Wesley Publishing Co., 1996), chapter 14, pp. 208-218.

10. For an earlier draft of this analogy, see John G. Sullivan, *To Come to Life More Fully* (Columbia, MD: Traditional Acupuncture Institute, 1990), pp. 197-200. I adapt the analogy from Arthur J. Deikman, *The Observing Self* (Boston: Beacon Press, 1982), pp. 103-104.

11. Those who like the "WURT formulation" might think of the three levels as WURT "Y" (a surface way), WURT "Z" (a deeper, more observing way), and WURT Omega (the deepest level of seeing and being — a oneness with the all).

12. Those who prefer the "WURT formulation" may think of the letter Y in WURT-Y as itself a symbol of the "horns of a dilemma" (either-or, oppositional) thinking. Call the Observing Self "WURT-Z." (In drawing the letter Z itself, we can see a movement from the surface: the horizontal line at the top, moving down the diagonal to another level — the horizontal line at the bottom of the Z.) To "go to Z" is to awaken the observer in us, to see and be from this larger sense of self. Only from WURT-Z do we begin to understand more adequately what I have called the "Four Beginnings."

13. Philip Kapleau, *The Three Pillars of Zen* (Boston: Beacon Press, 1967), p. 311. Modified for inclusive language.

14. Quoted in Nancy Wilson Ross, *The World of Zen* (New York: Random House Vintage Books, 1960), p. 271. See also Frederick Franck, *Echoes from the Bottomless Well* (New York: Random House Vintage, 1985), p. 91.

CHAPTER FOUR

Ethics as a Way

Seek what is
good for the whole
and
fair to each participant-part

The path of transformation begins with practice. Practice begins with the Wisdom Chant:

There are at least TWO ways to relate to anything —
a small-minded way and a large-minded way.
Choose large mind.

The process of transformation is not value-neutral. The process is value-driven from the start, asserting that some ways of living are more worthy than others — for example, to enact kindness over cruelty, reconciliation over revenge, respect over prejudice, justice over exploitation, love over hate.

How can we tell good practice from bad, constructive actions from destructive ones? Here is where ethical criteria are needed — criteria open to revision, yet sufficiently grounded in the nature of living systems to give effective guidance. Wherever we speak of growth and deepening, we are in the terrain of the normative, the ethical. We can enter this land in a cultural trance, or we can bring to light the assumptions we are already using and take their measure.

In fact, we are not entering the realm of ethics and value for the first time. We have been in this realm all along. The very notions of small mind and large mind are normative ones, carrying clear value criteria as I use them. Thus, a small-minded way of relating or a small-minded conversation is one that promotes unnecessary suffering and reduces creative possibility for our common life. A large-minded way of relating or a large-minded conversation is one that reduces unnecessary suffering and promotes creative possibility for our common life.

In the introduction I proposed the following mission for a revitalized ethics:

To come to life more fully
so as to act more wisely and more effectively,
to reduce unnecessary suffering, and
to promote creative possibilities for our common life.

"Reducing suffering and promoting possibility for our common life" — this provides our first ethical criterion. Furthermore, we can expand the last phrase, "our common life." I would say that care for our common life involves seeking "what is good for the whole and fair to the participant-parts." This provides a second intertwined ethical criterion.

Wholes and parts. As seen in the last chapter, wholes stretch from the interpersonal through the institutional to the interconnectedness of life on the planet, what the Zen master Thich Nhat Hanh calls "interbeing."[1] Transformation is not complete unless and until it seeks *what is good for wholes of various sizes* — interpersonal to planetary. Transformation is not complete unless and until it looks to *what is fair to all the participants involved.* In the planetary context, the participants include the human ones and all the other beings that co-inhabit our world. Thus, the scope of ethics is as wide and deep as the wholes and parts that make up our world.[2]

Explicit ethical criteria are needed now more than ever as we stand at a crucial juncture in world history. Our most widely-shared paradigm influences the corporate culture of our key institutions, and it filters down to how we see ourselves and our relationships. *We are standing between worldviews.* The modern worldview began to crystallize in the Renaissance and grew to full strength in the last century. Despite having gained much from this modern, industrial worldview, we are now seeing its destructiveness "writ large." Given our world population and our advanced technology, we see that following the logic of our reigning paradigm is relentlessly "turning global village into global pillage." In 1994, David Orr made the point in an especially striking way:

> If today is a typical day on planet earth, we will lose 116 square miles of rain forest, or about an acre a second. We will lose another 72 square miles to encroaching deserts, the results of human mismanagement and overpopulation. We will lose 40 to 250 species, and no one knows whether the number is 40 or 250. Today the human population will increase by 250,000. And today we will add 2,700 tons of chlorofluorocarbons and 15 million tons of carbon dioxide to the atmosphere. Tonight the earth will be a little hotter, its waters more acidic and the fabric of life more threadbare. By year's end the numbers are staggering: The total loss of rain forest will equal an area the size of the state of Washington; expanding deserts will equal an area the size of the state of West Virginia; and the global population will have risen by more than 90,000,000.[3]

A decade later, the picture has not markedly improved.[4]

Our behavior flows with a clear logic from fundamental principles embedded in our reigning paradigm or worldview. For example, if global business operates on the sole imperative to "maximize short-term profits for shareholders alone," the results will be global pillage indeed. A number of businesses are aware of this consequence and realize that transformation with an ethical compass calls for reversal of this state of affairs — moving from a "short-term" to a "longer-term" perspective, expanding what counts as "profits," and broadening "shareholders" to a much larger sense of "stakeholders." Indeed, to envision a sustainable and perhaps regenerative future calls us explicitly to invoke ethical criteria to measure what we do. It calls us, for example, to deepen our understanding of what is Good for the

Whole and Fair to the Participant-parts, applying that measure to the global worldview, to institutional culture, and to interpersonal ways of constructing who we are.[5] The challenge is immense; the timing is urgent. Quite literally, our lives depend upon it.[6]

Yet before proceeding, we need to continue revisioning ethics, the reason being that ethics presently has a bad name. To many it stands for restraint, often dogmatically imposed without appeal to reason or evidence or defensible value criteria. Even where ethics is seen as being in service of bettering our common life and hence presenting vision or ideals to live by, ethics can seem either too little or too much for our tastes. To rehabilitate ethics as a dimension of transformation, a story must be told. To some extent, this story echoes what we learned in our recent visit to the Analogy of the Lake.

Key Distinctions: The Three Houses

We are working at the intersection of ethics and spirituality. Looking at that intersection under the aspect of ethics, we can distinguish the Pre-ethical, the Ethical (in at least two modes), and the Trans-ethical.[7]

1. The First House — the Pre-ethical

Here we are in a place where, in Thomas Hobbes's words, life appears as "solitary, poor, nasty, brutish and short."[8] Here, people appear as barbarians; life is perceived as "under threat." In such a situation and mode of understanding, one group assaults another group and we encounter "violence writ large." Think of the murder, rape, pillaging and burning in East Timor. Or the obscene "ethnic cleansing" in Bosnia and Kosovo. Think of the Nazi death camps or the Russian gulags. Such situations are pre-ethical in their insensitivity and cruelty. In this first house, when you think of ethics, you yearn for basic order and minimal decency. Imagine that you are about to be mugged. You want your assailant to stop. Outer conduct is good enough. If the assailant runs away because he mistakenly thinks aid is at hand, if he stops because he is afraid of punishment, well...you are relieved and ask no more.

2. The Second House — the Ethical

Here we start with fundamental decency — an *ethics of minimal duties.* In entering the second house, we perceive that good outward behavior is largely assured. Yet we begin to realize that such behavior is not enough, especially when that outward behavior is motivated solely by extrinsic factors — such as reward and punishment, praise, and blame. Conformity based solely on *what is imposed from without* will vanish like the mist when authority is elsewhere. When the cat's away, the mice will play. So in the second house, we seek more.

The second house brings mind and heart into the picture. The next step is to see the point and purpose of certain patterns of life — to learn what helps persons and communities to flourish and what does not. The next step unfolds an *ethics of aspiration.* Here, moral imagination expands, empathy and compassion are fostered, mind and heart are respected. We learn to be open to reason and evidence, willing to accept feedback and revise our views when needed. Here, care increasingly enters. We cultivate what is good for the whole and fair to the participant parts. We extend our circle of care, acting to reduce surplus suffering and promote creative possibility for our common life. Our embodied attitudes and actions are grounded in insights regarding the true nature of things. We see ethics as reminding us of the best conditions (as we thus far understand them) for life among others.

3. The Third House — the Trans-ethical

In the third house, there is mysticism, a total experience of oneness. When one is in deep mystical experience, all distinctions fade. In this context, ethics disappears because others disappear. In this house, we hear the poem of Rumi:

> *There is a field beyond right and wrong.*
> *Let's meet there.*
> *When the soul lies down in that grass,*
> *the world is too full to talk about.*
> *Ideas, language, even the phrase each other*
> *doesn't make any sense.*[9]

From the vantage point of mysticism, ethics can be seen as a second or third best. Lao Tzu and Chuang Tzu critique ethics from the stance of the mystic.[10] Yet the Buddhist Eightfold Path includes the ethical with the meditative. The Sufis remind us, "You cannot find God by seeking, but only the seekers find him." Ethical cultivation is a needed foundation of mysticism. When the mystic returns to life among others, ethics also returns — to give us ways to check the authenticity of so-called "masters," to help us remember when we forget.

Three houses: the house of the pre-ethical and, in a sense, the prehuman.

the house of the ethical, the house of the human in its becoming

the house of the trans-ethical and, in a sense, the trans-human

With all of this said, let us return to the ethical.

ETHICS FROM A WESTERN PERSPECTIVE: MINIMAL ETHICS vs. ETHICS OF ASPIRATION

I suggest we use a traffic light model to gain a sense of minimal ethics, and then, of a fuller ethics. Imagine a traffic light tipped onto its side. We have three circles in three familiar colors:

As children know, RED says "Stop!" Think of the RED as reminding us of *what is good for the whole* — but in a minimal way. Think of red as blood and blood as a reminder of harm. Think of it as a signal to avoid or reduce the harm to the whole. "At least, do no harm," the Hippocratic oath reminds physicians. RED reminds us to stop and remember that acts and policies have consequences.[11] In assessing their consequences, RED asks us to reduce harm to the whole.

As children know, GOLD says "Caution!" Think of the GOLD as reminding us of *what is fair to the participant-parts* — but in a minimal way. Live by the gold of the Golden Rule — at least in its minimum version. The great Rabbi Hillel uses the negative (or "do not") version of the Golden Rule when saying, "Do not do to others what you would not have them do to you. The rest is commentary. (Now read the commentary.)" Do not demean people. Do not treat beings of worth as if they were things to be used. In other words, avoid or reduce golden rule unfairness.[12]

As children know, GREEN says "Go!" Think of the GREEN as reminding us to take responsibility for our actions — at least minimal responsibility. Responsibility in a minimal sense means recognizing that we, as adults, act *knowingly* and *willingly* and, when our actions cause harm to the whole or unfairness to parts, we must *own up to that fact.* In other words, we agree to be held accountable for what we do. Such a view of ethics, which includes an interior side — knowing and willing — alters how we view a person's blameworthiness. Whatever diminishes our knowledge (e.g., ignorance or deception) can diminish our responsibility. Whatever diminishes our freedom to choose (e.g., force or threat of force) can diminish our responsibility. The green of minimal ethics requires us to take at least minimal responsibility for our actions.[13]

Thus, an Ethics of Minimal Duties viewed on the traffic light model looks like this:

RED of BLOOD, of HARM	GOLD of GOLDEN RULE UNFAIRNESS / FAIRNESS	GREEN of MINIMAL RESPONSIBILITY
RED	GOLD	GREEN
at least, do no harm	at least, do not demean	at least, do not evade responsibility
Reminder that **Actions have CONSEQUENCES**	Reminder that **Persons and other beings with intrinsic worth have RIGHTS**	Reminder that **PEOPLE BEAR RESPONSIBILITY**

The "traffic light" analogy helps us recognize the dimension of the ethical, thus aiding us to make wiser ethical decisions. For a taste of this process, see appendix VIII, "Six-Step Model for Ethical Policy Decision Making," and appendix IX, "Ethics and the Tradition."

The story in the House of Ethics is one of development. First, norms are seen as imposed from without and as emphasizing what NOT to do. In small-minded ways of thinking and acting, an individual orients to rules in reward/punishment, praise/blame fashion. When I am in this mode of thinking, I orient to the rules in terms of their effect on me; I see norms in terms of how they help or harm me.

Gradually I come to understand that I am not the center of the world; I exist in the midst of others who are themselves centers of worth. Furthermore, we share meaning and value and purposes. We overlap in interests and concerns, overlap in what we consider meaningful and valuable. We are individuals and embedduals,[14] embedded in friendships and family relationships, dwelling within institutions and other forms of organized life, a part of the web of all life on the planet — partly sharing and partly diverging in our meaning-making and value-generating.

As we advance to moral maturity, we internalize to various degrees what was earlier external only. At best, we begin to explore the point and purpose of the norms we inherit. With teaching and luck, we grasp ethical criteria and then measure the inherited rules and rights in terms of these criteria. For example, does such and such a rule truly reduce unnecessary suffering and promote possibility for our common life? Is such and such a norm good for the whole and fair to the participant parts? Some inherited rules we set aside; others we recommit to — not because others tell us to, but because we have found that they have a basis in what serves the community and is fair to all participants. We come to see more and more what cultivates compassionate and respectful living among others. We tend to anchor our norms in the nature of things — the nature of community and the nature of persons. This, of course, gives criteria for judgment and revision of judgment.

One of the great women saints of Islam, Rabbia, said, "I refuse to serve my lord as a laborer seeking his wage." Here is a wonderful example of going from external to intrinsic norms, going beyond reward/punishment, beyond praise and blame thinking. Surely, there is a breakthrough here — to ethics as a way, on the way to further deepening. Once we pass this threshold, we enter what I am calling an Ethics of Aspiration.[15] To understand the further possibilities, let us return to the traffic light in a more pastel coloring — a softer red, gold, and green.

Again, the RED and GOLD are going to direct us to what is good for the whole and what is fair to the participant parts. Yet here, I go beyond the minimum. I begin to identify with the units larger than myself — my one-to-one relationships and the corporate systems within which I dwell. I come to care for them and wish to maintain and enhance them. I am my relationships. I am in them and they are in me. On the institutional plane, I am, for example, the university I serve as professor. I am in that university and it is in me. More widely still, I identify myself with the Great Family — all humankind and all in the plant and animal kingdoms — all my kin who make up the web of life. I am in this web of interconnection and it is in me.

Think of a softer RED — the RED of awakened heart, the heart of each community or communion in which I dwell. In an ethics of aspiration, I ask: How can I, with others, be of service to the various communities in which I live and breathe and have my being? How can I, with others, awaken the heart of each community and call it to its deep roots and its expanded possibilities?

Think of a softer GOLD — the gold of the deep nature of each being, the gold of each person or animal or plant. In an ethics of aspiration, I ask: How can I, with others, respect and honor the unique contribution of each being I encounter in the dynamic web of life? How can I, with others, listen to the deep gift of each form of life that comes to me? Let us ask not "What is wrong? How can I fix it?" Rather, let us ask "What is possible here and now? How can we co-create it?"[16]

Think of a softer GREEN — the green of responsibility as response-ability, the ability to choose my response. Think of the green as commitment to the practice of living large. In an older frame, this would be seen as developing the virtues — developing loving, compassionate, and wise attitudes and actions. Here, green calls us to become a deeper person, to become a practitioner for life in two senses — to act for the sake of the widest and deepest understanding of life, and to practice doing this for a lifetime.

Thus, an Ethics of Aspiration viewed on the traffic light model looks like this:

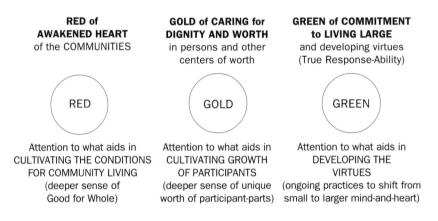

RED of AWAKENED HEART of the COMMUNITIES	GOLD of CARING for DIGNITY AND WORTH in persons and other centers of worth	GREEN of COMMITMENT to LIVING LARGE and developing virtues (True Response-Ability)
RED	GOLD	GREEN
Attention to what aids in CULTIVATING THE CONDITIONS FOR COMMUNITY LIVING (deeper sense of Good for Whole)	Attention to what aids in CULTIVATING GROWTH OF PARTICIPANTS (deeper sense of unique worth of participant-parts)	Attention to what aids in DEVELOPING THE VIRTUES (ongoing practices to shift from small to larger mind-and-heart)

A few words on the shifts that are involved: In moving to an ethics of aspiration, external compulsion fades and we see what serves in the nature of things. Alastaire McIntyre notes the shift with an example, which I will render in my own words.[17] Suppose you are a chess master and have a niece and nephew in whom you sense a hidden talent for chess. To encourage them, you say, "I will give you five dollars if you will play chess with me, and another five dollars if you win. Furthermore, I will play at a level that will make it possible (though not a sure thing) for you to win." Thus far, the motivation is external or extrinsic to the task. Imagine time passing and your nephew and niece coming to love the game more and more. Now the center of gravity for their motivation shifts to the game itself — the nature of the game, the great moves, etc. So too, our reference shifts when we develop what the ancients called "virtues" — good habits of mind and heart that issue in good actions. We focus more and more on the nature of communities and the nature of the participants that make up those communities. This is part of "coming to life more fully so as to act more wisely and more effectively."

The ancients also knew that virtue at its highest had an effortless quality about it and a joyousness. To cultivate what connects us, and to provide aid to persons and other forms of life so they can flourish — how wonderful. And for those who arrive at this point (even for moments), it becomes paradoxically "nothing special" — simply what humans do when they are at their best!

Let me summarize two aspects of the movement from minimal ethics to an ethics of aspiration.

First we move from *extrinsic motivators* (reward/punishment, praise and blame) to *intrinsic guides*. By "intrinsic guides," I mean criteria such as what is good for the whole and fair to the participant parts. Such criteria encourage us to investigate the nature of things, especially the nature of wholes and parts, communities and the participants in them. Such criteria invite us to investigate what allows communities, organizations, etc., to flourish, and to investigate what allows persons (and even other centers of worth) to flourish. The move from extrinsic motivators to intrinsic guides allows for an ethics that is revisable — one that is called to shift in accord with our own and our fellow humans' growing understanding.

Second, we move *from "me" to "we"* as we heed the call to participate in and take responsibility for units larger than ourselves. This means "owning" our relationships as part of who we are, "owning" our organized enterprises as part of who we are, "owning" our place on the planet as part of who we are. I am reminded of an experience at a meeting: A newcomer to the group often prefaced his remarks with "This is what you ought to do." A friend asked him, "What is this 'what YOU should do'? Aren't we together in this?" Little by little, the new member's language shifted. "This," he came to say quite naturally, "is what we should do."[18]

Extrinsic to intrinsic guides. Outsider to insider point of view. These two movements belong together.[19]

Here we are at the edge of the ethical where it is moving toward the trans-ethical. This terrain we shall explore in Part

Two. Before that, however, I want to share the same basic movement in a different framework — one that aids us in moving from a linear model to a cyclical or spiral one.

ETHICS FROM AN EASTERN PERSPECTIVE

Consider first the symbol of yin-yang:

Yin-Yang Symbol

YANG

Upward
and
Outward
Movement

YIN

Downward
and
Inward
Movement

The yin side is dark like nighttime, yet there is a dot of light; the movement is descending, moving downward and inward. The yang side is light like daytime, yet there is a dot of darkness; the movement is rising, moving upward and outward. In a 24-hour day, evening into night is yin; morning into day is yang. In a year, autumn and winter are yin; spring and summer are yang. Both polarities are needed as in breathing in (yin) and breathing out (yang).

Next, let us turn to the Three Phases of the Buddhist Eightfold Path and overlay them on the yin-yang symbol, as below.

Three Phases of the Eightfold Path

CONDUCT PHASE
(In Sanskrit, *Sila* Phase)

MEDITATION PHASE
(In Sanskrit, *Samadhi* Phase)

INSIGHT/RESOLVE PHASE
The Insight/Resolve Phase
or Knowing/Loving Phase
deepens into a Phase of
Wisdom/Compassion
(In Sanskrit, *Prajna/Karuna* Phase)

In fact, the Eightfold Path is best seen as ongoing and hence a spiral path — starting with a phase of insight and resolve, then entering into the phase of ethical action (the yang or "breathing out" phase), and then into the phase of meditative deepening (the yin or "breathing in" phase).

At each turn, we gain deeper insights and are inspired to live them out. From insight and resolve, we move naturally into the conduct phase. In other words, we move out into action in the world. We seek to act more wisely and more effectively for the sake of aiding our own and others' spiritual deepening. Because we are attuned to the Way, outward action prompts inward reflection. We enter into the meditative phase, returning to ourself and our source. This prompts new insights and expands our hearts, inviting us again to act in the world in wiser and more compassionate ways. And the cycles continue.

Here is a chant to help us remember the Eightfold Path:

Knowing, loving — here we go now	steps 1 & 2 *insight/resolve phase* (moving to wisdom/compassion)
Speaking, acting, right vocation	steps 3,4,5 (yang) *conduct or ethics phase*
Steady, mindful, concentration	steps 6,7,8 (yin) *meditation phase*

— Repeat, again and again —

The *insight/resolve phase* has an aspect of knowing/realizing, and an aspect of committing to a larger way — one, I would say, that seeks what is good for the whole and fair to the participant-parts. At its highest and deepest, wise understanding (prajna) is wedded to compassionate caring (karuna).

The *ethical or conduct phase* focuses on how we speak and act and make our living and life.

The *meditation phase* focuses on being steady in daily practice — on stilling the small mind within us and invoking the observing self; on living more and more mindfully, in contact with the Great Mystery as Source and Goal.

In early turns of the wheel, we are moving — in a larger sense
— *from the pre-ethical to the more fully ethical.* Thus, at the start,
the *insight* might be that all is not well, that I am suffering and
causing suffering — that, perhaps, I am addicted and have no
freedom. The resolve may be to undertake a program of recovery
— say, a Twelve Step Program.[20]

The ethical action steps include *speaking* about what is
happening in a different way: confessing the state I am in and the
harm I have caused and am causing; acknowledging (to myself
and others) that I have a problem; admitting that I cannot handle
this problem on my own, that I need help; asking for such help.
The *actions* include inventorying my life: allowing true sorrow
and remorse to have voice; asking forgiveness of those I have
harmed; making amends where possible. The *right vocation* or
right livelihood involves seriously looking at the work I do and
how I do it, making sure that my way of earning a living does not
conflict with my work of recovery. If I am an alcoholic, I may
need to change my profession from being a bartender. I might
also have to change my patterns of relaxing — where I go and
the persons I go with.

The meditative steps introduce steady, ongoing practices to
remember my insight and strengthen my resolve — meditation,
prayer, spiritual reading, reflective journaling, etc. I also am
invited to find ways to support others and to be supported in
stabilizing a new life.

In the middle turns of the wheel, we are moving *within the
ethical* — moving, as I would say, from a minimal ethics to an
ethics of aspiration.

Consider the *insight/resolve phase.* Here, the phase of insight
and resolve flows out of ongoing practice such as this book
recommends: deepening what it means to dwell in interconnection;
bringing more understanding and more compassion to each
encounter; staying rooted in the present and remembering the
source; aligning to wider purposes and shared responsibility. All of
this begins with practice — with distinguishing in the moment
between small mind and larger mind-and-heart, and choosing large

mind again and again. Such practice changes situations and changes the practitioner. Practice deepens into a path with a heart — a way of thinking and feeling and acting more wisely, with gratitude and loving kindness, with compassion, balance, and joy.

As an example, think of a particular friendship. The whole is the friendship moving through time. You and your friend are the participants. You gain insight into this friendship — insight into what makes this friendship flourish, what keeps it healthy, and what tends to put it into dis-ease; insight into how to tend this unique friendship; and insight into the unique natures of the parties within it. What am I learning about friendship and about myself as friend and the other as friend in this relational field? On the basis of a growing understanding, what commitments am I called to undertake — commitments that move me from extrinsic motivators to intrinsic guides, and from an outsider to a participant point of view? In a general way, both parties in the friendship are called to practice a way of living large.

Consider next the *conduct phase:* "speaking, acting, right vocation." In speaking, we might emphasize what connects us. We might learn to "think friendship first and then you and me." We might speak in ways that keep in mind the mission and values of the friendship. In acting, we might more and more take responsibility for our own actions as they affect the friendship and the people in it. In shifting our way of living, we might notice more and more when we are coming from unity and sufficiency and when we are coming from separation and scarcity.

Consider last the *meditation* phase: "steady, mindful concentration." Here, we seek to put in place daily practices that keep us awake and alert. Here, we seek to become more attentive to what we say and do, how it is received by the other, and how all of that strengthens or weakens relational bonds. As we come more and more from the source, we see how this friendship is embedded in wider and wider circles of life. We develop reflective practices "to come to life more fully so as to act more wisely and more effectively — to reduce unnecessary suffering and to promote creative possibility for our common life."

All of this, as a friend and colleague says, is not a "one-walk dog."[21] Having a dog in a city means walking the dog each day.

So moving from minimal to aspirational ethics is not a "one-walk dog." Part Three offers specific practices to sustain this advance on a daily basis.

CONCLUDING COMMENTS

Aspirational ethics leads us to the door of the third "house" — the trans-ethical. We shall enter that house in Part Two. Before we do, let us consider a comparison offered by therapist and Zen teacher David Brazier — a comparison worth considering as we climb the mountain of aspirational ethics and look over the valley toward the mountain of spirituality. He claims to be contrasting Western ethics and Zen Buddhist ethics. I believe that he is closer to contrasting two stages in ethical development. Here is how he puts it:[22]

WESTERN ETHICS	ZEN BUDDHIST ETHICS
Tends to see individuals as selfish and in need of restraint for sake of social living	Tends to look to ethics as a part of a practice and a path that is liberative
Often appears as restrictions imposed from without	Tends to see the precepts as integral to the path — perhaps even as revealing how the bodhisattva lives (Think how one with spiritual depth lives.)

True, ethics in the West appears restrictive and extrinsic, but this is only in the first stages of ethical development. A deeper way to look at Western ethics is to see how people can internalize both the conduct and the reasons for the conduct, how they can move from a minimal ethics to an aspirational one.

Think of it in this way: When I do not know who I am, I tend to manipulate you. When I wake up to the fact that (as the Buddhists might say) we are "not one, not two," then I serve what joins us together and you and myself. Furthermore, I do this with dignity and joy and a sense of humor. Liberated by the real for service to the real, I am at home in the world, engaged in the dance, grateful and celebrating life. At this stage, I am open to a still larger context. Some call it the trans-ethical, others "the higher reaches of ethical living."[23] We shall simply name it "spirituality."

References

1. See Thich Nhat Hanh, *Interbeing: Fourteen Guidelines for Engaged Buddhism,* third edition (Berkeley, CA: Parallax Press, 1998). Also see his *The Heart of Understanding* (Berkeley, CA: Parallax Press, 1988).

2. As we shift into the emerging ecological paradigm — as we come from inter-connection and see in a more relational manner — we will become aware in a new way of wholes and parts. See Peter Senge, C. Otto Scharmer, Joseph Jaworski, Betty Sue Flowers, *Presence: Human Purpose and the Field of the Future* (Cambridge, MA: Society for Organizational Learning, 2004). They write: "For Goethe, the whole was something dynamic and living that continually comes into being 'in concrete manifestations.' A part, in turn, was a manifestation of the whole, rather than just a component of it. Neither exists without the other. The whole exists through continually manifesting in the parts, and the parts exist as embodiments of the whole." p. 4.

3. See David W. Orr, *Earth in Mind: On Education, Environment, and the Human Prospect* (Washington, DC: Island Press, 1994), p. 7.

4. In more recent years, collection and publication of key data has been restricted. Carbon dioxide emissions have increased. Population growth has lessened somewhat, with AIDS and other diseases playing a part. However, other costs are emerging. For example, climate-related deaths and climate-related pressure on insurance companies have increased significantly. (Personal communication with David Orr, Elon University, Oct. 8, 2004)

5. For an example of clear use of ethical criteria to envision and enact a sustainable future, see Karl-Henrik Robèrt, *The Natural Step Story: Seeding a Quiet Revolution* (Gabriola Island, British Columbia, Canada: New Society Publishers, 2002).

6. See Jack Miles, "Global Requiem: The Apocalyptic Moment in Religion, Science, and Art," 50th anniversary keynote address, Cross Currents Consultation, Association for Religion and Intellectual Life. Printed in *Cross Currents,* 50, no. 3 (Fall 2000), pp. 294-309; www.crosscurrents.org/milesrequiem.htm.

7. This distinction of an X and a pre-X, and a post- or trans-X, can be found in Lawrence Kohlberg's work on moral development. See his *Essays on Moral Development. Vol I. The Philosophy of Moral Development: Moral Stage and the Idea of Justice* (San Francisco: Harper and Row, 1981). For Ken Wilber, see any of a range of his books from *The Spectrum of Consciousness* (Wheaton, IL: Quest Books, 1977) and *The Atman Project* (Wheaton, IL: Quest Books, 1980) to such recent works as *The Marriage of Sense and Soul* (New York: Random House, 1998), *Integral Psychology* (Boston: Shambhala, 2000), and *A Theory of Everything* (Boston: Shambhala, 2000).

8. See Thomas Hobbes, *Leviathan,* edited Richard Flathman and David Johnston (New York: WW Norton, 1997). Hobbes wrote the Leviathan in 1651.

9. Here I blend translations of Coleman Barks and Robert Bly.

10. See, for example, Lao Tzu's *Tao Te Ching,* chapters 18, 19, and especially 38.

11. Those familiar with ethical traditions will recognize utilitarian themes here. That acts or policies have consequences, and that such consequences should be assessed by their impact on social utility, are themes associated with Jeremy Bentham and John Stuart Mill, among others. For an introductory survey of these doctrines with critique, see James Rachels, *The Elements of Moral Philosophy,* fourth edition (New York: McGraw-Hill, 2003).

12. Following Kant, I take personhood as the foundation for rights; yet there is more to be said. "Persons have rights" is shorthand only. Other beings certainly have degrees of inwardness, degrees of awareness, sensation and freedom. For example, think especially of whales and dolphins. They too have worth in their own right and do not exist solely to be used by humans. Native peoples saw all beings as having a certain intrinsic worth. So we might say that there are wholes to be respected and parts of wholes to be respected. Bioregions and other ecosystems deserve our respect. These are complex questions dealt with in environmental ethics. Again, see Rachels on Kantian or rights-based ethical systems.

13. Consider a mentally retarded youth who sees neighborhood children playing "cowboys and indians" in a field. Wanting to join in, he sees a handgun lying in the field, picks it up, and shoots a little girl. The death of the innocent girl is a great harm and violation of her rights, yet the boy is not ethically responsible. The classic doctrine (in ethics, and at some points, taken over in law) is that responsibility and hence blameworthiness is a function of acting knowingly and willingly. To the extent that knowledge is lessened by ignorance, deception, fraud, etc., ethical responsibiity is lessened. To the extent that freedom is lessened by coercion, force, etc., ethical responsibility is lessened. To see the contrast, imagine a competent adult who is seeking revenge against a hated rival, and knowingly and willingly with full deliberation kills the same young girl, the granddaughter of his foe. Here, there is ethical responsibility. For more, see discussions on ethical and legal responsibility (culpability) and on informed consent.

14. The term "embeddual" comes from developmental psychologist Robert Kegan. See his *The Evolving Self* (Cambridge, MA: Harvard University Press, 1982), p. 116.

15. The distinction I am making here is different from a distinction between a minimal ethics of duty and an ethics of supererogation. Here, a distinction is made between actions that are prohibited or required in a framework of minimal decency, and actions that are praiseworthy but not required by minimal ethics — acts of heroic virtue. For heroic virtue, think of actions such as jumping into a river to save a drowning child when the risks are high (but not foolishly so) and the chance of success uncertain. My ethics of aspiration does not focus on heroic virtue nor, more generally, on what is "above and beyond duty." My framework goes beyond "duty" in another sense — more qualitative than quantitative. For the use of ethics of aspiration, I am more indebted to the legal philosopher Lon Fuller. See his *The Morality of Law,* revised edition (New Haven, CT: Yale University Press; 1977). Again, I am not drawing the distinction in the way Fuller does.

16. This question arises out of my work with colleagues at Tai Sophia Institute for the Healing Arts. I am not sure who first formulated it. For more on enhancing possibility, see Rosamund Stone Zander and Benjamin Zander, *The Art of Possibility* (Boston: Harvard Business School Press, 2000).

17. See Alastaire McIntyre's classic, *After Virtue,* second edition (Notre Dame, Indiana: University of Notre Dame Press, 1984).

18. For more on the power of this shift, see the above-mentioned *Art of Possibility,* the Twelth Practice, "Telling the WE Story," pp. 181-196.

19. In his later work, Lawrence Kohlberg speaks of "ideal role maintaining" and "ideal system maintaining" perspectives as defining his stages three and four. I prefer "ideal role maintaining and enhancing" and "ideal system maintaining and enhancing" perspectives. In my view, the "ideal" pertains to the criteria: what is good for the whole and fair to each participant-part. For more on Kohlberg's development, see my "Kohlberg's Progress Toward Understanding the Moral Life" (unpublished Ph.D. thesis, University of North Carolina at Chapel Hill, 1982; available University Microfilms, Ann Arbor, Michigan).

20. For more on the Twelve Step Program, see appendix v.

21. I owe the term to Dianne M. Connelly at Tai Sophia Institute for the Healing Arts.

22. See David Brazier, *Zen Therapy* (New York: John Wiley & Sons, 1996). I have put in chart form what Brazier discusses on pages 36 and following.

23. The term "trans-ethical" is a term at home in the thinking of Ken Wilber. The "higher reaches of ethical living" is a phrase used by Roger Walsh in his *Essential Spirituality* (New York: John Wiley & Sons, Inc., 1999). See pp. 143-144.

PART TWO

The Ecological / Spiritual Steps

A Cosmic Context

CHAPTER FIVE

The Great Pattern in Space —
Interbeing and the Impulse to Care

...And I have felt
A presence that disturbs me with the joy
Of elevated thoughts, a sense sublime
Of something far more deeply interfused,
Whose dwelling is the light of setting suns,
And the round ocean and the living air,
And the blue sky, and in the mind of man:
A motion and a spirit that impels
All thinking things, all objects of all thought,
And rolls through all things.[1]

— WILLIAM WORDSWORTH

Begin with the Oneness. Begin with what joins us together. We are both wholes unto ourselves and participant-parts in wider contexts. "Holons" is the word Arthur Koestler invented to speak of realities that are both parts and wholes. We are "holons," relational beings all the way down and up.

Wordsworth writes of "a motion and a spirit that...rolls through all things," and of "the round ocean and the living air." The flowing of water, the invisibility of air — these are images of a subtle force that the ancient Chinese called *ch'i*. The Chinese saw all beings as composed of this dynamic force, flowing like water, subtle and vital like the breath.

The breath of the Earth is the atmosphere. Wherever we are, we are living in a "sea of air," joined in the interchange of breaths. This interchange links us air-breathing animals with the plants and trees which offer oxygen.[2] Poet Gary Snyder captures the grand sweep in his "Prayer for the Great Family." Here, he expresses gratitude to Mother Earth, to Plants, to Air, to Wild Beings, to Water, to the Sun, and to the Great Sky.[3] I shall use the term "The Great Family" to represent all nature, nonliving and living, including the human ones.

While Wordsworth speaks of "a motion and a spirit that...rolls through all things," Chief Seattle speaks of the web of life, saying, "We do not weave the web of life, we are merely a strand in it. Whatever we do to the web, we do to ourselves."[4] Buddhists speak of "mutual co-arising" — the whole and the parts arise together. Indra's net symbolizes this interrelationship of all things:

Far away in the heavenly abode of the great god Indra,
    there is a wonderful net,
a net hung by a cunning artificer in such a manner
    that it stretches out infinitely in all directions.
In accord with the extravagant taste of deities,
    the artificer has hung a single glittering jewel
    in each "eye" of the net.
Since the net is infinite in all dimensions,
    the jewels are infinite in number.
There hang the jewels, glittering like stars of the first magnitude,
    a wonderful sight to behold.
If we now arbitrarily select one of those jewels for inspection
    and look closely at it, we will discover
    that in its polished surface
there are reflected all the other jewels in the net,
    infinite in number.
Furthermore, each of the jewels reflected in this one jewel
    is also reflecting all the other jewels —
an infinite reflecting process ever occurring.[5]

How beautiful! Every jewel reflects the whole from a unique place in the net. In a mysterious way, every jewel reflects every other jewel and is reflected back by them. The whole is in the part and the part is in the whole — deep interconnection, what the modern Zen master Thich Nhat Hanh calls "interbeing."[6]

Native peoples find it natural to dwell in interconnection — in kinship with all beings and the regions in which they dwell. Why do we find it so difficult? What happened to make something once natural now strange?

EXPLORING THE MODERN WORLDVIEW

Somewhere, somehow, we began to live as if we were separate, alone, and in danger.[7]

–KABIR EDMUND HELMINSKI

Somewhere, somehow, our culture began to live as if we humans were separate, alone, and in danger.

When did that happen? In the West, some 500 years ago — let us say around 1500 CE, at the beginning of the modern world. Think of the rise of modern philosophy and science. Think of the movements toward democracy and a new view of economics. All start from the individual, from the part rather than the whole. All start from separateness. And with the separateness comes a disintegration of community, a new aloneness, the struggle of all against all. Then arises a chilling feeling of danger — felt danger reinforcing self-interest and self-defense. "We are born alone and we die alone," declares the tough-minded saying, proclaimed with fearsome certainty.

"Somewhere, somehow, we began to live as if we were separate, alone and in danger." Separate. Alone. In danger. And yet ... the words "as if" alert us to the lie.

We are not born alone. We are born into a family or into the arms of other caregivers. If this were not the case, we would not survive. We learn to "recruit care."[8] The great child psychologist, W. E. Winnicott, remarked, "There is never just a baby."

Nor do we die alone. In the end, we seek those who love us. And when we die, there is an empty space for those who loved our changing face. A unique presence is no longer a part of the dance.

So the words "We are born alone and die alone" are, at best, a half-truth; at worst, a destructive lie. We are discovering the price we pay when we elevate "being separate, alone, and in danger" to a dogma. We construct a deadly certitude. We issue a license to kill. "Power over" replaces "partnership with."[9]

When we begin from separateness, we see ourselves and others as "skin-encapsulated egos." These separate entities are real. "What joins us together" is less real, something created by acts of the will, perhaps formalized in a contract.[10] Under this view, the motto or mantra for relationships turns out to be "for as long as we meet each other's needs" — a view useful in some contexts, disastrous in others.[11]

If the deepest reality is *separateness*— in particular, my *separate self* — then the ultimate measuring rod will be *self-interest*. Of course, in thinking of my self-interest, I can be wise or foolish. I can focus on short-term or longer-term gains. I can be manipulative or non-manipulative. Yet, even when I seek mutual gain or "win-win," I am looking at relationships as a vehicle to satisfy two self-interests. With self-interest as basic, relationships become highly vulnerable. The mantra haunts me: "for as long as we meet each other's needs." We go from ME to THEE to a weak sense of WE. How might we reverse this order of proceeding?

Beginning with What Joins Us Together

Suppose we start from a deep sense of connectedness. Think of a tapestry. Here the "knots" are intertwined threads connecting one place in the tapestry with another — until all are seen as part of the whole.

We may notice a very small area of the tapestry, notice how one small area connects with the next. This is similar to observing a one-to-one relationship, say, two colleagues in a work setting who have achieved a true partnership.

We may focus on a larger part of the pattern where many interweavings connect to form an intermediary design. We might think of an organization — say a college or corporation. We might see this, at its best, as a partnership of partnerships.

Finally, we may look at the tapestry as a whole, glimpsing something of the full design. This might be like observing the pattern of all life on the planet.

Different orders of magnitude. Differences of scale. Think of the smallest unit as a one-to-one relationship with the potential to become a partnership. Think of intermediate scales as potentially partnerships of partnerships. Finally, we come to the whole tapestry — mysterious and ever-changing. At this point in time, the planet earth is the widest horizon of our common experience. Yet, the earth itself is part of a much larger universe. And, from a mystical perspective, the universe itself is a part of the Great Mystery. At each region we find wholes that are parts of larger wholes until we reach all that is.

The point is this: *starting from interconnection means seeing that we are already intertwined.* We are already related as mirrors of the mystery, members of the Great Family and of the Human Family. Such a sense of prior interconnection means starting with a much stronger sense of WE. Then, in the light of that pattern of relationships and their possibilities, we respect the other and ourself — *from WE to THEE to ME.*[12]

Spend a moment to appreciate the magnitude of this reversal:

The Way of Separation goes from ME to THEE
    to a weak sense of WE.
The Way of Interconnection goes from a strong sense
    of WE, and, within that relational field,
        moves to THEE and also to ME.

As appendix VII shows, this strong sense of WE is a new way to think — a new vision of *how part and whole intertwine.* A way of neither dependence (whole over part) nor independence (part over whole), it brings a new sense of interdependence. Coming from dynamic interconnection allows us to recover much of the wisdom tradition without losing the gains of modern times.

INTERCONNECTION AND THE WISDOM TRADITIONS

The wisdom traditions — West and East — begin from a oneness. In my analogy of the lake, I proceeded in an Eastern manner. The descent was a path of letting go — letting go of our surface self and learning to dwell more freely and fully at the depth. Or better, letting go of restrictive small-mindedness and coming back to life in larger mind, with a remembrance that at depth we are already one.

Here, I wish to consider the viewpoint of the West as manifest in the three "religions of the book" — Judaism, Christianity, and Islam.

The roots of the Way of Interconnection are present in the Hebrew Scriptures.[13] Jesus speaks of the Two Great Commandments and says they contain the entire law and the prophets.[14] Islam deepens them still further.[15] The Two Great Commandments are:

> Love the Lord your God with all your heart, with all
>   your soul, and with all your strength.
> Love your neighbor as yourself.

All about love. Yet notice the order of proceeding. Start first with love of the deepest source of unity. Then love your neighbor as you love yourself.

How can this speak to us today? Suppose we were to see God at the heart of all that joins us together — as Unity itself, as that which sustains every union containing the seeds of wholeness, health, and holiness. Perhaps then we might say with deep respect:

> Love *That Which Deeply Unites Us* with all your heart, with
>   all your soul, and with all your strength.
> Love your neighbor as yourself.

This is welcome encouragement. Start with the Way of Interconnection — with that which unites us at all levels. Then see the other as neighbor and oneself as equally worthy. See neighbor and self as intertwined in relational fields-within-fields.

The West suggests an order of loving that begins with unity. The East suggests that we let go of surface illusions to dwell in an already existing oneness.[16] Either way, we are encouraged to begin from our unique place in the Great Pattern, the Great Web, the Net of Indra, the Nest of Interbeing.[17]

INDRA'S NET REVISITED

Think of yourself in Indra's multidimensional net. You are a nodal point where billions of threads join. You are like a starburst — expanding from a center in all directions. Each thread, each ray of light is a relational field linked to another nodal point. And on and on.

In this picture, "who you are" and "where you are in the pattern" point to the same thing. You are the sum total of all the relationships you have ever had. And every other nodal point (knot or jewel) is also the sum total of all the relationships it has ever had.

In poetic language, you are a jewel that reflects all other jewels and is reflected by all other jewels. So am I. Each of us reflects the entire universe from a point of view.

The gentle Zen master Thich Nhat Hanh invented the term "interbeing." He writes:

> If you are a poet, you will see clearly that there is a cloud floating in this sheet of paper. Without a cloud, there will be no rain; without rain, the trees cannot grow; without trees, we cannot make paper....So we can say that the cloud and the paper *inter-are*. "Interbeing" is a word that is not in the dictionary yet, but if we combine the prefix "inter-" with the verb "to be," we have a new verb, inter-be.[18]

Thich Nhat Hanh points out that if we look even more deeply into the sheet of paper, we will see sunshine and the logger and all that sustains the logger; and we will see ourselves, too, since we are now in relationship with the paper. To see each being as an interbeing can help us break out of our delusion of separateness. Each jewel is surely an interbeing. Any two interbeings are already interconnected in the great web.

Nor is that all. Imagine in each of the jewels all the levels of the lake analogy in miniature. I have in me inward depth as well as outward reach. On the surface, I tell stories generated by fear and desire. At the mid-level, I can experience the observer-in-me. I can see and hear and feel with open heart. At the depth, I have intimations of a oneness beyond words — of a no-self that is, at the same time, unified with all. And what is true for me is true for every other jewel in the net. Each has an inward side and can be contacted at different levels.

Here is a profound paradox. I live in a field of relationships that is both vast and simple. Vast — in that interbeing is linked to every other interbeing in the net or web or tapestry. Vast — in that every jewel can mirror all the levels of the lake. Simple — in that heaven is in a grain of sand and eternity is in each hour, as William Blake reminds us.

Let me present the web as a meditation phrased in the first person so that each person can say the words herself or himself.

A MEDITATION

I am born into a family in a place and time. Before I could speak, my mother held a space for me. "You are daughter to me, or, you are son to me," she said, and smiled. I feel this relational field in which we both dwell. I open my heart. I send loving awareness and blessing to her.

I call to mind my other close family relationships — with my father, with my sister or brother, my grandmother or grandfather. And on and on. I open my heart and send loving awareness and blessing to each of these relationships and the people in them.

I realize that the complex interweaving that is my family is part of the larger tapestry of humankind since the beginning. I too can say with the Roman poet, "I am human and nothing human is alien from me." I am brother or sister to all human beings — from the most glorious to those with heart sealed shut. I am brother or sister to all human beings — from those who commit crimes against humanity to those saints who show us the highest reaches of the human heart. I open my heart and send loving kindness to all the human family.

I realize that the whole human family is part of a larger tapestry. That tapestry includes all the plants and animals whose interlocking system of exchange has created a habitable earth. They are our elders. They continue to weave the web of which we are but a part. We belong to this larger family. With St. Francis, I can call all the beings of the more-than-human world my brothers and my sisters. I open my heart. I send loving kindness to all these elders.

I look out into the night sky and I begin to glimpse how vast the tapestry is. The net of Indra extends through hundreds of millions of galaxies to the edge of the expanding universe. I am born into the great matrix — into the life conditions on this planet in this galaxy in this universe. I open my heart to it all. I bring loving awareness to all interbeings in the manifest universe. May all be well.

Finally, I may bring my consciousness to the "inside of the inside" and the "outside of the outside" of all things. I bring my consciousness to touch the Mystery itself — the Mystery that has many names and no name, that is closer to me than I am to myself, that is present at every point in the web, encompassing all that is. I open my heart to the Mystery — hidden and revealed, vast and simple. I send loving awareness to the One, to Unity itself.

LOVE, COMPASSION, AND WISDOM[19]

We are already connected at the deepest levels — as mirrors of the mystery and members of the Great Family. Recognizing this, our hearts open and gratitude appears — gratitude for being in life together, for the ancestors and the children, for the beauty of the earth, for the presence of mystery.[20]

From such belonging and gratitude comes a reinforced sense of the largeness of life. From such belonging and gratitude comes an impulse to care for all interbeings.

Living from interconnection offers a remedy for what the Buddhists call the three poisons: *greed, hate,* and *delusion.*

1.   *Greed Overcome Through Love.*

Greed is solely about the enhancement of myself. Love is an impulse to wish the other well, to forward the other's growth, to give rather than take. When we experience ourselves as profoundly interconnected, will not love arise naturally?

In small mind, we often confuse love with sentimentality and caring with meddling. Great love — possible when the wisdom eye is opened — is seeing that I am so intertwined with the other that I am able to love them no matter what. My loving them gives them the utmost space for them to flourish.

2. *Hate Overcome Through Compassion*

Hate is a desire to diminish the other. Compassion is a way of feeling with another — feeling with them their suffering, and wishing that they be free of suffering. When we experience ourselves as profoundly interconnected, will not compassion arise naturally?

In small mind, we often confuse compassion with pity and even condescension. Great compassion — possible when the wisdom eye is opened — is seeing that I am so intertwined with the other that I stand in their place and feel the hurt, yet also know there is a larger view. When I stand thus with the other in the larger relational field, then I may gift the other with a sense of living larger too.

3. *Delusion Overcome Through Wisdom*

Delusion is the result of ignorance. Wisdom is a way to see clearly from the heart — to see and to hear and to feel in the widest and deepest way. When we experience ourselves as profoundly interconnected, when we see ourselves and others as manifesting all the levels of the lake, will not wisdom arise naturally?

In small mind, we often confuse wisdom with knowledge or even with information.[21] Great wisdom is also great compassion and great love. When I see clearly who I am, I also know who you are; and I realize how deeply we are intertwined. And, in moments of grace, perhaps I also glimpse *namaste*, so beautifully explained in these words:

> In India, when we meet, we often say *namaste,* which
> means, I honor the place in you where the entire
> universe lives. I honor the place in you of love, of light,
> of truth, of peace. I honor the place in you, where, if you
> are in that place in you, and I am in that place in me,
> there is only one of us.

References

1. William Wordsworth, "Lines Composed a Few Miles Above Tintern Abbey," on revisiting the banks of the Wye during a tour, July 13, 1798.

2. For a beautiful reflection on our interbeing with trees, see Thom Hartmann, *The Last Hours of Ancient Sunlight: Waking Up to Personal and Global Transformation* (New York: Harmony Books, 1999), chapter entitled "The Death of Trees," pp. 46-54.

3. See "Prayer for the Great Family" in *Turtle Island* by Gary Snyder (New York: New Directions Book, 1969, 1974). Synder mentions that he composed this invocation "after a Mohawk prayer."

4. Chief Sealth (or Seattle) delivered a speech to his people, the Duwamish, in 1854. Dr. Henry Smith took notes. In 1970, screenwriter Ted Perry adapted Smith's version of the speech. For the Perry version, see John Seed, Joanna Macy, Pat Fleming, and Arne Naess, *Thinking Like a Mountain: Towards a Council of All Beings* (Philadelphia, PA: New Society Publishers, 1988), pp. 67-73.

5. This is my version of the story, arranged to suggest poetry and with some very minor modifications from the account given by Francis H. Cook in his article, "The Jewel Net of Indra," in J. Baird Callicott and Roger T. Ames (eds.), *Nature in Asian Traditions of Thought* (Albany: State University of New York Press, 1989), p. 214. The image occurs in the Avatamsaka Sutra. For a fuller treatment of this teaching, see Francis H. Cook, *Hua-Yen Buddhism: The Jewel Net of Indra* (Penn State University Press, 1977).

6. See, for example, Thich Nhat Hanh, *Interbeing: Fourteen Guidelines for Engaged Buddhism,* 3rd edition (Berkeley, CA: Parallax Press, 1998).

7. Kabir Edmund Helminski, *Living Presence* (New York: Jeremy P. Tarcher/Perigee Books, 1992), p. 50.

8. See Robert Kegan, *The Evolving Self* (Cambridge, MA: Harvard University Press, 1982).

9. Riane Eisler uses this formulation in her book *The Chalice and the Blade* (San Francisco: Harper and Row, 1988), especially chapter 8.

10. The great scholar of the English common law, Sir Henry Maine, once remarked, "The difference between the medieval world and the modern world is the difference between status and contract." In a world defined by status, one's claims on others and duties to others are founded in long-standing custom, and flow from one's place in the web of organized life. In a world based on contract, one's rights and

duties are founded on contract (or the law seen as a kind of contract) and flow from the fact that one is an individual.

11. Hugh and Gayle Prather are attuned to the dangers of this way of speaking. See their book, *I Will Never Leave You* (New York: Bantam Books, 1996).

12. This is not meant as a return to the past but as a move forward. As a caution, think of three phases in human history: a pre-modern period with emphasis on the collective, a modern period with emphasis on individuality, and a post-modern period where we attempt to articulate frameworks capable of allowing us to take the best from what went before and avoid some of the limitations. See appendix XVII.

13. See Deuteronomy 6:4 — famous as the beginning of the Sh'ma: "Hear, O Israel, the Lord, the Lord our God, the Lord is One. And you shall love the Lord your God with all your heart, and with all your soul and with all your might." See also Leviticus 19:18 on love of neighbor.

14. See Mark 12:29-31; Matthew 22:37-40; Luke 10:25-28.

15. See the Koran 5:73 and 21:25. The first Shahadah — "There is no god but God" — accentuates the Oneness of the Real, of God. Islam sees all prophets as coming with the message of oneness, of *tawhid*. See Sachiro Murata and William C. Chittick, *The Vision of Islam* (New York: Paragon House, 1994).

16. The Hindu sages see a unity beneath the infinitely diverse manifestations. The Buddha awakens to a consciousness beyond dualisms, yet is able to recognize the forces of greed, hate, and delusion. Confucius sees the way of large-minded person as mirroring the way of the heavens. Lao Tzu presents the Tao as the pattern that runs through all things. See my earlier book, *To Come to Life More Fully* (Columbia, MD: Traditional Acupuncture Institute, 1990), chapter 1, for more on striving and letting go.

17. Ken Wilber exchanges the image of hierarchy for the image of nest. See his *Integral Psychology: Consciousness, Spirit, Psychology, Therapy* (Boston: Shambhala, 2000) and other recent writings. Where he speaks of "The Great Nest of Being," I prefer to say "The Nest of Interbeing," using Thich Nhat Hanh's more expressive term.

18. See Thich Nhat Hanh, *Peace Is Every Step* (New York: Bantam Books, 1991), p. 95. See also Thich Nhat Hanh's *Interbeing: Fourteen Guidelines for Engaged Buddhism* (Berkeley, CA: Parallax Press, 1998).

19. Here, I draw on the work of David Brazier. See his *Zen Therapy* (New York: John Wiley & Sons, 1996), especially chapters 17, 18, 19.

20. On gratitude, see the wonderful work of Brother David Steindl-Rast, *Gratefulness: The Heart of Prayer* (Ramsey, NJ: Paulist Press, 1984). I return to this theme in chapter 9.

21: As in T. S. Eliot's lines, "Where is the wisdom we lost in knowledge? Where is the knowledge we lost in information?" I might ask further, "What happens when even information transmutes into free-floating opinion? How will we find our way home?"

CHAPTER SIX

The Great Pattern in Time —
Co-creating the World in Its Unfolding

Heaven is my father and earth is my mother
and even such a small creature as I
find an intimate place in its midst.
That which extends throughout the universe,
I regard as my body.
That which directs the universe,
I regard as my nature.
All people are my brothers and sisters and all
things are my companions.[1]

— WEST WALL INSCRIPTION FROM THE OFFICE OF CHANG TSAI,
AN 11TH-CENTURY ADMINISTRATOR IN CHINA

In the last chapter, we recognized how deeply we are interwoven with all of life. We are "interbeings." Ancient teaching reminds us "we form...one body with heaven, earth and all the myriad things."[2] In this spirit we can repeat the words Chang Tsai inscribed on his office wall: "That which extends throughout the universe I regard as my body."

In this chapter, we turn from space to time — to see the Great Pattern in movement, to watch how nature works, to collaborate in the world's unfolding. If we do these things, we can also say with Chang Tsai, "That which directs the universe I regard as my nature."

Where do we stand to experience this expanded sense of time and movement? The Navajo, it is said, suggest that *we see ourselves standing in the midst of seven generations*. According to this teaching, when we are about to make a decision, we should ask two questions: "Will this honor my parents and their parents and their parents? Will it benefit my children and their children and their children?" This is the clue we need. First, we open ourselves to generational time and stand between the ancestors and the children.

Now, let us expand the picture beyond generational time, even beyond the epochs of humankind. Think of "earth time" (some 4.5 billion years) within the time of the universe (some 15 billion years). From this vantage point, suppose we think of ourselves as a species — the human ones who arrived late in the development of life on earth. Let us stand, representing our species, in the midst of the time of earth's unfolding. In this role, let us call to mind the beings of the three times — past, present, and future.

First, call to mind our "ancestors" — humans, yes, but also all the living and nonliving beings that have made earth a habitable place for us: mountains and rivers and prairies, flowers and grains, fields and forests, animals and fish and birds, insects, bacteria and other microorganisms. They are all our elders, as native people well knew. When we act, are we honoring all our ancestors — human and more-than-human?

Next, call to mind our contemporaries, especially humans of recent generations who are inflicting great harm on the planetary web — harm to fellow humans, yes, but also harm to other species, and harm to the very conditions of life. Stand in solidarity with all the beings of earth at this historical moment, acknowledging the harm and seeking possibilities to go forward together.

Lastly, call to mind all the children of all the creatures whose future is at risk. We, the human ones, number more than six billion and have an advanced technology. We can, for the first time, damage irrevocably the very conditions for life. We are destroying ecosystems that took billions of years to develop. Can we find a way of going forward together for the sake of all the children?

Surely, we make a start when we acknowledge that we are already in motion, already involved in the earth's unfolding, and that we are now, as a species, behaving much as a cancer to the earth, growing at the expense of the whole.[3]

SPACE AND TIME: THE WEB IS BEING WOVEN STILL

From a Buddhist perspective, whole and part arise together. The whole is not the same reality without the part, and the part is not what it is without the whole. The upshot of this perspective is truly remarkable: The order in the macrocosm is more like an artistic than a logical order.[4] In a "logical order" the parts can be replaced without altering the whole. In an "artistic order," on the other hand, the parts cannot be replaced without altering the whole. For example, *this* production of *this* play with *these* actors before *this* audience on *this* day cannot be done again.

When we understand interconnection as an artistic order, we realize that we are not replaceable parts. The total web, woven in space and time, would be different if we had not been born. If we had encountered different relationships (or even if we understood those relationships differently), the whole would have been constituted differently. There is then, something momentous in the choices we make, the traces we accumulate, the hopes and fears we project.

We arise from unity. In the beginning of the universe, all things are present (in potential), present in what has been called "a single, if multiform, energy event."[5] Elements are made and galaxies arise in the first ten billion years. Over the next nearly five billion years, the earth forms and transforms, producing the conditions for life to emerge, and inventing new ways to sustain life. Life develops feeling and consciousness, deepening the inward side of things. Finally, in a blink of cosmic time, we the human ones appear and our story begins. We generate language and art and culture. And our own story unfolds in the midst of the earth's story, in the midst of the universe story.[6] Such is the sacred story we now can tell.

In such a vast story, we encounter two kinds of time — cyclic time (day and night, the seasons) and transformative time (when novel and, in a sense, irreversible, developments unfold). Key transitional points include the forming of elements, galaxies, and planets; the development of life, consciousness, self-reflection; and, in the human story, a sequence of cultural stages.[7] The sciences have given us an enriched creation story. To understand how this view from science can make a difference, let us look at creation stories more generally.

CREATION STORIES

A creation story — what Thomas Berry calls a functional cosmology — is more than a series of events. It is a way of invoking "a world of meaning and value" — a world big enough to live in. We need such stories to illumine the mind, enkindle the heart, and cause movement in the unknown places within us.[8] To touch us deeply, such stories are expressed in a mythic way and performed in a ritual way. The myth gives meaning to the ritual, and the ritual acts out the myth — proclaimed and enacted, designed to enter our bodies, minds, hearts, and spirit.

Here is a creation story of a nomadic tribe:[9]

Once upon a time, in a time before time, in a time that was and is and always will be, a god entered our world. This god entered by descending, by coming down the pole at the center of the world — the pole that links earth and heaven. Arriving here, the god made chaos into cosmos, creating a dwelling space suitable for humans and other beings.

What was done "in that (timeless) time" is done always. Always the earth is being created. Always the god is arriving at the center. Always the god, like the light and warmth of a campfire, creates a habitable space that holds off the darkness. We, the human ones, find the pattern of our work in the example of the god.

Now, this tribe was nomadic, so it carried with it a sacred pole. Wherever the pole went became the center — a moving center, like a pillar of light illuminating the darkness. This pole-in-movement marked the boundaries of what was considered ordered and safe, and what was chaotic and dangerous. The pole created a moving horizon, opening new spaces before it and leaving hospitable spaces behind it.

In the net of Indra, each jewel is a center reflecting the universe from its own place, and, simultaneously, is reflected by every other center. Think now of every center in movement — shifting and changing, caught in forgetfulness but carrying the capacity for wakefulness, accumulating the past and forming the future.

These early images prefigure modern insight. The pattern shifts and moves. The whole evolves. The new science of complexity explores how, when a number of beings are in a set of relationships under certain conditions, something surprising can emerge.[10] A new "being" or "interbeing" can be born. When conditions are neither too frozen nor too chaotic, a new emerging whole can arise that is not preordained and not predictable by us. The drama contains room for improvisation. A whole can truly be greater than the sum of its parts.

So the pattern itself evolves. The tapestry is woven and rewoven and continues to surprise and delight. Emergent "holons" arise in unexpected fashion. On the material level, for example, hydrogen and oxygen come together in a certain way and form a new being, "water," with properties beyond either of the partnering elements. On the organic level, certain changes in the underlying gene pattern give rise to different life forms. On the human level, two humans — two meaning-makers and value-shapers — can come together in ways that allow a new reality to arise, resulting in new forms of partnership, new collaborative organizations.

We are now seeing the earth itself as a self-organizing, self-sustaining interbeing. Brian Swimme and Thomas Berry speak of the Universe Story and offer a telling of that story that honors science, art, and spirituality.[11]

What is to be learned? From the perspective of space, *lessons of deep interconnection*. From the perspective of time, *lessons of collaboration*.

Lessons from the West — The Universe Story and a Commitment to Partner the World in Its Unfolding

A recent student of mine told me that the Universe Story painted for her such a vast horizon that she stopped using the term "God." The word seemed too small — or at least her notion of mystery seemed too small. Yet a new sense of awe and gratitude had arisen for her. If she re-owns the old name, it will be to point to a much larger, more mysterious presence — a larger God.

This, perhaps, is always a first lesson: letting go and standing in a wider world; dwelling in the largeness of awe and gratitude.[12]

What can be noticed about the universe unfolding over 15 billion years or more? Some writers point out three themes:

1. Differentiation, complexity, surprising novelty
2. Communion, harmony, deep interconnection
3. Interiority, intensity, mystery.[13]

The first two themes offer a creative tension: diverse, ever-surprising possibilities held together in a deep communion. I have been inviting us to begin from that communion, from that unity, from that which joins us together. "E pluribus unum" — out of many, one. The ancients would honor both movements: From the one came the many as a "breathing out." From the many, we return to the one as a "breathing in."

The last theme looks to a growing capacity for inwardness — sensitivity, consciousness, reflective awareness — the capacity, perhaps, for perceiving a depth dimension to all things. I have presented each jewel in the net as having within it some analogue to the three levels of the lake: (i) a surface appearance, (ii) a more inward functioning, (iii) a depth connection to the source and to the whole. This is my way of speaking of this dimension of inwardness.

Phrase it as we will, the first lesson is one of awe and humility — as if we were looking up at a star-filled sky, as if we were astronauts gazing back at our home planet suspended in space. And there is a new appreciation of how long it took for the earth web to be woven: over four billion years. Against such reaches of time, we can appreciate even more the irreplaceable qualities of every species and of every eco-region that is part of the tapestry. Once gone, they will not be again.

Thomas Berry urges us to take the earth as our teacher. We are grounded, he says, in "the dynamics of the earth as a self-emerging, self-sustaining, self-educating, self-governing, self-healing, and self-fulfilling community of all the living and nonliving beings of the planet."[14] Hence, "the earth is itself the primary physician, primary lawgiver, primary revelation of the divine, primary scientist, primary technologist, primary commercial venture, primary artist, primary educator, and primary agent in whichever other activity we find in human affairs."[15]

Consider the timespan of the universe and the time of the earth. As we struggle to comprehend such reaches of time, we find new ways to learn from the earth — to learn:

- ways of honoring diversity as bringing creative gifts to the whole,
- ways of sustainable living,
- ways of prizing the local as well as the global,
- ways of simplifying our lives so we take less in quantity while experiencing lives richer in quality.

The shift certainly requires that we slow the speed and volume by which "we move natural resources through the consumer economy to the junk pile or the waste heap."[16] It requires a new shared sense of what is meaningful and valuable, and a new commitment to collaborative action in service of all beings in the Great Family.

LESSONS FROM THE EAST — THE BOOK OF CHANGES AND A COMMITMENT TO CHOOSE LARGE MIND

One of the oldest of the Chinese wisdom texts is the *I Ching*. The Chinese character pronounced "ching" means book, or better, a classic. The character written as "I" in English (pronounced *e,* as in the word "bee") is usually translated as "changes"; yet the character means both change and constancy. So the book is about *changes that proceed in a way that is relatively constant.* This includes changes that recur (seasons) and changes that set a new framework (as when a child becomes an adult). In both kinds of change, there are lessons to learn.

A. *Picturing Change*

The *I Ching* is the first book to represent everything as a form of energy or *ch'i.* The energy manifests itself in two generic aspects — the upward-and-outward energy called "yang," and the downward-and-inward energy called "yin."

In a 24-hour period, we see the *upward-and-outward YANG energy* from dawn through the brightness of day until the evening.

We see the *downward-and-inward YIN energy* from dusk through the darkness of night until dawn.

In a year, yang energy predominates in spring and summer; yin energy predominates in autumn and winter. In human relationships, yin and yang show up in receiving and giving, listening and speaking, being and doing.

The *I Ching* symbolizes yin energy as an open line (— —) and yang energy as a continuous line (——). All of "the ten thousand things" — all beings-in-situations — can then be represented as different combinations of yin and yang energies.

How is this done? The *I Ching* (anticipating abstract art) represents each situation as a "six-story house," or hexagram.[17]

HEXAGRAM

(A "six-story house"
ready to receive a
yin or yang line on
each floor)

On any "floor" or position in this six-story house, imagine that the lights can be on (yang) or off (yin). In other words, on any floor or position, you can write a yin line or a yang line. This gives 64 hexagrams — 64 pictures of diverse situations in life.[18]

Next, imagine the 64 hexagrams on a border or frieze around the top of a room. They are pictured on the wall in numerical sequence: Hexagram 1, Hexagram 2, Hexagram 3 … all the way to Hexagram 64. This gives us one picture of changing situations.

However, there are further possibilities. Suppose that, as in a laser show, a laser beam might be sent from any hexagram to any other. For example, a laser beam from Hexagram 1 is sent across the room to Hexagram 14 — or from Hexagram 17 to 53, or on and on. In other words, in addition to proceeding in a sequence of 1, 2, 3, … on to 64, we also add changes from any hexagram to any other. Many more possibilities. A sophisticated device to represent the world in process.[19]

B. *Living Wisely with Change*

We are no strangers to change. More and more, we experience our lives as moving at a faster and faster pace. How can we live wisely in such a fast-moving stream? This question returns us to the fundamental distinction we first met in chapter 1 — the distinctions between events and how we relate to the events. This distinction was discovered at some point in the evolution of the Book of Changes. The distinction became central to Confucius and his school. This distinction gave rise to the possibility of using the *I Ching,* not for fortune-telling, but as a true wisdom text.[20]

A situation — what is happening — is represented by a hexagram. But wisdom resides not in *what* is happening but in *how we relate* to what is happening. Will we understand and respond in small mind or large mind, foolishly or wisely? A wise investor can make money whether the stock market is going up or going down. A wise person can live in large mind whether life is on the ascent or on the decline, whether things are going according to plan or not.

Remember the Wisdom Chant: "There are at least two ways to relate to anything — a large-minded way and a small-minded way. Choose large mind."

From the vantage point of large mind, we can see two difficulties with using the *I Ching* in a fortune-telling mindset:

First, in the fortune-telling mindset, we tend to see situations dualistically — good or bad, fortunate or unfortunate. But the Chinese word for crisis or transition is composed of sub-characters: one is the character for "danger, beware"; the other, the character for "opportunity." Hence, any situation brings with it both danger and opportunity. Some situations come with the *danger* side forward — the death of a loved one, a divorce, the loss of a job. Even here, after the grieving abates, new opportunity arises. Some situations come to us with the *opportunity* side forward. For example, a TV personality comes to tell us we have won the sweepstakes. Yet even here danger lurks — we may forget who we are and lose our center. So breaking out of a small-minded fortune-telling approach keeps us flexible and open, seeing all events as both danger and opportunity.

Second, a fortune-telling mindset encourages us to be passive and to downplay our power to make choices. We may think that the future will unfold as it will, that there is nothing to do but wait. Such passive yielding to fate is a far cry from living the spirit of the Wisdom Chant.

In large mind, once we realize we have a choice, we begin to notice which choices open up life and which choices close down life. We see how we produce surplus suffering and how we reduce such suffering. An ethical stance becomes possible — a way to reduce unnecessary suffering and promote constructive possibilities for our common life.

The challenge is to take this wisdom way, and, using the perspective of evolutionary time, apply it to our present situation. We as a species again are seeing how interwoven we all are. We as a species hold the power to co-create our future. In both local and global contexts, how can we care for the whole and be fair to each participant-part? The wisdom way points to collaboration in large contexts and partnership in one-to-one encounters.

LARGE MIND, ECO-SPIRITUAL MIND, ONENESS MIND

The Navajo taught us that we stand in the midst of seven generations. The Navajo taught us to ask, "Will this honor the ancestors, and will this serve the children?"

We stand as a species in the midst of the Great Family within earth time, within cosmic time. Will our actions honor the "ancestors" in the human and more-than-human sense? Will our actions serve the "children" of all life-forms on our planet?

To think of ourselves in this way is to come to large mind, eco-spiritual mind, oneness mind — not only in space but also in time. What practices arise from and support this expansive mind? Consider the practices of *gratitude* and *grieving*, the call to a *change of heart* and to *collaborative service*.

First, as we consider these practices, *call to mind the beings of past time,* our ancestors. Recall the passage at the beginning of the chapter:

> *Heaven is my father and earth is my mother*
> *and even such a small creature as I*
> *find an intimate place in its midst.*

> . . . .

> *All people are my brothers and sisters*
> *and all things are my companions.*

Suppose we think that "even such small creatures as we, the human species," are daily being welcomed into our world by the other forms of life. All of these forms of life co-created the conditions which allowed us to emerge. They are co-creating for us the conditions in which we can survive and prosper. If we begin to grasp this basic fact, we can practice a wider sense of gratitude — gratitude, as Gary Snyder says, to the Great Family: gratitude for the long time it took for the web to be woven, gratitude for all who weave it still, gratitude for all that has been. And we come to a new realization: these conditions for life are now in our hands.

Second, *call to mind the beings of the present time,* our contemporaries. Think of ourselves and other humans of recent generations who are inflicting great harm on the planetary web. Sit with that harm, vividly mindful of the plundering of resources, the extinction of species, the polluting of air and soil and waters. What are we doing to ourselves and to all the forms of life that co-sustain this wondrous world? Surely, there is grieving to be done — an immense grieving — as we hear the suffering of the earth. John Seed and Joanna Macy do this in a ritual they call the "Council of All Beings." [21] Here, some humans take on the role of animals or plants or even ecosystems like rivers or forestlands. They give these beings a voice with which to speak to us, the human ones.

If we listen to our suffering brothers and sisters, we shiver to realize that the lives of our own and other species are in our hands. We can, for the first time, damage irrevocably the very conditions for life. To recognize even a small fraction of the devastation we have wrought produces a deep grieving. [22]

Third, *call to mind the beings of the future times,* our human children and the children of all the beings who companion us. They call us to a change of heart-and-mind — to a change in how we think and feel and act as individual interbeings, and in our partnerships and larger organizations.

The ancient traditions speak of repentance: "metanoia," a change of direction — the direction of our lives. Such a turnaround has three features: First, *acknowledge before others what we are doing.* Second, *let the harm and sorrow touch us — grieve with others.* Third, *make a commitment to repair the damage so far as possible and to live in more wholesome ways.*[23] These commitments need to be undertaken in solidarity with others.

With others, we commit to learn from the earth better ways to live our common life —

- ways to honor creative diversity within a deepening understanding of our oneness,
- ways to honor the inward mystery of ordinary things,
- ways to respect the resources of the earth,
- ways to simplify our needs,
- ways to care for what we use and return what is left over, thus allowing the earth to reuse it.

Since the task is a collective one, the invitation is to learn new ways of collaboration, new ways to co-create the world in its unfolding. Such ways seem to be less a striving to fix things and more a process of simplification so that nature can heal itself and us. Will we simplify our lives — to honor the ancestors and to serve the children?

> In the next century
> or the one beyond that,
> they say,
> are valleys, pastures.
> we can meet there in peace
> if we make it.
>
> To climb these coming crests
> one word to you, to
> you and your children:
>
> *stay together*
> *learn the flowers*
> *go light* [24]
>
> – GARY SNYDER

References

1. Quoted in Thomas Berry, *The Dream of the Earth* (San Francisco: Sierra Club Books, 1988), pp. 14-15.

2. Ibid., p. 15. Berry is quoting the words of Wang Ming-yang, a Chinese thinker of the early sixteenth century.

3. I take the image from Peter Russell. See his book *The Global Brain* (Los Angeles: J. P. Tarcher, 1983).

4. See David L. Hall and Roger T. Ames, *Thinking Through Confucius* (Albany, NY: State University of New York Press, 1987). Also see Roger Ames's article, "Putting the *Te* back into Taoism," in J. Baird Callicott and Roger T. Ames, eds., *Nature in Asian Traditions of Thought: Essays in Environmental Philosophy* (Albany, NY: State University of New York Press, 1989), pp. 113-144.

5. Berry, *The Dream of the Earth,* pp. 45-46.

6. We go from matricentric to patricentric epochs, from the time of the great classical religions and philosophies to the modern scientific, technological, industrial epoch. Finally, we begin to see the possibility of an emerging ecological epoch. For these five cultural epochs, see Berry, *The Dream of the Earth,* pp. 93 and 101-105; also chapters 5 and 11. For a fuller exposition of where we stand now, see Thomas Berry's more recent book, *The Great Work* (New York: Bell Tower division of Random House, 1999).

7. See Brian Swimme and Thomas Berry, *The Universe Story* (San Francisco: HarperSanFrancisco, 1992). Also see Berry's earlier book, *The Dream of the Earth,* p. 93.

8. The phrase "illumine the mind and enkindle the heart" is an echo of theologian John S. Dunne.

9. The tribe is the Arunta tribe, the Achilpa. They called their divine being "Numbakula." See Mircea Eliade, *The Sacred and the Profane,* trans. by Willard R. Trask (New York: Harcourt, Brace and Company, 1959), pp. 32ff.

10. See, For example, M. Mitchell Waldrop, *Complexity: The Emerging Science at the Edge of Chaos* (New York: Touchstone Division of Simon and Schuster, 1992), and Stuart Kauffman, *At Home in the Universe: The Search for the Laws of Self-Organization and Complexity* (New York: Oxford University Press, 1995).

11. See Brian Swimme and Thomas Berry, *The Universe Story.*

12. I think of Matthew Fox in his book *Creation Spirituality* (San Francisco: HarperSanFrancisco, 1991), pp. 17ff.

13. Thomas Berry speaks of differentiation, communion, and subjectivity (earlier he used "interiority"). Alfred North Whitehead spoke of complexity, harmony, and intensity. I add surprise, deep interconnection, and mystery.

14. Berry, *The Dream of the Earth,* p. 107.

15. Ibid.

16. Berry, *The Dream of the Earth,* p. 7.

17. At times, the representation is more complex and is pictured as one house or hexagram changing into another. I am using *The I Ching or Book of Changes,* Wilhelm/Baynes translation, third edition (Princeton, NJ: Princeton University Press, 1967), Bollingen Series XIX.

18. Mathematicians have been fascinated by the *I Ching,* which they see as seeking to describe the world in binary notation. The formula for generating all possibilities of six places with two states in each place is given by 2 to the sixth power, or 2X2X2X2X2X2.

19. All the hexagrams have a nature significance, for example, sky and earth, fire and water, mountain and lake in the changing seasons. And all the hexagrams also have a social significance in terms of family relationships and relationships in organizations such as a kingdom. Hence the hexagrams are immensely suggestive and speak to the imagination.

20. The *I Ching* can be read in three ways, I believe. First, it has been (and still is) used as a fortune-telling device. I shall discuss the issues I have with using it in this manner. Second, it can be read as a wisdom text from a wisdom mindset. This is the approach I am taking. Lastly, it can be read in the light of synchronicity, the doctrine that nothing happens by chance. Carl Jung was interested in the *I Ching* at this level. But one need make no commitment to such a doctrine to read the *I Ching* in the wisdom way.

21. See John Seed, Joanna Macy, Pat Fleming, and Arne Naess, *Thinking Like a Mountain: Toward a Council of All Beings* (Philadelphia, PA: New Society Publishers, 1988).

22. Joanna Macy and Molly Young Brown share dozens of exercises allowing us to mind what we are doing. See their *Coming Back to Life: Practices to Reconnect Our Lives, Our World* (Gabriola Island, BC, Canada: New Society Publishers, 1998).

23. See Dante with respect to the three aspects of repentance: confession, contrition, and satisfaction. Dante Alighieri, *The Divine Comedy: Cantica II: Purgatory,* trans. Dorothy Sayers (New York: Penguin Books, 1955), Canto IX with commentaries, pp. 134-142.

24. This excerpt is from a poem by Gary Snyder titled "For the Children," which appears in his *Turtle Island* (New York: New Directions, 1974), p. 86.

CHAPTER SEVEN

An Inclusive Spirituality

Have I told you lately that I love you?
Have I told you there's no one above you?
Fill my heart with gladness
take away my sadness
ease my troubles, that's what you do.

. . . .

There's a love that's divine
and it's yours and it's mine
and it shines like the sun.
At the end of the day we will give thanks
and pray to the One.

Have I told you lately that I love you? [1]

—VAN MORRISON

How mysterious is the whole in its largest manifestation. Call it
Nature or Tao. Call it God or "All That Is." Call it simply, with Van
Morrison, "the One." Are there not moments when, in our deepest
partnerships, we sense ourselves caught up in the oneness and
experiencing it as love?

How mysterious is the deepest nature of each part, each
"interbeing" in the net. Each jewel reflects the entire net. Each jewel,
in its own fashion, contains all the levels of the lake — surface,

midway down, and the depth; an outward appearance, an inward nature, and a connection with the whole. Every relationship, entered deeply, can manifest the spirit.

The modern Irish troubadour, Van Morrison, sings in such a way that love for the human beloved and love for the Great Mystery interfuse: "There's a love that's divine, and it's yours and it's mine, and it shines like the sun. At the end of the day, we will give thanks and pray to the One."

DWELLING IN ONENESS, DWELLING IN LOVE

What habits of mind-and-heart will aid us to live mindfully? Consider these possibilities:

coming from deep interconnection,
committing to collaboration with the earth's unfolding,
dwelling in oneness,
sensing the unity as love.

Coming from *interconnection,* we see "Heaven is my father and earth is my mother... All people are my brother and sisters, and all things are my companions."[2]

Committing to *collaboration* with the earth, we see that how we speak, act, and live has an impact on the conditions for the continuance of life. We are co-participants in the unfolding of the Great Pattern. We can be asleep or wakeful, enslaved or free, in small mind or large mind, operating for the sake of some persons only, or operating for the sake of all.

Dwelling in *oneness,* we begin to see large mind as remembering the oneness and acting so as to sustain and enhance the well-being of the whole.

When we experience large mind as partnership mind, eco-mind, oneness mind, then all our practices take on a dignity. All work is world work. All learning is learning from the earth. All living is a form of loving — practicing partnership, committing to collaboration, dwelling in grace and gratitude all our days.

RELIGION AND SPIRITUALITY

Religion and spirituality are like sex and intimacy. One can have sex without intimacy and intimacy without sex. Yet when sex and intimacy dance together, the result is glorious.[3] Likewise, one can have religion without spirituality and spirituality without religion. Yet when they dance together, the result is glorious.

The outer side of religion can be defined through four C's: Creed, Code, Cult, and Community Organization.[4] Spirituality goes beyond these things to taste a deeper life, to experience oneness and to act from that place. Spirituality begins with mystery: we are more than we can know and we know more than we can say.[5] I think of spirituality as the *practice of living mindfully and being open to mystery* — this to be done in a framework that honors both mind and heart, that has place for paradox, and that recovers a deeper sense of all life.[6]

Spiritual practices lie at the core of the great religions and "ways of being," West and East. These practices invite us to "taste and see" for ourselves. In fact, there is a remarkable convergence in the testimony of those who have taken the experiential path.

To introduce religion and spirituality gives permission to discuss the Great Mystery and to speak of the ultimate as God or Tao. Religion, like all things powerful, is open to use and abuse. Throughout history some of the best and worst of human endeavors have taken place under the mantle of religion. Some have been burned badly by the religion of their childhood and no longer walk in its ways. If spirituality is a love for the whole, then one need not be religious to be spiritual and one need not be spiritual (even in this open sense) to care for the world in its unfolding. However, when the very conditions for life on the planet are at stake, we need the support of all who are of good will. Hence, if a narrow view of science and technology conspire to wreak ecological destruction, so too a narrow view of religion conspires to blind us from the demands of ecological and social justice. Here as elsewhere, the invitation is to go larger and the invitation is to all.

GOD AND OUR IMAGE OF GOD

What does it mean for a person-as-part to love the whole? Again and again, humans have personified the whole — the largest horizon that they encounter, the deep mystery in which they dwell. Perhaps whatever we love takes on "personal" qualities.

In the scriptures of the West, it is written that God created us (the human ones) in God's own image and likeness. We humans return the favor by "creating" God (or more properly, our image of God) in our own image and likeness. Perhaps better, we "create" God in the image of what we see as the best qualities we can imagine. This can be valuable. *Whatever God is, God must be better than the best of humans* (that is, more forgiving, more compassionate, and so forth). If one's image of God is less than the best of humans, then that image is an idol, "too small a god." Persons who realize this must, in conscience, reject that image. They have a choice: either to become an atheist or to find a larger God. It is in service of finding a larger God that I undertake a brief excursion into the realm of mystery.

According to the wisdom traditions, all of the "sizes" of wholes are enfolded by a mystery smaller than the small and larger than the large — a mystery that constantly goes beyond our conceptions of it. Hence it is important to distinguish between the whole — the mystery — and our conception of it at any time in our own cultural development.[7]

SHIFTING IMAGES OF THE WHOLE

The native or first peoples see everything as having spirit. Many go on to name the Whole. They call "What joins all things together" by the name "Great Spirit" or some variant. The One and the many are honored.[8]

In the time of the Goddess, the Spirit is represented as the Great Mother. Birthing and sustaining life is a key power. In later language, we would say that the Spirit is thought of as immanent, deeply intertwined in the earthly world. To align with the Spirit is to respect and care for all beings, to join the dance of life, to sustain the fruitfulness of unfolding nature.[9]

With the rise of Western world religions, the Spirit is pictured as an independent, self-sufficient father figure in the sky. Such religions draw a strong line between Creator and creatures. The relation of Spirit to the world is represented as a strong dualism: spirit vs. matter, the changeless vs. the changing, independence vs. dependence, etc.

In this viewpoint of traditional Western theism, God creates and sustains the world; however, because of the values of the time, a certain image of God takes hold:

- Because independence is valued above dependence or interdependence, God is seen as sovereignly *independent* of the world.
- Because what is unchanging is valued above what is changing, God is seen as basically perfect in the sense of *changeless* and *unaffected by the creation.*
- Because keeping good order is valued above increasing enjoyment for all, God is seen as a *"cosmic moralist"* — rewarding and punishing behavior to uphold a certain moral order, or, at least, is seen as primarily concerned with the moral attitudes and actions of persons.
- Because masculine strength and the ability to control are the marks of a leader in this period, God is seen as *male,* as *controlling,* often as *legitimizing the status quo.*[10]

A curious mix is created when this traditional picture is placed alongside the dominant view of the modern age. On the one hand, matter, nature, the body, and the feminine are devalued. On the other hand, self-interested economics, extreme individualism, and material tokens of success are overvalued.

Today, we are revaluing interdependence, change and development, the enjoyment or happiness of all beings, and collaborative persuasion. In light of this, we would expect a larger notion of God to emerge as well, one that exhibits a new balancing of immanent and transcendent features, that emphasizes interdependence and positive change, and that sees leading in a new light.[11]

If we are deeply interconnected and we are in movement, should not our image of the One likewise not be separate, but deeply interconnected with all being? And should not our image of the One likewise be in movement?

In the picture I have been sketching, the whole is seen as a self-organizing, self-sustaining "interbeing" capable of generating surprising new emergent configurations. In our time, perhaps the Spirit can best be represented by *the whole in its unfolding,* the image of a process within and beyond the world. This process evokes wonder and surprise even in God, as parents can be surprised by their child's potential. Here Spirit is identified with the impulse toward the True, the Good, and the Beautiful, as inviting all beings to co-create the next steps. Here God might be seen as the "inside of the inside of everything," coming to understand the web from within each jewel.[12] God might be seen as persuading to the good rather than controlling and coercing, just as love wishes the good of the other and is sympathetically attuned to the other's sense of that good. God might be seen as truly affected by the suffering of creation, truly participating in the happiness of all beings, and truly inspiring us to co-create what is possible and positive at every step. And, since the world is not yet what it will be, we can also think of Spirit as transcending any particular moment in the world's unfolding.[13]

ONENESS AND LOVE

Lawrence of Arabia tells of meeting an elderly Bedouin in the desert. The Bedouin said, "The love is from God and of God and towards God."[14] Suppose we were to say the love is from the whole and of the whole and towards the whole. In any relationship, if we think first of *what joins us,* there are larger possibilities than either of us might imagine — possibilities of a harmony we might call love. In any relationship, we already stand within the Great Pattern, already held by the mystery, already flowing with the power of the whole.

This is significant for our practice. *We are "from" and "toward" a reality larger than any of us.* "From" a larger reality in the sense of being sustained moment-to-moment by the creativity of the whole. "Toward" in the sense that we are called to live larger — for the sake of the larger good, for the sake of our common life, for the sake of the world in its unfolding.

To align with the Spirit on this emerging view would be *to come from a sense of the whole, to participate in the evolving whole, and to contribute to the rise of surprising emergents.* Everywhere is the center; everywhere is the source of abundance. We can align with the unrestricted impulse to know and love in ever widening and deepening ways.[15] Knowing moves toward wisdom (prajna). Loving moves to ever more inclusive circles of loving kindness (maitri), compassion (karuna), and sympathetic joy (mudita).

Coming from interconnection, committing to collaboration, and remembering oneness shifts everything.

To and fro. From and towards. From the prior oneness to the new manifestations of larger oneness — like a baby rocked at night, hearing a soft lullaby, a child who then will grow and act on its own; like a ship in a safe harbor in a gentle sea, which then will set out on adventurous voyages. What a difference it makes to come from oneness, to be sustained in oneness, and to be urged on to oneness in forms ever new.

In these last three chapters we have focused on the entire weaving — in space, as interconnection; in time, as collaborative co-creation; throughout, as enveloped in mystery. In the next chapters we shall explore these principles as applied in one-to-one relationships. We shall look at life as partnership and explore how to bring our partnerships to life more fully. For each partnership possesses its own kind of unity and holds its own place in the Great Pattern. Each partnership is already in movement and comes to life in collaboration. Each partnership is a part of the Great Mystery. Indeed, in the relational field of the two, Van Morrison's words come back to their original context. We sing with him again:

> *Have I told you lately that I love you?*
> *Have I told you there's no one above you?*
> *Fill my heart with gladness*
> *take away my sadness*
> *ease my troubles, that's what you do.*
>
> . . . .
>
> *There's a love that's divine*
> *and it's yours and it's mine*
> *and it shines like the sun.*
> *At the end of the day we will give thanks*
> *and pray to the One.*
>
> *Have I told you lately that I love you?*

References

1. "Have I Told You Lately," song with words and music by Van Morrison from his 1989 CD, *Avalon Sunset*. The song is copyright 1989, Essential Music (administered in the U.S.A. by Rightsong Music, Inc.). Note that the verse beginning "There's a love that's divine" has two versions. First, it is sung: "There's a love that's divine and it's yours and it's mine like the sun. At the end of the day we should give thanks and pray to the One." Later, it is sung: "There's a love that's divine and it's yours and it's mine and it shines like the sun. At the end of the day we will give thanks and pray to the One."

2. Inscription from the office of an 11th-century Chinese administrator. See References, chapter 6, no. 1.

3. This insight I owe to my wife, Gregg Winn Sullivan.

4. By creed, I mean the belief system. By code, I mean the ethical teaching. By cult, I mean the forms of prayer and worship. By community organization, I mean the structure of governance of the religious body.

5. The notion that "we can know more than we can tell, and we can tell nothing without relying on our awareness of things we may not be able to tell" is from Michael Polanyi, *Personal Knowledge* (New York: Harper Torchbooks, 1964), p. x. See also Polanyi's smaller book, *The Tacit Dimension* (Garden City, NY: Doubleday, 1966), p. 4.

6. Spirituality is always redressing prior imbalances for the sake of moving to larger mind-and-heart. Thus, in our time, spirituality is engaged in recovering "the body, nature and place." This project of recovering the knowing body, the creative cosmos, and a complex sense of place is presented in Charlene Spretnak, *The Resurgence of the Real: Body, Nature and Place in a Hypermodern World* (New York: Routledge, 1997), especially chapter 1. See also Sallie McFague, *The Body of God: An Ecological Theology* (Minneapolis: Fortress Press, 1993).

7. In one sense, this is another example of the fundamental distinction discussed in chapter 1 — the distinction between *something* and *our way of understanding and responding* to that something. In another sense, the case of God is unique. To make the point in an Eastern fashion, God is not one of "the ten thousand things" — God is not a thing at all. Or in a Western frame, there are not all created things plus one more, God. See my discussion in *To Come to Life More Fully,* chapter 7.

8. This view found in the East and West, North and South has been called animism. The view, we might say, emphasizes immanence and honors diverse manifestations of the numinous. Yet such a view can also turn deadly and cruel, as scholars such as Mircea Eliade have noted again and again. For a contemporary revisioning, see Freya Matthews, *For Love of Matter: A Contemporary Panpsychism* (Albany, NY: State University of New York Press, 2003).

9. On this, see Anne Baring and Jules Cashford, *The Myth of the Goddess: Evolution of an Image* (New York: Penguin Viking Arkana, 1991); Riane Eisler, *The Chalice and the Blade: Our History, Our Future* (San Francisco: Harper and Row, 1987); Shirley Nicholson, ed., *The Goddess Re-Awakening: The Feminine Principle Today* (Wheaton, IL: Theosophical Publishing House Quest Book, 1989); and Merlin Stone, *When God Was a Woman* (New York: Harcourt Brace Harvest Book, 1976) — originally published in Great Britain under the title *The Paradise Papers*. For a critical perspective, see Ken Wilber, *Sex, Ecology, Spirituality: The Spirit of Evolution* (Boston: Shambhala, 1995).

10. I am relying here on one exposition of process theology. See John B. Cobb, Jr., and David Ray Griffin, *Process Theology: An Introductory Exposition* (Philadelphia, PA: Westminster Press, 1976). See especially the Foreword for the characterization of traditional theism as (1) God as Cosmic Moralist, (2) God as the Unchanging and Passionless Absolute, (3) God as Controlling Power, (4) God as Sanctioner of the Status Quo, and (5) God as Male. All are positions rejected by process theology.

11. Such a view, called process theology, did arise in the 1920s in the work of Alfred North Whitehead. See his *Religion in the Making* (New York: Macmillan Company, 1926), *Science and the Modern World* (New York: Macmillan Company, 1926), and his masterwork, *Process and Reality* (New York: Macmillan Company, 1929). Scholars of many faiths have carried forward this work, and variations have emerged. See the overview in Cobb and Griffin, *Process Theology*, Appendix B: A Guide to the Literature, pp. 162-185. However, so far as I can judge, these views have hardly touched the work of the churches or synagogues or mosques.

12. The characterization of God as "the inside of the inside" of everything is from Alan Watts.

13. The view here proposed is one that stands with process theology on a number of issues. See Cobb and Griffin, *Process Theology*, mentioned above.

14. See T. E. Lawrence (Lawrence of Arabia), *Seven Pillars of Wisdom* (Garden City, NY: Doubleday, 1935), pp. 355-356. The quote is a favorite of John S. Dunne. He first discusses the passage in his *Reasons of the Heart* (New York: Macmillan, 1978; reprinted Notre Dame: University of Notre Dame Press, 1979), p. 1. The quote is a leitmotif in Dunne's subsequent writing.

15. The impulse to unrestricted knowing and loving is a theme developed by Bernard Lonergan. See his *Method in Theology* (New York: Herder and Herder, 1972). Also David G. Creamer, *Guides for the Journey: John MacMurray, Bernard Lonergan, James Fowler* (Lanhan, MD: University Press of America, 1996), and Mark J. Dooley, *The Place of the Heart in Lonergan's Ethics* (Lanhan, MD: University Press of America, 1996). The phrase "The Good, the True and the Beautiful" comes from Plato. However, note that Ken Wilber looks to the differentiation of morals, science, and aesthetics, and the need to integrate them as prefigured in Plato's phrase. See Ken Wilber, *Integral Psychology: Consciousness, Spirit, Psychology, Therapy* (Boston: Shambhala Press, 2000).

PART THREE

The Existential Steps

Uniting Ethics and Spirituality Through a Set of Concrete Practices

CHAPTER EIGHT

A Focus on Practice —
One-to-One Relationships Revisited

I have a feeling that my boat
has struck, down there in the depths,
against a great thing.
                    And nothing
happens! Nothing… Silence…Waves…

— Nothing happens? Or has everything happened,
and are we standing now, quietly, in the new life? [1]

– Juan Ramón Jiménez

We live at the intersection between time and the timeless. Spirituality calls us to the present, to the source, to our deep interconnection. Ethics invites us to carry this experience of interbeing into action, promoting, at all levels, what is good for the whole and fair to the participant-parts.

Consider the great web of life — woven and being woven still. A close-up view of this tapestry reveals that we are woven into all sorts of *one-to-one relationships*. These relationships are holons — wholes unto themselves and parts of larger wholes. A middle range view reveals that those relationships take their place in *larger organized systems* — from families through institutions to nations and international organizations. Each of these living systems is a holon — a whole unto itself and a part of larger wholes. The widest-angle view, the view of earth from space, allows us to see ourselves interwoven with *all beings on this planet*. Yet the planet with all its forms of life is again a holon — a whole itself and a part of a much larger universe.

We act in expanding rings — from interpersonal fields, to institutional fields, to the planet itself as a field of activity within the cosmos. The wisdom traditions hold out a picture of nested contexts and say "As above, so below." A simplified picture might be:

Macrocosm = the planetary whole with all its participant parts
Mesocosm = an institutional whole with its participant parts
Microcosm = an interpersonal whole with its participant parts

Transformation, at this time in history, means we think first of the whole and then the participant parts. The notion of "living large" is the motivational link between ethics and spirituality. The notion of "practice" is the action link between the two. Hence, practice — recognizing when we are in small mind and shifting to larger mind-and-heart — has a new character in these new times. Such transformational practice will move us:

- from focus on separate substances to relational wholes;
- from operating from scarcity to operating from sufficiency;
- from focus on the short term to the longer term — at least to intergenerational time;
- from sole emphasis on the seen-only to recognition of seen and unseen (more subtle) qualities;
- from leading as "superiority over" to leading as "collaboration with."

How can such shifts be reinforced again and again? My own work with both university students and adult learners for more than a decade has convinced me of the value of two invitations:

Invitation one: I invite us to start by rethinking one-to-one relationships — seeing each relationship as a whole unto itself and as a part of larger wholes, seeing first the relational field and then the parties within the field. *We begin with one-to-one relationships as our first field of practice.*

Invitation two: I invite us to recover some ancient wisdom. The Chinese acupuncture tradition speaks of five key energy systems or functions.[2] In this healing art, the individual body is seen as a complex energetic system. For certain purposes, this body-mind-spirit organism is seen as a self-regulating system, analogous to a politically organized community (kingdom or commonwealth). This encourages us to think of a set of functions for the well-being of the organism as analogous to a set of governmental ministries or cabinet offices. I recommend that we think of *five key functions for coming to life more fully,* and that we apply such functions to *relationships* — the smallest unit larger than the solitary self.

A Preview — Five Functions for Life Among Others

Once upon a time, in a land far away yet near at hand (as we shall soon see), there was a kingdom. Five ministries served this kingdom. Although all five operated simultaneously throughout the year, the five were named for different seasons. The executive function was held by the Ministry of the Summer Sovereign. The First Minister (counselor and diplomat, similar to the American Secretary of State) was called the Autumn Minister. The Winter Minister dealt with resources, especially human resources and, even more especially, learning as a resource. The Spring Minister, like a Minister of Defense, was responsible for skillful strategy — to protect the well-being of the realm.

Think of the four ministries facing one another across a vast central square. The Summer Sovereign's palace is on the south side facing the Winter Ministry on the north; the Autumn Ministry of Diplomacy is on the west side facing the Spring Ministry of Defense on the east. In the center of the square, there is a round building — a granary, a center for the distribution of food. This fifth ministry is called the Harvest Ministry of Earth's Abundance.

What can we learn from these five ministers? How might we apprentice to each and develop specific practices to bring our relationships to life more fully?

From the **central Harvest Ministry of Earth's Abundance**, we can learn (a) how to appreciate life, coming from a sense of abundance, and (b) how to nourish all who serve the relationship, giving simple gifts.

From the **Summer Ministry of Heart's Direction**, we can learn (a) how to name the relationship, remembering its nature and special tasks, and (b) how to call to collaborative service all officials and citizens of the realm for the sake of all given to their care.

From the **Autumn Ministry of Diplomacy**, we can learn (a) how to acknowledge situations exactly as they are (with their surface difficulties and deeper possibilities) and (b) how to let go of what no longer serves.

From the **Winter Ministry of Resources** (especially the resources to foster learning and leadership, creativity and collaboration), we can learn (a) how to practice deep listening in unknowing, seeking compassionate understanding, and (b) how to practice inquiry in unknowing — like a Wise Fool — to discover new learning.

SUMMER MINISTRY OF HEART'S DIRECTION
Heart as Sovereign / Sovereign of Awakened Heart

TYPE OF
PARTNERSHIP

family relationship
work relationship
friendship

SPRING MINISTRY
OF DEFENSE
Warrior / Strategist

AUTUMN MINISTRY
OF DIPLOMACY
Diplomat / Sage-Counselor

WINTER MINISTRY OF RESOURCES
Minister of Deep Waters / Wise Fool

Picture the partnership as a bowl or boat, floating in the ocean — the four ministries above are on the rim of the bowl or boat; a fifth ministry, the Late Summer Ministry of Earth's Abundance, is in the center, underneath the bowl or boat of partnership:

LATE SUMMER MINISTRY
OF EARTH'S ABUNDANCE

From the **Spring Ministry of Defense**, we can learn (a) how to open options for effective action, and (b) how to take skillful steps in a timely manner.

This section of the book introduces these practices in the service of bringing one-to-one relationships to life more fully. To "apprentice" to these ministries enables transformative practice in a way similar to, for example, Stephen Covey's seven habits of highly effective people.[3] In what follows, I offer ten practices to bring relationships to life more fully.[4]

RETURN TO RELATIONSHIPS

You and I
have so much love
that it burns like a fire,
in which we bake a lump of clay
molded into a figure of you
and a figure of me.
Then we take both of them,
and break them into pieces,
and mix the pieces with water,
and mold again a figure of you,
and a figure of me.

I am in your clay.
You are in my clay.
In life, we share a single quilt.
In death, we will share one bed.[5]

— KUAN TAO-SHENG

The poem is about married love. About life and death. A single quilt, one bed. A relational field in which the fire bakes the partners and breaks them and reshapes them again and again.

The relational field in which the partners dwell is a part of the Great Pattern; yet it has its own nature, its own tasks, its own type.

Marriage is but one example of such a relational field containing two parties. I have proposed that we take such *one-to-one relational fields* as the fundamental unit of interconnection.[6] This will be our *focus for practice*.

ONE-TO-ONE RELATIONSHIPS ARE OF DIFFERENT TYPES, HAVING DIFFERENT TASKS

Focus now on three generic types of one-to-one relationships — *friendships, family relationships,* and *work relationships* — and then expand the range of each.[7]

In the *friendship category,* consider all one-to-one relationships that have the potential to become friendships — from strangers (and even enemies), to acquaintances and neighbors, to deep friendships over time.[8] The basis here is that we share a oneness as members of the Human Family and members of the Great Family. We have a fundamental value and dignity, even when we forget this core insight.

In the *family category,* consider relationships such as spouse to spouse, mother/father to daughter/son, the relationships of brothers and sisters, and the whole range of family ties such as aunts, uncles, cousins, stepchildren, grandparents, grandchildren, etc.

In the *world of work beyond the family,* consider leader-follower, employer-employee, teacher-student, doctor-patient, salesperson-customer, government official-citizen, lawyer-client, as well as colleague-colleague, and on and on. Here we are primarily concerned with life in organizations larger than the family. Consider, for example, governmental, economic, religious, educational, or voluntary organizations.

In an older day, we would have said that each relationship has its own nature. Today, we are aware of cultural variations. Even so, we can speak of relationships being of different types. We can notice that different types look to different tasks.

Each of our core relationships — friendships, family relationships, work relationships — is *partly discovered* and *partly created.* Each is partly discovered because the world's poetry still echoes convincingly about these fundamental relationships. Each is partly created and re-created because over time we gain new insights and correct old oversights.

We may move from culture to culture. We certainly grow through different stages of life. With each change of life conditions, it is open to us to ask:

- What is the shape of this friendship now?

- What does it mean to be spouses in this new phase of our marriage?

- What does it mean to be mother or father to a son and daughter now that they are grown?

- How can I understand being "a son" to my mother and father now that they are in their eighties?

- What does it mean to be brother and sister now that we think so differently?

- What is required of us as colleagues now that we have new roles in a changing organization?

Relational fields — partly discovered and partly created. How can we bring them to life more fully?

FROM RELATIONSHIPS TO PARTNERSHIPS

Under the model of separateness, the individual is primary. In such a world of individuals, we can create single or double satisfaction.

Manipulation brings only single satisfaction. I will "win" even at others' expense. I am willing to go against their will and best interest, using deception and/or coercion. I treat them as if they were things to be used, without intellect and without the capacity to give free consent. In manipulating others, I refuse to see them as equal, rational, and free. I only care about what I want.

Cooperation brings double satisfaction. Consider "cooperation" as a process whereby people join together to achieve a shared task *for the sake of their individual self-interests.* Cooperation is a form of "win-win" or mutual gain. The individual self is still the measuring rod. Yet, independent worth is given to each party, and the goal is to meet the needs of each party.

Cooperation is a great achievement. Yet something more is possible if we shift from a model of separation to a model of interconnection.

Suppose we come from a model of interconnection. Then, even in a simple relationship, we can appreciate three realities: the relational field and the two parties within it. For example, consider a marriage and the two spouses. A partnership, in my sense, will serve all three.

I think of partnership as a process whereby two people join together to achieve a shared task for *the sake of a unit larger than either, a unit that also includes the parties within it.*[9] The orientation is toward a true "we," which is not reducible to several self-interests. This opens the way to *triple satisfaction,* bringing care for the relational field and care for the two parties within it.[10] My mantra for this profound shift of orientation is "Think partnership first, and then you and me."

To summarize: In this view, a relational field is itself a reality. A relational field has its own nature, its own type and tasks, its own conditions for health and wholeness. True partnership is possible when both parties orient to a reality larger than either, when both tend the relationship and the parties within it.

THINKING IN IMAGERY

Think of the relationship — the potential partnership — as a boat floating on the sea. The boat of a *friendship,* a *family relationship,* a *colleagueship in common work.*

- The boat of the partnership is itself a unity, a wholeness, something more than simply the two persons within it.

- The boat has a unique history for each couple. When that history is healthy, think of the boat as a synergy extended through time.

- The boat resonates with the experience of others who have undertaken similar partnerships.

- The boat is sustained by the elemental realities of the natural world, realities symbolized by fire, air, water, and earth.

- The boat is sustained, as well, by the web of living interbeings — plants and animals and humankind. These too, like an ocean, support every partnership.

Other ways of looking at the relationship include thinking of it as a *bowl,* or a *garden,* or a *polity* (e.g., kingdom or commonwealth). Each image opens us to think of the relational field itself as a reality. For example, the garden provides conditions for the plants within it to grow. A commonwealth sets conditions through which its citizens will flourish. In each instance, the relational field needs care as well as the beings within that field.

Two steps, then: first, to see each relationship as a potential partnership; second, to utilize the set of practices to care for the many partnerships in our lives.

A Framework for Embodying Practices

What does it mean to shift to a partnership way? What does it mean to "Think Partnership First"? Here are four images and a rhyme:

> *Bowl, boat and garden plus kingdom I see.*
> *Think partnership first, and then you and me.*

Think of the bowl of a partnership and the people within it — people who are creating the holding environment and being created by that environment.

Think of the boat of a partnership, already in movement, going somewhere.

Think of the garden of a partnership and the trees within it — the garden needing attention as well as the individual trees, the total system producing and sustaining conditions for growth.

Think of a partnership as a mini-kingdom or commonwealth — an organized form of life structured to pursue goals larger than individual purposes, structured to realize shared visions, shared dreams.

For simplicity, think here of a potential partnership as a boat floating on the sea — sky above, sea and seabed below. Think of the two partners within the boat.

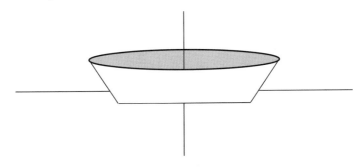

A storyteller might begin by saying: "There are four ministries or functions for life. They surround the boat of any relationship no matter how the boat maneuvers. We honor these four. And we honor a fifth ministry connecting earth and heaven, sustaining and nourishing all that arise between them."[11] Here we think of four healing functions, like orbs, surrounding the boat, and a fifth in the center and beneath.

From above, the picture would look like this:

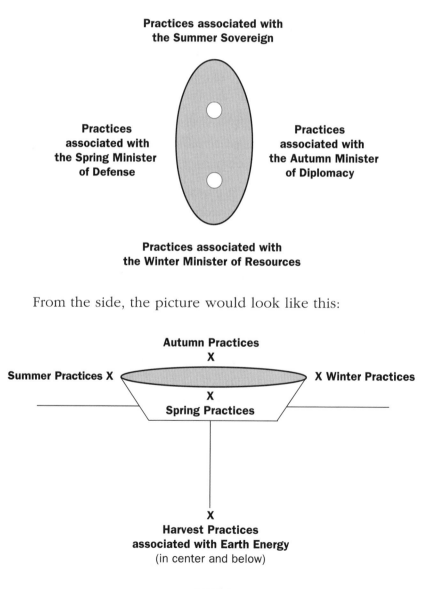

**Practices associated with
the Summer Sovereign**

**Practices
associated with
the Spring Minister
of Defense**

**Practices
associated with
the Autumn Minister
of Diplomacy**

**Practices associated with
the Winter Minister of Resources**

From the side, the picture would look like this:

**Autumn Practices
X**

Summer Practices X

X Winter Practices

**X
Spring Practices**

**X
Harvest Practices
associated with Earth Energy**
(in center and below)

Recall that a one-to-one relationship can be imaged as bowl or boat or garden. We also can think of the relationship as analogous to a politically organized community — call it a mini-kingdom or commonwealth. Then imagine the healing centers as ministries to a kingdom or commonwealth of that relationship. In what follows, I devote a chapter to the earth ministry, and then a chapter each to the summer, autumn, winter, and spring ministries. Each ministry will teach us ways of bringing potential partnerships to life more fully.

There is a value to introducing the healing functions under archetypal images associated with seasons. For me, archetypes are super-enriched images and symbols. Each person draws from the superabundant meaning the insights that serve at the moment. But each archetype is far richer than anyone can ever fully articulate. We can return to these ministries and ministers (to use the political analogy) time and time again, just as we can return to the seasons time after time. Always new insights await us. Stereotypes, on the other hand, are super-impoverished images and symbols; they reduce complex realities to one or two simple dimensions.[12]

Instead, choose archetypal thinking. Think of the relationship as bowl or boat or garden. Think of the relationship as mini-kingdom or commonwealth. See the functions for wholeness as archetypes — ministers to a kingdom. Apprentice to each of the archetypes and learn to embody practices that promote health and wholeness. These practices are very specific ways to shift from *small mind (reactive and ego-centered)* to large mind *(proactive and partnership-centered)*. Apprenticing to the five ministers allows us to take on a range of practices, to become practitioners to each of our partnerships, to care for each partnership and the partners within it.

This is a worthy aim. Since we have been thinking of a partnership as a boat floating upon the sea, we may appropriately close this chapter with a French prayer from medieval times:

> Lord, help me...
> Because my boat is so small,
> And your sea is so immense.[13]

References

1. The poem, "Oceans," is by Juan Ramón Jiménez. See Robert Bly, ed., *The Soul Is Here for Its Own Joy: Sacred Poems from Many Cultures* (Hopewell, NJ: Ecco Press, 1995), p. 246.

2. These systems are associated with the four seasons: summer, autumn, winter, and spring, plus a fifth season, late summer or harvest season — one that we can also represent in the middle of the circle. My experience is with the five-element or five-phase system of acupuncture as taught at Tai Sophia Institute in Laurel, Maryland. See Dianne M. Connelly, *Traditional Acupuncture: The Law of the Five Elements,* 2nd ed. (Laurel, MD: Tai Sophia Institute, 1994) and my own earlier book, *To Come to Life More Fully* (Columbia, MD: Traditional Acupuncture Institute, 1990).

3. The reference is to Stephen Covey, *The Seven Habits of Highly Effective People* (New York: Simon & Schuster, 1989).

4. Those acquainted with the acupuncture tradition will know that there are four officials associated with what I am calling the Ministry of Heart's Direction. There are two officials associated with each of the other four ministries. I am simplifying the twelve officials to ten practices and then applying them, not to the body personal, but to the body interpersonal. For more on the twelve officials, see J. R. Worsley, *Classical Five-Element Acupuncture, Vol. III: The Five Elements and the Officials,* privately printed by J. R. and J. B. Worsley, The Worsley Institute of Classical Five-Element Acupuncture, 1998.

5. Kuan Tao-Sheng (A.D. 1262–1319), a painter and calligrapher, was the wife of Chao Meng-fu, also a painter and calligrapher. The poem is titled "Married Love," translated by Kenneth Rexroth and Ling Chung, *The Orchard Boat: Women Poets of China* (New York: McGraw Hill, 1972). The poem is also reprinted in Robert Hass and Stephen Mitchell, eds., *Into the Garden: A Wedding Anthology* (New York: HarperCollins, 1993), p. 13.

6. I am learning to see "individuals" as the sum of all their relationships and what they have made of these relationships over time. Thus an individual person is best seen as an "interbeing." Yet in a culture of separation so used to starting with the individual, I believe there is value in beginning by considering the relational field and the two focus points within it.

7. Those familiar with Eastern thought will recognize the imprint of Confucius's five key relationships: (1) Friend-Friend, (2) Spouse-Spouse, (3) Mother/Father-Son/Daughter, (4) Older Brother/Sister-Younger Brother/Sister, (5) Leader-Follower. Notice that numbers 2, 3, and 4 refer to family relationships, while number 5 refers to a relationship in the world beyond family, yet task-centered nonetheless. For Confucius, of the five, only friendships are not defined by duties or tasks.

8. As mentioned above, Confucius sees friendship as a relational field that is not structured by duties. Here the partners are equal in the sense that what is

given and what is received are the same. Confucius sees family relationships and those in the world beyond family as structured by duties or tasks to be done. In such relationships there is also reciprocity; but what is given and what is received is not, for Confucius, the same in kind. What the parent as parent offers the child is not the same as what the child offers the parent, although both wish to see that the child becomes a responsible adult. Aristotle makes a similar point in *The Nichomachean Ethics.*

9. In a sense, partnership is an application of collaboration in the relational field of two. "Collaboration," as I am using the term, is a process whereby several people join together to achieve a shared task or goal *for the sake of a unit larger than the parties — yet including the parties within it.* When the relational field embraces two parties, I speak of "partnership" and triple satisfaction. Of course, collaboration can occur in units larger than the relational field of two — for example, in a college or corporation. Then the relational field of college or corporation is taken as a reality in itself. We are invited to care for conditions for wholeness in respect to the larger unit, as well as care for the participants within the organization or larger holon. When coming from interconnection, we are always oriented to "more than single and more than double satisfaction." See appendix vii.

10. Don Edward Beck and Christopher C. Cowan, in their book *Spiral Dynamics: Mastering Values, Leadership, and Change* (Cambridge, MA: Blackwell Publishers, 1996) speak of "win-win-win." Although there are substantial differences between how they use "win-win-win" and how I use "triple satisfaction," still the similarities bear noting. Their "third" is the spiral dynamic they discuss throughout their book.

11. In our lake analogy, the power of nourishing life arises from the deep oneness, from the "ever-present origin," in Gebser's phrase. See Jean Gebser, *The Ever-Present Origin,* trans. Noel Barstad and Algis Mickunas, revised edition (Athens, Ohio: University of Ohio Press, 1991).

12. For more about archetypes, see appendix x.

13. See Robert Bly, ed., *The Soul Is Here for Its Own Joy,* p. 112.

Chapter Nine

Earth at the Center —
Practices Arising from Abundance
and Gratefulness

From earth's good harvest,
receiving and giving,
we share simple gifts
that make life worth living.

———

'Tis a gift to be simple, 'tis a gift to be free.
'Tis a gift to come 'round where we ought to be.
And when we are in our place just right,
we'll be in the garden of love and delight.
When true simplicity is gained,
to bow and to bend we will not be ashamed.
To turn, to turn, 'twill be our delight,
'til turning, turning, we come 'round right.[1]

Think of the season of late summer, the season of harvest, of harvest received and harvest given, shared, distributed. The yin-yang symbol appears in this season as a dance of receiving and giving.

Among the ancient Chinese, this season is correlated with the energy of earth — the fertile soil grounding life and nourishing life.[2]

If we think of a relationship as a bowl or a boat upon the sea, then we can picture the earth energies below the bowl or boat, extending upwards. In many restaurants in China, the table has in the center a revolving platform on which food is placed, a built-in "lazy Susan." This device allows the food to rotate, allows all to be served. In like fashion, the practices associated with earth provide a thoughtful tending that grounds and nourishes our relationships and those within them. We receive in abundance, and we share simple gifts.

Reflect on the key image of food: food — received from the good earth in harvest time; food — given for the nourishment of all. We receive food for our bodies, our emotional well-being, our minds, and our spirits. Having food to eat and food to share is a primal cause of gratefulness.

Food harvested. Think of the round fullness of a harvest moon. In the harvest, all forms of life have a part to play. The harvest is truly an affair of the family — the human family and the Great Family.[3]

Food stored. Think of barns well-stocked for the winter; of goods made ready, preserved and stored on kitchen shelves. This also is an aspect of the earth's function — to put aside, to save and have ready, to make sure there is enough.

Food distributed and shared — distributed over great distances, and distributed across a dinner table. Think of a Christian Eucharist (the word means "thanksgiving"). Think of a Jewish Sabbath meal or a Passover meal. Think of the place of food in all the great holidays and holy days. Food distributed and shared — how deep an image of hospitality, of generosity, of courtesy, of kinship.

INTRODUCING EARTH PRACTICES: COMING FROM ABUNDANCE AND ABLE TO NOURISH LIFE

Reflect now on receiving and giving: receiving abundantly and responding gratefully; receiving gratefully and sharing freely; and, in the largest context, *receiving* from creation and *giving* to creation. From this basic power for life, we are invited to perform two key functions.

1. To show gratefulness for life, living from a sense of abundance,
2. To nourish all — by thoughtful tending and simple gifts,

for the sake of our relationships and all they serve.

Think of a time in your own life when you were truly grateful, when you knew yourself as gifted and a gift. Spend a few moments savoring that experience of gratefulness or great-fullness. A time when "all was well and all manner of thing was well."[4] What images come to you when you recall such a time? What sounds or songs? What tastes or textures? What emotions?

If we invite a number of people to share out of this fullness, we shall sense and hear the harvest functions, the gifts of earth, spoken by many voices. Each person contacts different aspects of these energies or functions or gifts. In fact, the ancient healing arts encourage us to see arising out of each season an official or minister in a kingdom or commonwealth. So, before looking at specific practices in more detail, it is useful to look at these personified archetypes of the "earth" or "late summer" energy.

Archetypes of the Earth Ministry and the Earth Minister

Receiving and giving, gratefulness and the giving of simple gifts — the image of earth in harvest time. How might we imagine a person embodying the energy and gifts of this season? How might we imagine a servant leader — a minister or official in charge of practicing gratefulness and nourishing all within the kingdom or commonwealth? How might we learn to embody these qualities so as to serve the common good — whether the common good of the smallest community (a one-to-one relationship), or an institution, or the planet itself? Here are some ways the "Ministers of Earth's Bounty" might appear:[5]

First, these functions for life can be personified as a *Grateful Giver of Simple Gifts.* Think of offering a cup of tea to someone in distress, caring for a child, bringing a meal when there is a death in a family, visiting an old person in a nursing home. Simple gifts, thoughtful tending to all levels — body, mind, heart and spirit.

Second, these functions for life can be personified as a *Good-*

natured Mother — good-natured and down-to-earth, not a perfectionist; content to be a "good enough" mother; content to be a giver of simple gifts;[6] skilled at receiving and giving, like a mother who receives from her child and gives in return — neither keeping score nor subtly manipulating, but offering unconditional positive regard; a love "no matter what" — seen simply as being a parent, as loving one's child. The Buddha says we should treat each being as a mother treats her only child. No wonder, then, that many see this minister as a good-natured mother.

Third, these functions for life can be personified as a *Sage Entering the Marketplace of the World* with hidden compassion. In the Zen tradition, there is a series of ten pictures illustrating the process of enlightenment in terms of an oxherd and his or her ox. The tenth picture depicts the enlightened one, looking fat like a Buddha, entering the marketplace of the world, serving life — yet unpretentious, almost hidden.[7]

About such enlightened ones, the commentary accompanying the pictures notes, "Even the wise cannot find them....They go their own way, making no attempt to follow the steps of earlier sages. Carrying a gourd, they stroll into the market; leaning on a staff, they return home. They lead innkeepers and fishmongers in the Way of the buddha."[8]

The accompanying poem proclaims:

...barefooted, they come into the market place.
Muddied and dust-covered, how broadly they grin!
Without recourse to mystic powers,
withered trees they swiftly bring to bloom.[9]

Here is another guise of the Earth Minister, going his or her way almost unseen.

The words *humus* (or soil), *humor,* and *humility* all come from the same root. All shed light on this season and ministry with its associated practices.

First, *humus:* of the earth, down-to-earth, earthy — muddied and dust-covered. There is an aspect of the Wild Man or Wild Woman here — connected with spontaneity, sexuality, and nature.

Next, *humor:* "How broadly [the enlightened ones] grin!" Gentle humor is itself a simple gift — helping us to see ourselves as human, to put things in perspective, to make life manageable.

Lastly, *humility:* a knowledge of our true size, an appreciation for the human condition, a sense that we are all in life together.

Again and again, we step into the place of this season and minister, live from a sense of abundance and offer the functions of *gratefulness* and *nourishment.*

PRACTICING GRATEFULNESS AS A WAY

The harvest energy of earth reminds us: We do not live in a world of scarcity. We need not speak the language of lack. We come from abundance. Together, we have enough and we are enough. "Enough for our need, not our greed," as Gandhi said.

Gratefulness or "great fullness," as the Benedictine monk Brother David Steindl-Rast puts it, "is the full response of the human heart to the gratuitousness of all that is."[10] This widest of horizons — all that is — is gratuitous in that we are not owed it. We do nothing to deserve it. We receive it as pure gift, and the heart's response is gratefulness or "great fullness." Cultivating this response is the first practice of the harvest season or the earth phase.

How can gratefulness become a deep theme in our lives and a source of service?

Much earlier, I mentioned the Sufi saying: If the pickpocket meets the saint, all that pickpocket sees are pockets." In other words, a "pickpocket" conversation is too small a conversation

SMALL-MINDED "GIVING" Language of Lack and Complaint	LARGE-MINDED SERVICE Language of Abundance and Request
Egocentric Concerns	Concern for Triple Satisfaction
I do not have enough.	We have in ourselves and our relationships all that we need.
I/We are inadequate.	We are sufficient for what is before us.
I am right to complain.	I will shift from complaint to request.
I will keep score.	I will share abundance.

for us to see the saint in others or in ourselves. We need to shift to larger conversations.

All the ministers preside over enlarged conversations. The Earth Minister urges us to notice and let go of the *language of lack*. The Earth Minister coaches us to replace a *conversation of scarcity* with a *conversation of abundance*. The chart on the previous page illustrates how we may achieve this shift.

The Earth as Minister, as serving the community, offers a set of practices: Come to large-mindedness through a sense of abundance. Notice your internal and external conversations. Shift from *language of lack* to *language of abundance*. Shift from *language of complaint* to *language of request*.

Rumi has a marvelous poem:

Today, like every other day, we wake up empty
and afraid. Don't open the door to the study
and begin reading. Take down a musical instrument.

Let the beauty we love — BE — what we do.
There are hundreds of ways to kneel and kiss the earth.[11]

PRACTICING THOUGHTFUL TENDING: EMPATHY AND WHAT IS NEEDED

The emotion associated with Harvest Season is *empathy*.[12] Empathy is not the same as sympathy. Sympathy often connotes "feeling sorry for someone." Empathy is standing in the place of the other, sharing the other's way of seeing and feeling, and, at the same time, having the capacity to distinguish wants and needs.

Acting out of empathy need not mean "fixing things." At times, it may mean supporting another to find a way through. We may lack the power or right to intervene ourselves. We can, however, remain present. Thus, thoughtful tending and true service requires practical wisdom and certain self-disciplines.

In true service, there is no sense of superiority. No desire to obligate the other. No "keeping count or keeping score" — how much you are getting vs. how much you are giving. In true service, there is the *abundance* of shared harvest, the *gratefulness* for our common life, and *generosity* of spirit. Thoughtful tending serves partnerships and those within them in accord with our best sense of their true nature, present stage, and free unfolding.

When we dwell in a conversation of scarcity, we never have enough — not enough money, not enough energy, not enough time. In such a conversation, we see generosity as expending scarce resources, see ourselves and others as "skin-encapsulated egos" and go back and forth — trapped in a selfishness vs. altruism ping-pong game. The common result is the complaint, "When will there be time for me?"

In coming from prior unity and seeking triple satisfaction, we let go of this mindset and open the way to liberation.

American psychologist James Mark Baldwin observed, "Every genuine act of self-sacrifice is an act of self-enhancement." I would add that the "self" we sacrifice is not the "self" we enhance. We sacrifice a small-minded, egocentric self; we enhance a large-minded, partnership-centered self.

A senior vice president of a large corporation was fond of saying to those he worked with, "I will never do anything TO you. I will never do anything FOR you. I will gladly be in partnership WITH you."

The grateful giver of simple gifts, the wise mother, the one who enters the marketplace and helps in invisible ways — these images remind us of some of the richness of this ministry.

ON RECEIVING AND GIVING

Recall the small verse with which I began this chapter:

From earth's good harvest,
receiving and giving,
we share simple gifts
that make life worth living.

The earth ministry provides a training in receiving and giving, without causing further unnecessary suffering.

Recall that the causes of surplus suffering are the three poisons: attachment, aversion, and ignorant delusion. Here, attachment means a kind of compulsive "hanging on, trying to incorporate the other, giving the other no space." Aversion is a fearful "pushing things away, rejecting them, not wanting to understand them." Delusion is identifying with these likes and dislikes, and falsely believing that is all we are.

Love (Sanskrit: maitri) overcomes clinging, suffocating attachment because love is "allowing the other to be other, without stipulation or restriction."

Compassion (Sanskrit: karuna) overcomes aversion because empathy is "deep understanding of what is other as though from the inside."[13]

Wisdom (Sanskrit: prajna) overcomes ignorance and delusion by understanding what is real and what is not, what reduces suffering and promotes possibility and what does not.

To receive without clinging or expecting more, without aversion to what was given or in what manner — is this not skillful receiving? To give without clinging or incorporating, without resentment and counting the cost — is this not skillful giving? Thus, the three poisons and their antidotes provide ways to measure our skillfulness in this arena.

The Earth Minister nourishes all on the levels of body, mind-heart, and spirit. For such nourishing to be thoughtful tending and not unhealthy entrapment, this minister must also have awareness of how "food" is abused.[14] For example:

To receive what is unhealthy; to receive the healthy compulsively; to reject the healthy through aversion; to identify with unskillfulness as "that's the way I am or it is." Are these not some of the ways we miss the mark in receiving?

To give what is unhealthy; to give what is healthy with manipulative motives; to refuse to give what is needed through fear of rejection; to identify with a pattern of giving as adequate when it is simply "the way we have always done it." Are these not some of the ways we miss the mark in giving?

Yet at times we do manage to receive with grateful heart, and we do manage to give gifts with generous heart. We have some skill in these human arts already, and we can deepen our practice.

SOME TEACHING STORIES

We teach and are taught by our students. As they have stories to tell of their own practices, we receive these stories and give them away again.[15]

One of my university students, Matt, had been doing some

service-learning as part of an ethics course. He was tutoring a fourth-grade student, Paul — a student labeled "at risk." This is what Matt told me he learned: "There was something about Paul that I noticed every Tuesday when I saw him waiting for me, as though this meant something to him. I worked with him and encouraged him. Strange as it may seem to you, he was the one person I felt responsible to most of this semester. I didn't feel responsible to you or for coming to class. I didn't feel responsible for my education or to my parents, who were paying for it. I didn't even feel responsible to myself. But I did feel responsible to Paul, and I thought of how he would feel if I failed to show up." A simple gift — given and received and returned.

FOR ONGOING PRACTICE

To live lightly on the earth,
to be aware and alive,
to be free of egotism,
to be in contact with plants and animals,
starts with simple concrete acts.[16]

Whatever the Late Summer Minister offers is offered as *nourishment*. A cup of tea. An empathetic ear. A warm hug. A sympathy card. A phone call to say hello to one who has been ill. An offer to see to it that loved ones are cared for. Words meant to bring hope where there was despair.

Pick a relationship — a potential partnership. Ask yourself: How may I serve this partnership — this day?

1. **Begin with gratitude, gratefulness, great-fullness.**

2. **Notice and shift *language-of-lack-and-complaint* to *language-of-sufficiency-and-request*.**

3. **Practice thoughtful tending and the giving of simple gifts.**
   Do at least three simple, thoughtful acts each day.

A good beginning — and, when done with good heart, it is enough. "Satis est," Latin for "It is enough." Satis-faction: to make it enough. Triple satisfaction: to tend the partnership and the couple within it so that — for here and for now — it is enough.

> *Either hoeing the garden*
> *or washing bottles at the well,*
> *making soup for a sick man*
> *or listening to someone else's child,*
> *studying books, stacking logs,*
> *writing to the local paper*
> *or pulling that stubborn lamb*
> *into our world, I hear*
> *the song which carries my neighbor*
> *from one doing to the next:*
> *Earth feeds us out of her empty bowl.*[17]

The words of the familiar song echo still:

> *When true simplicity is gained,*
> *to bow and to bend we will not be ashamed.*
> *To turn, to turn, 'twill be our delight,*
> *'til turning, turning, we come 'round right.'*

References

1. The old Shaker song, "Simple Gifts."

2. When the ancient Chinese texts deal with the *energies as five,* they have two ways of representing the fifth energy, that of earth. One arrangement emphasizes space and structure; the other arrangement emphasizes time and movement.

   In the temporal arrangement, late summer is quite naturally placed on the circle of the seasons between summer and autumn. This mode of representation emphasizes time — time for harvesting, storing, and distributing earth's bounty. However, in the structural or "kingdom" imagery, the earth energy is placed in the center.

   For the acupuncture tradition, the earth energy is manifested on two meridian systems: one associated with the spleen and the other associated with the stomach.

3. See Gary Synder's poem "Prayer for the Great Family," fashioned after a Mohawk prayer, in Allan Hunt Badiner (ed.), *Dharma Gaia: A Harvest of Essays in Buddhism and Ecology* (Berkeley, CA: Parallax Press, 1990), pp. 193-194.

4. The phrase echoes Julian of Norwich. It also sounds in the final lines of T. S. Eliot's *Four Quartets.*

5. In the acupuncture tradition, these personifications of the energy systems are often called "officials." I prefer the terms "minister" and "ministry." For more, see my earlier book, *To Come to Life More Fully* (Columbia, MD: Traditional Acupuncture Institute, Inc., 1990), chapter 6, pp. 75-87. For further detail, see Professor J. R. Worsley, *Classical Five-Element Acupuncture, Vol. III: The Five Elements and the Officials* (privately printed by J. R. and J. B. Worsley, The Worsley Institute, 1998).

6. Dr. James D. Glasse, then president of Lancaster Theological Seminary, gave a graduation speech at Elon College in North Carolina on May 20, 1973. He spoke of three kinds of people in religious organizations: First, the *Eggheads* — those who take a very intellectual approach to doctrines, codes of behavior, and the rest of life. Next, the *Snake Handlers* — those who crave strong emotional experiences: to testify, to weep, to shout with joy, etc.; and last, the *Fish-fryers* — those who do not consider themselves intellectuals and who are uncomfortable with public display of high emotions. If, however, you need someone to fry fish or do chores at a community supper, they are ready and willing to be of service. They are one example of givers of simple gifts.

7. In the East, there is the figure of Kwan-yin (Kannon, in Japan) — "she who hears the cries of the world," a figure of immense compassion. Kwan-yin is certainly another image of the Earth Minister, yet I choose the oxherd from the Zen Oxherding Pictures to emphasize the hidden aspect of the this minister.

8. Philip Kapleau, *The Three Pillars of Zen* (Boston: Beacon Press, 1967), p. 11. Modified for inclusiveness.

9. Ibid. Also modified for inclusiveness.

10. Quoted in M. J. Ryan (ed.), *A Grateful Heart* (Berkeley, CA: Conari Press, 1994), p. 1. The quote is from David Steindl-Rast, *Gratefulness, The Heart of Prayer* (Mahwah, NJ: Paulist Press, 1984).

11. See *The Essential Rumi,* trans. by Coleman Barks with John Moyne, A. J. Arberry, Reynolds Nicholson (San Franciso: HarperSanFrancisco, 1995), p. 36. Here I have used the word "afraid" for "frightened" (as in a Bly translation), and the word "earth" for "ground." The capitalization in the next to last line is also mine.

12. The emotions traditionally associated with the five elements or phases are these: for summer (fire), *joy*; for late summer (earth), *empathy*; for autumn (air/metal), *grief*; for winter (water), *fear*; and for spring (wood), *anger.*

13. The quoted materials in this and the previous four sentences are taken from David Brazier, *Zen Therapy* (New York: John Wiley & Sons, 1996), pp. 91-93, with small modifications.

14. David Brazier examines eating disorders in terms of the three poisons: compulsive eating as a form of attachment; anorexia as a form of aversion; and bulimia as a form of ignorant confusion with its perplexity and fixed ideas. See ibid., p. 89 and following.

15. The teaching stories from students that I share are true; the names, at times, are changed.

16. Gary Snyder, *Turtle Island* (New York: New Directions, 1974), quoted in Kazuaki Tanahashi and Tensho David Schneider, editors, *Essential Zen* (San Francisco: HarperSanFrancisco, 1994). I am responsible for dividing this prose sentence as a poem.

17. Peter Levitt, quoted In *Essential Zen,* p.33.

CHAPTER TEN

Practices of Summer Energy —
Following and Leading from
Awakened Heart

Naming our union
its nature we see;
think partnership first,
then you and me.

Having learned to receive in gratefulness and to give simple gifts, we are ready to explore the seasons of summer, autumn, winter, and spring, and the ministries associated with them. We begin in summer, apprenticing to the ministry of the heart.

Summer suggests the warmth of the sun — sun, fire, and the heart. In summer, as a season, there is maturity, joy — and yes, the promise of partnership, even of love. Personified, this season can be thought of as the Minister of Heart's Direction, or the Sovereign of Awakened Heart.[1] The emblem of the Sovereign is the Fiery Sun — Life, Light, and Warmth, touching all.[2]

Remember the slave who became king — in an instant he went from slave to free and from citizen to sovereign. In the ministry of the heart, this is our challenge as well: to become free and to care for the community. Becoming free, we enter into large mind, into partnership mind-and-heart. Remembering interconnection, we bring heart's direction to the smallest community, the relational field of two.

Coming from interconnection, large mind becomes leadership mind; open heart becomes a place where oneness and love can be felt. The heart "leads" by staying in contact with the already existing largeness. The heart reminds us that we are already in relational fields, in potential partnerships, in the Great Pattern. *This call to large, joyful, partnership mind-and-heart is the first function of the Summer Sovereign of Awakened Heart.*

The heart speaks the most intimate truths. We are and have always been in relationship. Realizing this, we can name our relational field: as friend-to-friend, or lover-to-lover, or spouse-to-spouse, or parent-to-child, or coworkers in a worthy work. *The second function of the heart is to name and cultivate and ennoble the whole.*

The yin-yang symbol in this ministry appears as following and leading. For the ancient Chinese, even the Sovereign had first to be a follower — following "the mandate of heaven." Even the Sovereign had to follow the deepest sense of what is good for the whole and fair to the parts. Only then, as in the story of the slave who became king, can the Sovereign remember what is important and lead from the heart with kindness, justice, and compassion.

As we apprentice to the Summer Sovereign, we are invited to perform two key functions:

1. To call to Large, Joyful, Partnership Mind-and-Heart, inviting us to transform relationships into partnerships;

2. To name, cultivate, and ennoble each partnership, evoking the great "FOR THE SAKE OF" —

for the sake of the partnership and all that it serves.

We discover and declare that we are already a bowl, a boat, a garden, a commonwealth. We discover and declare that all, at base, is in good order. The question to ask is not "What is wrong, and how can we fix it?" Rather, the question to ask is "What are the possibilities now, and how can we co-create them?"[3] The heart is there to remind us of these things — to bring heart to all our partnerships; to ennoble them; to trace their best nature; to call to highest service; to elevate interconnection to love; to enkindle abiding joy. All of this is associated with the season of summer, the Summer Sovereign, and the practices of the heart.

THINKING PARTNERSHIP FIRST

When we live from the space of the heart's ministry, we know that we are not "separate, alone, and in danger." We come from prior interconnection. We orient to "what joins us together." We remain open to the inspiration of the heavens. As we take on the practices associated with this season and archetype, these questions come to the fore:

- What are we about together?
- What type of partnership are we examining?
- What is its task or mission?
- What is it at its best or at its depth?
- What are the deep values it rests on, the vision it promotes, the virtues it requires?
- How can we encourage the basic values and virtues so that the partnership may be a place of peace and joy and service?

Consider these verses:

Held by the Oneness
as vast as the sea,
think partnership first,
then you and me.

Naming our union
its nature we see;
think partnership first,
then you and me.

In the tradition of the American Indians of the Plains, each household had a symbolic shield or emblem that represented this unit. In appendix XI, I give an exercise for making a shield for a partnership.

"Naming our union its nature we see." This is especially important where the same two people are co-participants in several gardens, several mini-kingdoms. In the family, we may be husband and wife and parents to our children — two bowls, gardens, kingdoms. At work, we may be colleagues, and we may be friends as well — two bowls, gardens, kingdoms. To make a shield for each is useful work. If we merge gardens or kingdoms, how can they flourish? On the other hand, once the sovereign-in-us names the partnership and gives a sense of its nature and mission, the other ministers (or functions for life) stand ready to assist. We can then bring each partnership to life more fully.

A New Sense of Leadership

Max DePree, in his book *Leadership Is an Art,* writes: "The first responsibility of a leader is to define reality. The last is to say thank you. In between the two, the leader must become a servant and a debtor. That sums up the progress of an artful leader."[4] In our context, the first responsibility is to define the reality of the partnership — its type and task, its mission or fundamental vision, its basic values and virtues. This function falls to the Summer Minister.

In a mythic way of speaking, we are invited to apprentice to the Ministry of Heart's Direction so as to learn how to care for our partnerships — with fairness and mercy, with vision and with heart. Think of how Merlin trained the young Arthur in the kingly virtues. Think of how the great Lady of Avalon trained young women in those queenly virtues that hearken back to the time of the Goddess.[5]

One caution: leadership, in this model, is *functional, not positional.*

Think of a kingdom as in the story of the slave who became king. Here, and in larger organizations in general, different people occupy different positions (roles, offices). One might hold the position of Summer Minister of Heart's Direction; another, the position of Autumn Minister of Diplomacy; a third, the position of Spring Minister of Defense. This view sees leadership as *positional* only.

In our view, leadership is also *functional.* Each person must be able to supply any of the functions of any of the ministers. This is why we apprentice to each of the ministries — to learn to give the gifts of each as needed.

Put differently, all the ministers lead, but by offering different gifts. We become practitioners to the relationship by learning to presence whatever "shows up as missing."[6] The idea is that a partnership (seen as a kind of organism) has all the needed functions for life and is oriented to health and wholeness.[7] However, this or that function for life may "show up as missing." The seeds are there, but need nurturing.

Suppose that one of the partners notices that a sense of direction is showing up as missing in the partnership. Then, with skill, that person can stand in the place of the Ministry of Heart's Direction and help call the partnership to largeness. Perhaps one of the partners stands in the summer energy of the heart and says, "We have been friends for a long time. At the moment, we are going through a rocky time. The surface waves are frightening and unpredictable. Yet we are good friends. The bowl of our friendship is solid. Our friendship has been through many seasons. We have built a world together. For the sake of that friendship, for the sake of all whom our friendship serves, can we not find a way to go forward together?" That is a speaking from the Ministry of Heart's Direction.

LESSONS FROM THE CHINESE

In the Confucian tradition, "living large" and "leading from the heart" are intertwined. One grows as a person in order to be a noble, healing presence to all the relationships of our life.[8] But what does it mean to "rule from the heart" in the highest way? Let us begin re-imaging "leader" with help from the Chinese character *zhi*.

The Chinese ideogram *zhi* has a number of senses:

to rule, to direct, to administer, to govern;
to heal, to treat, to take care of;
to judge offenses, to punish. [I would add, to prune.]

The ideogram is composed of two primary images: a river and a mouth.

The first image is a river — flowing water. The banks guide the water. They may even shift to do so. The banks provide a principle of limitation in service of the river fulfilling its nature as river. "Let the river be river," we say. In like fashion, when we stand in the warmth of the heart as minister, we learn to guide each partnership to fulfill the tasks originating from its nature — for example, the distinctive qualities of friendships, family relations, and colleagueship in diverse types of work.[9]

The second image — a mouth — reminds us of the importance of speech, of language, of skill at saying what is in one's heart. From this ministry, we speak to call forth the nature and highest mission of a partnership. We speak for the sake of the whole and all it serves. We speak with warmth and joy.

How are healing and governing related? In the ancient traditions, nature is the healer. The medical practitioner simply partners the person who is suffering so as to aid her to come to life more fully, to reduce unnecessary suffering, and to bear what must be borne. When we companion others in this way, we help them find their gifts, find their work and worth, and come into life again. Here, healing is a call to remember who we are in our partnerships and in ourselves. Not by accident do the terms "health," "wholeness," and "holiness" come from the same root. To think of the *ruler as a healer* is an aid to reorient our thinking.

How are gardening and governing related? Once again, nature knows how to grow the garden. The gardener skillfully assists by recognizing the growth pattern of the various plants and what they need to flourish.[10] The good gardener needs patience and an appreciation of the seasons — not like the person who went out every morning to give the carrots a tug to help them grow![11] When we stand in the summer ministry of heart, we partly discover and partly create a space for people (and other creatures) to grow together. Under the image of gardening, the notion of *pruning* gives a different sense to "punishing." Pruning may be required for the sake of the health of the whole, not for revenge.

Again, notice the strong emphasis on nature in this view of leadership. The true ruler is a follower — of nature and the natures of things. To think of the *ruler as a gardener* is another aid to reorienting our thinking.

In the Chinese medical texts, the heart is the ruler of the totality of body-mind-spirit. The Chinese ideogram for the heart is represented as a bowl-like stroke with three dots above it. The heart is an empty vessel into which the spirits can come. The true leader is a follower of the way of nature.

In speaking of the heart as sovereign, the ancient texts see a dual function: sovereign as empty vessel — open to the heavens and wisdom traditions of earth; sovereign as expressive of the warmth of love — heart speaking to heart. Sometimes this dual function of sovereign is pictured as a couple, the *Queen and Consort* or the *King and Consort*. Then the sovereign aspect is seen as tending the task of receiving the highest inspiration of the heavens. The consort aspect is seen as making known the worth of the work to others in heart-to-heart fashion. To apprentice to this ministry is to learn both skills.

A MYTHIC WAY OF CONSIDERING THE SUMMER PRACTICES

Poet and storyteller Robert Bly speaks of three functions of the King or Queen:

> To bring order to the realm — putting first things first, keeping big things big and little things little;
> To encourage creativity;
> To bless — especially to bless younger men and women.[12]

When we stand in the summer ministry of heart, we realize anew what is primary and what is secondary. We glimpse what brings quality to this partnership. Recall the heart as life-giving.

When we stand in the ministry of heart, we celebrate creativity. We delight in new ways of expressing who we are together and the gifts we give and receive. Recall the heart as light-giving.

When we stand in the ministry of heart, we bless — from the heart to the heart — with warmth and genuine affection. The poet W. B. Yeats wrote: "And twenty minutes more or less, it seemed, so great a happiness, that I was blessèd and could bless."[13] In the exchange of blessings, our partnerships develop heart and soul. We come to know each other in the beauty of loving and being loved. Recall the heart as warmth-giving.

By contrast, wounded or evil kings and queens have lost sight of what is most important, and hence bring disorder. They are fearful of creativity and seek to crush it. They are not a blessing to the realm but a curse. Weak sovereigns fail through inability to order, inspire, and bless. Overbearing rulers, such as dictators, exchange partnership for power. This is a false order, one that perverts creativity and cannot bless.

Drawing on the Chinese medical tradition, I have stressed two key functions of the Summer Minister:

1. To call to Large, Joyful, Partnership Mind-and-Heart, inviting us to transform relationships into partnerships;

2. To name, cultivate, and ennoble each partnership, evoking the great "FOR THE SAKE OF" —

for the sake of the partnership and all it serves.

In these functions we see a way of ordering — of putting first things first, of fostering creativity, and of blessing those in the realm.

THE POWERFUL PHRASE, "FOR THE SAKE OF"

A friend of mine who is an acupuncturist was dealing with a patient who seemed to have given up on herself. He said to her, "If you were healthy, what would show up in your life?" She mentioned several things she deeply wanted to do. "Well, then," my friend continued, "for the sake of that picture of your life, will you continue to partner me in creating movement?" The patient opened up and began to make progress. My friend stood in the space of the heart's ministry and called to large mind, evoking the powerful phrase, "for the sake of."

In one of my workshops, a woman told me she had been battling bulimia for 18 years. "For her own sake" did not seem to be a big enough conversation. Then she thought, "Could I stop for the sake of my children and their children?" This was a big enough context for her to undertake the hour-by-hour road to recovery. She did stop, and was still free of bulimia when she repeated the workshop a year later. After that workshop she wrote to me: "Again, the work with the Ministers has had a dramatic and positive effect on my life. I have been in a wobble with my husband for the past two months. When I arrived home, we were able to find our sovereign…! Yippee!"

The heart as sovereign reminds us of the "kingdom" and how

all "kingdoms" stand between the ancestors and the children. Health and wholeness always prompt us to remain open to wider circles of life. Individuals who turn in on themselves become egocentric. Yet, couples also can turn in on themselves, creating, in D. H. Lawrence's phrase, an "egoism-of-two." Likewise, a family, an institution, a nation can turn in on itself.[14] Even the entire human race can turn in on itself and not recognize the claims of all life on the planet. The remedy is to keep widening our "for the sake of" until it encompasses all that is.

Whatever the size of the "whole," for its own health it must open out to still wider contexts — all the way to the realm of mystery, to all that is. My formula to keep this in mind is the phrase *for the sake of the partnership and all it serves.*

This orientation to a reality larger than ourselves is helpful in resolving conflict. We can say:

> This issue is not about me in the sense of *my* likes and dislikes, *my* current opinions and fixed positions.

> This issue is not about you in the sense of *your* likes and dislikes, *your* current opinions and fixed positions.

> This issue is about what enhances our partnership, enhances what we are about together.

> For the sake of this partnership and all it serves, can we rise to larger mind and true collaboration?

> For the sake of this partnership and all it serves, can we seek triple satisfaction, that is, health for the relational field and health for the two parties within the field?[15]

JOY AND THE ANATOMY OF THE HEART

Above all, the heart as minister is a *joyful presence.* When we see and act from the heart, for the sake of the whole, the call to large-minded mission and service is most alive. There is a joyous quality in this way of seeing. There is a joyous quality in this way of being.

Pierre Teilhard de Chardin said, "Joy is the most unerring sign of the presence of God." Is it not also the most unerring sign of a partnership alive to triple satisfaction — satisfaction for the relationship and satisfaction for both the parties within the whole? Is it not the most unerring sign of the summer minister-in-us, calling us to care for the whole from the heart?

Once, in a group, we were seeking to decide a troublesome issue. Feelings ran high. How should we decide this? An elderly woman spoke, saying, "We must decide from the highest mind and heart." Everyone echoed, "Of course!" There was a palpable freedom and joy in the room. The elder had spoken from the place of the Minister of Heart's Direction.

Joy comes from being reminded of who we are in our partnerships and in the love and service they make possible.

When we touch the oneness beneath all partial opposites, joy arises. The events of life come as they will — some to our liking, and others, not. As we relate emotionally to the events, happiness and sadness arise. Yet the source of joy is below these opposites. The source of joy is the oneness, the bowl of partnership that remains wondrous, even on days of tragedy.

FOR ONGOING PRACTICE

How shall we practice the functions of this ministry day-by-day? We already have learned from the Earth Minister how to come from interconnection, from sufficiency, and to practice gratefulness and the giving of simple gifts. Now we can add the gifts of the Summer Minister of Awakened Heart.

1. **Remembering the oneness, go to Large, Joyful, Partnership Mind-and-Heart.**
   Think partnership first, and then you and me.

2. **Name and celebrate each relationship as carrying the seeds of true partnership.**
   Once the task and nature of the partnership are spoken, expand the task and warm it — giving it soul.

3. **Act for the sake of the partnership and all it serves.**
   From the interconnection below and the inspiration above, let love and compassion serve all our kin.

In practice, we dwell in the energy of this Minister of Awakened Heart. We call ourselves and others to large mind and collaboration in joy. We understand how deeply we are intertwined, and allow love and compassion to arise. We name and ennoble each partnership, inviting the other seasons and ministers to give their gifts.

We began by naming the bowl of partnership. Later, we noticed that the Chinese character for heart is drawn as a bowl with three dots above it — a bowl open to the spirits. Such is the way of this ministry: following and leading from the heart.

References

1. In Chinese acupuncture, there are four meridians associated with this season and archetype: heart and heart protector, sorter and triple heater. In a mythic sense, all are seen as "members of the household of the sovereign." For more detail, see my book *To Come to Life More Fully,* chapter 6.

2. In the West, in Dante's *Divine Comedy,* the principle of wholeness is imaged as the sun with its threefold aspects of life and light and warmth. The polar opposite — the depth of evil, the lowest circle of hell — is imaged as dead and dark and cold.

   In the East, the Tibetan tradition speaks of the Great Eastern Sun: Great — because it is always there; Eastern — not in contrast to Western, but in the sense of always rising; Sun — as a natural source of radiance and brilliance in this world, which is the innate wakefulness of human beings. See Chögyam Trungpa, *Shambhala: The Sacred Path of the Warrior* (Boston: Shambhala Publications, 1984), chapter 6.

3. The root notions of this formulation I owe to my colleague, Dianne Connelly.

4. Max DePree, *Leadership Is an Art* (New York: Dell Publishing, 1989), p.11.

5. On Arthur, see the trilogy by Mary Stewart, *The Crystal Cave* (New York: Morrow, 1970), *The Hollow Hills* (New York: Morrow, 1973), and *The Last Enchantment* (New York: Morrow, 1979). See also Graeme Fife, *Arthur the King* (New York: Sterling Publishing, 1991). For a splendid introduction to the myth of Avalon, See Marion Zimmer Bradley, *The Mists of Avalon* (New York: Ballantine Del Ray, 1982).

6. I take this useful phrase from my colleague, Dianne Connelly.

7. A friend, Simon Mills, uses a term from physics and speaks of health as a strange attractor.

8. When the occasion for being sovereign arises, the large-minded person (chün tzu) can become a true ruler (wang). The small-minded person (hsiao jen), when the occasion for being sovereign arises, will become a hegemon or petty dictator (pa). See my *To Come to Life More Fully,* p. 148, for more.

9. Those who like acronyms might see task as T-O-N-E — the Task Originating from the Nature of the Enterprise.

10. See Harriet Beinfield and Efrem Korngold, *Between Heaven and Earth: A Guide to Chinese Medicine* (New York: Ballantine Books, 1991), especially chapter 2, "Philosophy in the West: The Doctor as Mechanic," and chapter 3, "Philosophy in the East: The Doctor as Gardener."

11. Peter Sellers's wonderful character, Chance Gardener, in the movie *Being There,* pays a backhanded compliment to the wisdom of gardening.

12. See Robert Bly and Michael Meade, *The Inner King and Queen,* two audiotapes available through Sound Horizons, ISBN 1-879323-05-2. Bly draws upon John Weir Perry, *Lord of the Four Quartets: Myths of the Royal Father* (New York: George Braziller, 1966). See also Robert Moore and Douglas Gillette, *King, Warrior, Magician, Lover: Rediscovering the Archetypes of Male Masculinity* (San Francisco: Harper, 1990) and their *The King Within: Accessing the Male Psyche* (New York: Avon, 1992). For the Queen, See Anne Baring and Jules Cashford, *The Myth of the Goddess: Evolution of an Image* (New York: Penguin Viking Arkana, 1991).

13. W. B. Yeats, *The Collected Poems of W. B. Yeats* (New York: Macmillan, 1956, 1979), stanza iv in "Vacillation," pp. 245-247.

14. Most of these egoisms have their own names. I think of nepotism, institutional isolation, nationalism, racism, sexism, ageism — even speciesism, where humans refuse to acknowledge the worth of life-forms other than human, such as plants, animals, and the bioregions which support them and us. For more on these issues, see appendix vi.

15. This principle of orienting to standards beyond this particular conflict and this set of personalities is recognized by those engaged in negotiation. See Roger Fisher and William Ury with Bruce Patton, 2nd ed., *Getting to Yes: Negotiating Agreement Without Giving In* (New York: Penguin Books, 1991); Roger Fisher and Scott Brown, *Getting Together: Building Relationships As We Negotiate* (New York: Penguin Books, 1989). We are simply deepening this principle by founding it in the nature of the enterprise (e.g., friendship, family relations, colleagueship in shared work) and recontextualizing in light of interconnection and the possibility of triple satisfaction.

CHAPTER ELEVEN

Practices of Autumn Energy — Acknowledging and Letting Go

Three times I bow,
letting go, letting be.
I honor the core, and
I set myself free.

Once upon a time, two Zen monks were returning to their monastery after a long journey. As they came upon a swift running stream, a lovely young woman came toward them from a grove of trees where she had been waiting. "Noble sirs," she said, "I am traveling to aid my mother who has fallen ill. She lives across the stream and to the south. But the stream is so swollen that I cannot cross for fear I shall be swept away. Will you help me cross, good sirs?"

The elder of the two monks nodded graciously, picked up the young woman and carried her across the raging stream. On the other side, he lowered her gently to the ground. The young woman expressed her thanks and continued on her way toward the south. The two monks wished her well and turned to the north to continue their journey home. Neither spoke for an hour. Then the younger of the two said to his companion, "I have been wondering — do you think that it is right and proper for us who are monks to touch a young lady, especially one so beautiful as she?" The elder monk smiled and said, "I lifted her up and put her down an hour ago. You are still carrying her."

This is a story about acknowledgment and letting go — the two functions of Autumn. The elder monk takes on both of those functions. He acknowledges the situation exactly as it is and lets go of small-minded patterns. An inner letting go precedes an outer letting go. The elder monk may have needed to let go of a way of responding — through desire or fear or confusion. Only then could he pick up the lovely young woman and put her down again.

INTRODUCING THE AUTUMN PRACTICES

Autumn as a season is on the arc of descent, its energy moving downward and inward. High summer is past and the harvest is in. The trees are aflame with color. The air has a chill, a bittersweet quality. Nature is letting go, simplifying, readying for winter. Personified, the Autumn energies are seen as a first minister of the sovereign, having qualities of a diplomat. The yin and yang can be seen in qualities associated with the Autumn phase of the cycle: *acknowledging* — a deep receiving of "how the situation is" in its surface and depth, and an action in the form of *letting go* of what no longer serves.

From this basic power for life, we are invited to perform two key functions:

1. To acknowledge the situation exactly as it is, with surface and depth features;

2. To let go of what no longer forwards life —

for the sake of the partnership and all it serves.

The Autumn Minister is fully in partnership with the Summer Minister. The Summer Minister *serves by promoting large, partnership mind* — large-minded purpose and possibility; the Autumn Minister *serves by letting go of small mind* — small-minded conversations, stories, ways of relating. Both capacities exist within us; both are needed.

THE AUTUMN MINISTER AS ARCHETYPE

The Autumn Minister resembles a *diplomat or wise counselor*. At her or his best, a diplomat possesses patience and the ability to *see things exactly as they are* — with their gifts and wounds, their surface difficulties, and their deeper possibilities. To see without blame, without needing to make anything different, AND to see the deeper possibilities in the situation.

The skilled diplomat begins with *honoring,* with a deep respect for all that people are and all they have accomplished. Such acknowledgment, far from being sentimental, is very realistic. The most realistic thing is to hold paradox. The paradox here is to be aware simultaneously of how things appear at surface and how things are at depth. Both are real — both need to be acknowledged.

In the medical texts, the Autumn counselor is the first minister of the Heart as Sovereign. This minister takes the mission and inspiration of the heart into all the parts of the "kingdom." When we stand with this minister, we become especially aware of the *worth of things invisible and hidden.* Throughout history, wise counselors have played multiple roles — as diplomat-advisors, as healers, and as seers of things visible and invisible.[1] There is a touch of the wizard here, and the shaman also — as Merlin was to the young Arthur, as the priestesses of Avalon were to the young women in their charge.

THE EMBLEM OF BOWING AND THE PARADOX OF CHANGE

I see bowing as the emblem of the Autumn Minister. In the bow, we find two functions of this minister — acknowledging things exactly as they are, and letting go of what no longer serves. When we bow to another, we deeply acknowledge the other. To do this, we need to let go — let go of all that prevents us from relating to the situation exactly as it is; let go of likes and dislikes, prejudices and preconceptions.

Letting go permits us to acknowledge. Acknowledging permits us to let go. Here we have a virtuous (rather than a vicious) circle. When we acknowledge a partnership and those in it, we find the power to let go of what is no longer needed. As we let go of what is no longer needed, we see more clearly the deep value of the real.

I often begin group work with a bowing exercise. We make small circles of six to eight persons. In these small circles, each person goes around, bowing in turn to each other person. The one bowing makes eye contact, bows, rises, and again makes eye contact before moving to the next person. Each person in the circle bows and is bowed to. Sometimes resistance comes up. A black man had to distinguish between serving and being servile before feeling free to bow with an open heart. Another colleague resisted bowing to people he did not like. "I cannot bow to people I do not respect," he proclaimed. I asked if he could bow to them, both in their surface manifestations and in their secret dignity as children of God. After a pause, he said he could and would. Later, he commented, "Sometimes you have to go deep, don't you?"

Acknowledgment of both surface and depth is a prerequisite of significant change. This manifests the paradox of change. *Only by affirming ourselves and others — exactly as we are — can we freely and truly change!* When we feel we are not all right exactly as we are, then we resist. We hold on, thinking "Who will I be if I allow myself to change?" We are caught between "I could not possibly change" and "I have to change." Whether we dig in our heels or shift behavior, we will do so because of external pressure. "I couldn't possibly" is at war with "I have to." Either way, we aren't free. Only when I know my deep worth can I freely change. Only when you know your deep worth can you freely change. Only when we both know the deep value of our partnership can we risk changing its form. Paradoxical, isn't it? Only by cherishing *the deep value that remains* can we let go of surface conditions in a timely and good-hearted manner. Such is the promise and experience of the bow. As the elder monk remarked, "I picked her up and put her down an hour ago. You are still carrying her."

BEGIN WITH ACKNOWLEDGMENT

Several years ago, I had a semester sabbatical and decided to take it at a neighboring university. I looked forward to time with friends in the university's department of education. One member of that department was a philosopher like myself. He was a master teacher, an older man who had been a gift to generations of students. When I first arrived, I scheduled a visit with him. I came to him full of enthusiasm, full of plans. On my every enthusiasm, on my every plan, he poured cold water. I was sharing deeply with this man, or so I thought. Yet all I felt from him was resistance and opposition, rejection of each initiative, criticism of every new direction I proposed. I left the meeting chastened, depressed, even angry. Was this to be my lot for a semester? How terrible!

At the end of that first week, still "carrying" the encounter with the older philosopher, I went to Maryland to co-lead an ongoing group. In the course of our work together, I told my discouraging tale. Uncertain and somewhat confused, I asked for coaching from the group. One of the group members responded, "John, did you acknowledge him? You tell us always to begin with acknowledgment, with the inner bow. Did you bow to him?"

With some sheepishness, I admitted I had not. The group had called me to awareness. When I returned to Carolina, I invited the elder philosopher to lunch. At lunch, I began by focusing on him — on who he was, what his life had been like, and the costs he had paid. I began by making an inner bow to this fellow human who was also a seeker. After that, everything changed. No opposition, willing collaboration, sharing of experiences and writings and references. Best of all, my encounter has become a teaching story. I witnessed firsthand the power of acknowledgment.

This story shows how the inner bow can be practiced when the other person is present. *Equally important is practicing the bow when the other person is absent.* Stephen Covey speaks of integrity and gives this simple instruction: "Do not talk about people behind their back in ways you would not speak to them to their face." This means letting go of small-minded conversations about friends, family members, coworkers — letting go of things we would not say to the other or would not say in that manner. So when the temptation arises to speak critically of folks in their absence, we can practice the bow. We can acknowledge and let go, acknowledge and let be.

To bow to a partnership or person or situation exactly as it is, with both its surface difficulties and its deep glory, is miles away from sentimentality. Such a bow comes from the real and takes us home to the real. Furthermore, the bow can take many forms. Here is a story about the gentle Japanese Zen monk Ryokan, a figure very much like Europe's St. Francis of Assisi.

> In Ryokan's village, a father had an unruly son. Not knowing what to do, the father brought his son to spend a day with the kindly monk. The day passed, but Ryokan could not bring himself to say a word of reproach. As Ryokan was getting ready to accompany the youth home, the young man bent down to aid Ryokan tie his sandals. At that instant, the young boy felt a tear and looked up at the saint who was silently crying. The young man, then and there, came to know his worth.[2]

Was not Ryokan's tear a form of bow? And did not the quiet acknowledgment allow the young man to let go of his traits?

LETTING GO AND LETTING BE —
LESSONS FROM THE BUDDHA

Once upon a time, a young boy was born in a faraway kingdom. His father, the king, named him Gautama Siddhartha. To ensure that the young prince would follow in his father's footsteps, the father devised a clever plan. He would give his son all that young men seek: wine, women, and song. The young Siddhartha could have all these pleasures; only one thing was forbidden — the young prince was not to venture outside the vast grounds of the palace.

Of course, this one forbidden thing preyed on Siddhartha's mind. So, on a series of nights, he went out of the palace with his charioteer.[3] What did he see? An old person. A sick person. A dead person. Also, he saw a monk.

Now, Siddhartha experienced both sides of life. He knew that besides youth, there was age. Besides health, there was sickness. Besides life, there was death. He realized that, at least for him, in the presence of suffering, this path of "self-fulfillment" was empty.

And the monk? Siddhartha learned that he had renounced the world in order to find peace. So Siddhartha became an ascetic and practiced self-denial for seven years. But he discovered that the path of self-denial did not work either. In the midst of denial, he imagined the other side. He still was not free.

So neither the path of self-fulfillment nor the path of self-denial was the answer. Neither dealt with suffering at its roots. With heroic determination, he resolved to sit beneath a banyan tree until he had broken through the hyphen of this "either-or/neither-nor." The breakthrough occurred, a middle way was found. Siddhartha woke up. After that, he became known as "the Buddha," which means "the one who woke up."

What did the Buddha discover? When prevailed upon to teach, he said: "I teach two things only: suffering and release from suffering." The release from suffering demands a certain letting go and letting be. That teaching is captured in the Four Noble Truths.

The first noble truth says, *"There is suffering (dukkha)."* Suffering comes in many forms. As I have mentioned earlier, I draw a distinction between *necessary suffering* and *unnecessary (or surplus) suffering.*[4]

Clearly, day by day, we do cause unnecessary, surplus suffering — to our partnerships, to others, and to ourselves. When we are asleep in our lives, we become "dukkha-causing machines"!

The second noble truth affirms, *"Suffering has its causes."* What are the root causes of surplus suffering? The Buddha lists them under three generic headings, often called the three poisons: *greed, hatred,* and *ignorant delusion.*

The three poisons can be formulated in diverse ways. We may speak of

Clinging	**Condemning**	and **Identifying** with this state of affairs as "who we are"
Liking	**Disliking**	and **Identifying** with the likes and dislikes by saying "that's just the way I am (or it is)"
Attractions	**Rejections**	and **Ignorance** of what is truly real

Notice that surplus suffering always involves an *emotional moving toward* (attraction), or an *emotional moving away* (repulsion), or *an imbalanced state* (ignorance or delusion or confusion).

The causes of unnecessary suffering lie in our small-minded ways of relating — our small-minded ways of *understanding* (labeling, interpreting); our small-minded ways of *responding* (liking, disliking, favoring and disfavoring and the resultant confusion). When we are asleep, on automatic pilot, we respond emotionally with attachment or rejection. Then our state of mind is confused, muddy like a pond when the water is stirred up. No wonder that we cannot see clearly or choose wisely. Furthermore, without inner work, we don't even know that our small-minded responses are creating surplus suffering. We are dangerously ignorant and stuck.

The third noble truth states: *"Remove the causes of suffering, and one will remove the suffering."* In other words,

1. Notice that we are causing surplus suffering by our clinging, condemning, and identifying.
2. Remove or reduce the suffering by letting go of these small-minded modes of relating.

If small-minded, ego-centered ways of relating cause surplus suffering, then a shift to larger, partnership-centered modes of relating can reduce such surplus suffering.

All this requires daily practice — and each of the seasons and their associated archetypes offer us specific kinds of practice. As we practice the gifts of each ministry, we realize that while practice does not make perfect, it does make a difference. Some habits of mind-and-heart open life, producing less surplus suffering and more possibility. Other habits of mind-and-heart close life, producing more suffering and less possibility. The need for practice — the need to discover for ourselves what works and what doesn't — leads to the fourth noble truth.

The fourth noble truth states: *"There is a Way to remove the causes (and thus remove suffering), namely the Eightfold Path."* I introduced the Eightfold Path in chapter four. There it gave a taste of ethics from an Eastern perspective. Here it appears in its place as the fourth noble truth. And the Four Noble Truths appear here in service of the Autumn Minister — the minister of acknowledging and letting go.

Recall that I introduced the eight segments of the path by way of a chant. The chant, to be repeated over and over, has eight beats to each line:

Knowing, loving — here we go now
Speaking, acting, right vocation.
Steady, mindful concentration.
[and again]
Knowing, loving — here we go now...

Think of the chant as a round. Round and round we go — day by day. A spiral path. As there are three lines for my chant, so the Eightfold Path has, as we have seen earlier, three recurring phases:

1. "Knowing and loving" refers to the *Understanding/ Response Phase,* which deepens into Wisdom/ Compassion (prajna/karuna).
2. "Speaking, acting, right vocation" refers to the *Conduct/Service Phase* (sila).
3. "Steady, mindful concentration" refers to the *Meditative/Stillness Phase* (samadhi).[5]

The Buddha's teachings are particularly valuable where we encounter highly-charged attachments or resistances, especially when we set those patterns in stone by identifying with them — by saying, in effect, "That's just the way I am," or "That's just the way he or she or it is!" or by asking, "Am I not justified in feeling this way?" Appendix IV locates the Buddha's teaching in service of releasing small-minded emotional responses.

Is it any wonder then that the teachings of the Buddha are prominent in the functions of the Autumn Minister? Perhaps we can imagine the Autumn Diplomat reciting them in this fashion:

1. There is unnecessary or surplus suffering.
2. I and others cause this unnecessary suffering through *clinging* (attachments), *condemning* (aversions), and *identifying* with these greeds and hates as if they were the whole truth of life.
3. To the extent I reduce my clinging, condemning, and identifying, to that extent I will reduce the unnecessary suffering I cause.
4. My practice involves an *understanding and response* component, a *conduct* component, and a *meditative* component (prajna/karuna, sila, and samadhi).

Sometimes, we need to let go of a person or thing. Say, for example, that Jane is in an abusive relationship. After failing to change the abuser, she may choose to let go of the person. Say that James is an alcoholic. He will need to let go of drinking alcohol. Sometimes we need to let go of a person or thing.

Far more frequently, however, what we need to let go of is *a way of relating*. This brings us back to the fundamental distinction between *what is happening* and *how I am relating to that*. Remember that how I "relate" has two components:

- my way of understanding the situation — how I put words to it, give it meaning, and then take my interpretation as "fact."
- my way of responding emotionally — my attachments, rejections, and identifications.

Sometimes we need to shift our speaking — we need to let go of one way of thinking and speaking, and adopt another (larger-minded) way of thinking and speaking. Such a shift is often called "reframing." Consider two examples:

Situation: I say, "My daughter is stubborn." My friend counters, "Isn't it wonderful how our children are creating their lives?" I see that what I have been calling "stubborn" can also be seen as "creating one's life." I shift immediately with no resistance to this "reframing."

Situation: Two women who are colleagues and friends pass each other in the hall at work. One is mumbling, jaws tight, with irritation, frustration, and anger written on her face. Her friend notices and says, "Well, that's one way to look at it!" and moves on. The first woman stops in her tracks, responding with a smile and outright laughter to her friend's very skillful nudge toward reframing.

At times, however, we experience the emotional aspect — our clinging or resisting — in full gale force. Then we meet any request to "reframe" as further cause for anger. In such states, the suggestion "just let it go" is downright infuriating. I can't let it go! I don't want to let it go! I dig in my heels and build further resistance. I generate additional objects of anger and additional justifications for the story I am telling. Remember my story of being locked out of my office

— the "Do you want a fight or a key?" story.

How can we break free? How can we let go of what no longer serves? How can we shift our ways of understanding and responding? Especially, how can we defuse the emotional charge?

A few strategies: "Chunk down" the issue: Could you let go of a part of the story you are telling? Could you let go of some of your resistance? Could you let go for a few minutes? Could you do this letting go with a larger "for the sake of"? — for the sake of our partnership and all it contributes? For the sake of the children? Could you let it go? Would you let it go? When? Here and now.

(For more on exercises in service of letting go, see appendix XII.)

ACKNOWLEDGMENT AND LETTING GO — THE PRACTICE OF MEDITATION

The Autumn Minister's skills of *acknowledging and letting go/ letting be* lie at the core of meditative mind-and-heart. Meditative mind, like the mirror-clear surface of a still lake, is spacious and open to reflecting whatever passes over it.[6] The following image is useful:

> *The wild geese do not intend to cast their reflection.*
> *The water has no mind to receive their image.*[7]

The geese fly over the clear surface. They are not seeking to affect the lake. They do not intend to cast a reflection. Simply, the geese are flying, and their reflection is passing over the lake. The lake is not greedy, not clinging. The lake does not seek the geese, does not "grasp" for them, does not seek to hold onto their reflection. The lake does not identify itself as "lake with reflection of geese." The lake is more than the passing reflections that now and again affect it.

In meditative mind, the geese may be sensations or emotions or thoughts. They enter the "mind space" and fly across it. Meditative mind, like the lake, dwells in silence and stillness. Meditative mind, like the lake, does not react to thoughts and emotions — it neither pulls thoughts and feelings into its space nor rejects thoughts or feelings when they appear. Thoughts and feelings enter as they will. They remain as they will. They exit as they will.

When we begin to meditate, we first notice thoughts or

emotional states casting a reflection in our mind.

- We notice "thinking" (fantasizing, judging, etc.), acknowledge that the thinking is present, then return our attention to the breathing.
- We notice emotional states (greed or possessiveness, fear and clinging, anger and rejection, etc.), acknowledge them, and return to the breathing.
- We notice sensations, acknowledge their presence, and return to the breathing.

Thoughts and emotional responses enter and exit. We return to the breathing, dwelling in the spaciousness of a receptive heart.

Meditative mind "acts by not acting" — it acts without causing static or defensiveness or tit-for-tat argument.[8] Who can walk through the world without leaving footprints? Who can wait until the muddy waters clear? Meditative mind acts by indirection and thus, is well. Meditative mind can welcome the trickster from the deep waters and smile.

The meditative way holds joy; it offers relief from striving so hard — relief from being so hard on others, on ourselves, on our partnerships. Our heart is naturally open and spacious. So let us soften the armor, dissolve the way we hold on too tightly, judge too quickly, identify too quickly — and bring a little humor to the human comedy.

Once upon a time in a far-off town, the synagogue was peaceful and filled with a special presence. Only the rabbi and the cantor and the janitor were present. All at once, the rabbi was caught up in fervor of prayer and prostrated himself before the scroll of the Torah, crying out, "I am nothing. I am nothing."

Never before had the cantor witnessed such fervor in the rabbi. Soon, the cantor too becomes caught up in the moment. He joins the rabbi, prostrating himself to the rabbi's left. He too cries out, "I am nothing. I am nothing."

Moved by the unusual piety of his rabbi and cantor, the janitor too comes forward, prostrating himself to the rabbi's right, and crying out, "I am nothing. I am nothing." At this point, the rabbi nudges the cantor and whispers, "Look who thinks he's nothing."[9]

Meditative mind can be as resourceful as the trickster in facing what is there — the outer and inner weather. "We cannot let go of anything we do not accept."[10] To become free, we have to allow the very thing that bothers us — allow it to be just as it is; notice how stories and emotions arise, and refuse to identify with them. As my friend and colleague Bob Duggan said to me: "Life is as it is. Upset is optional."

ACKNOWLEDGMENT AND LETTING GO — DEATH AND DYING; LOSS AND GRIEVING

Doctor Elizabeth Kübler-Ross devoted a span of her life to work with the dying. Her five stages of dying are well known. Yet they are worth revisiting because they illuminate another aspect of the Autumn Minister. The five phases are

Denial — "Not me."
Anger/Blaming — "Why me?"
Bargaining — "Me, but not now, later."
Depression — "Yes, me. Woe is me."
Acceptance — "I accept what is, and it is all right."[11]

These stages occur both in the persons who suffer directly and in the persons who tend them. The stages are no simple progression. I think of my own father's death and the crisscross path it followed. On one day, my father would be close to acceptance and wanting only time with my mother; the next day, he would be talking of going back to work.[12]

As we touch the preciousness of life, we come to realize that we must live with a broken heart, a heart that grieves.[13] The gentle monk Ryokan expresses one aspect of this by saying, "O that my priest's robes were wide enough to gather up all the suffering people in this floating world."[14]

What do we learn in moving into the sphere of autumn and performing the autumn practices? We learn that there is real evil in the world and in us — cruelty and injustice, abuse and forgetfulness — and this too must be acknowledged and owned. We learn to let go of our illusion that such destruction could not be happening yet again, or here, or with me. Little by little, we let go of the barriers of separation that armor the human heart, taking steps when the heart is ready.

In taking these steps, we observe the way we close off our heart by holding on to people and things and self-images; by holding on to belief systems that numb us to suffering; by holding on to easy recipes and sentimental slogans.

The philosopher Socrates believed that love of wisdom required that we practice the art of dying. Jesus pointed to the seed that must die in order for the plant to arise. The Prophet Mohammed said, "Die before you die." Unless we can let things go — let them be — how can we be present to them as they are, not simply as we would wish them to be?[15]

A Teaching Story

When Ben, a college-age student in my Quest for Wholeness class, returned from an Easter break, he told this story:

"My grandfather has been quite ill for a long time. My family worried that he was close to death, so everyone in the family decided to spend Easter at my grandparents' house. The first day, it was as if I put on my 'Quest hat': I noticed how the family was treating my grandfather. They were treating him, I thought, as a sick person only, always telling him not to exert himself, to get rest — things like that. I thought, 'Suppose we simply treat him as the person he is.' My brother and I talked it over, and decided we would treat him not as a patient in a sick role, but as James, our grandfather. We did. He became more animated with more color in his face.

"That night, in the cramped room we shared, my brother and I talked about what happened. We thought it might be a fluke, but resolved to continue. The next day he started off on the same plane where we left him the night before. We were in the sunroom talking and laughing and having a great time. Then other family members came in and (to our way of thinking) tried to put him back in the box. Wasn't he tired? Didn't he need a nap? 'No,' he said, 'I'm having a great time talking to these young lads. You all should be in here.'"

Ben reported that at the end of the visit, his grandfather took him and his brother aside. "That was the best family gathering I've ever had," he told them. "Thank you."

A story of letting go of one way of seeing. A story of acknowledging a grandfather in a different way.

FOR ONGOING PRACTICE

I think of autumn in my home region of New England, and of autumn in the mountains of North Carolina: The leaves turn. The air becomes chill. Change is in the air and in our bones. A letting go. A dying to summer and a hint of the onset of winter — bittersweet moments. How quickly life passes.

In light of this, how shall we live this day? How shall we practice the functions of the Autumn ministry day-by-day?

1. **Practice acknowledging situations exactly as they are.**

   Acknowledge the inner weather as well as outer weather. "Inner weather" refers to how I am telling stories, generating upset, and anchoring the lot by saying, "That's the way it is."

   Acknowledge both the surface and the depth dimension, seeing each partner as a jewel in Indra's net, as having all the levels of the lake within. See partnership in that way, as well.

2. **Practice letting go and letting be — the path of simplification.**

   Cultivate meditative mind — let our small-minded squawks have a place in the great spaciousness over the lake, but not become all that we are.

   Simplify life.

3. **Practice the bow — in many forms.**
   See the deep worth and beauty in our partnerships and the parties within them.

Die to the old, insufficient ways, and open to life more fully.

For the sake of our partnerships and all they serve.

The older monk said to the younger, "I carried the young woman and put her down an hour ago. You are still carrying her." With skill, perhaps the young monk too can allow himself to carry her, and also allow himself not to carry her — until all beings reach their home.

References

1. This ministry is associated with air and metal. The air above is subtle, rarefied, nearly invisible. Precious metal — say gold — within the earth is condensed, hidden, and of great value. Both air and metal are associated with autumn.

2. For more on Ryokan, See John Stevens, translator, *One Robe, One Bowl: The Zen Poetry of Ryokan* (New York: Weatherhill, 1977).

3. It is said that Siddhartha's charioteer was Lord Krishna in disguise — this makes the story even more mysterious.

4. The familiar Serenity Prayer echoes this distinction between necessary and unnecessary suffering. The prayer states: Grant me the *serenity* to accept the things I cannot change, the *courage* to change the things I can, and the *wisdom* to know the difference.

5. For a visual rendering of the Eightfold Path that accords with the five-element model, see appendix IV.

6. About meditation, I have learned much from vipassana or insight meditation. See Joseph Goldstein, *Meditation* (Boston: Shambhala Press, 1993); Joseph Goldstein and Jack Kornfield, *Seeking the Heart of Wisdom: The Path of Insight Meditation* (Boston: Shambhala, 1987); Jack Kornfield, *A Path with a Heart* (New York: Bantam, 1993); and Sharon Salzberg, *Loving Kindness* (Boston: Shambhala, 1995).

7. From Zenrin Kushu. Quoted in Nancy Wilson Ross, *The World of Zen* (New York: Random House Vintage, 1960), p. 258.

8. In the Taoist tradition, this is called *wei wu wei* — acting by not acting — as when a skilled group leader makes an intervention that goes in cleanly, without causing further turmoil or defensive behavior. See John Heider, *The Tao of Leadership: Lao Tzu's Tao Te Ching Adapted for a New Age* (New York: Bantam Books, 1986).

9. This is my retelling of a wonderful story I first came across in Ram Dass and Paul Forman, *How Can I Help?* (New York: Alfred A. Knopf, 1985), pp. 28-29.

10. Stephen Levine, *Healing into Life and Death* (New York: Doubleday, Anchor, 1987), p. 110.

11. See Elizabeth Kübler-Ross, *On Death and Dying* (New York: Macmillan, 1969); *Living with Death and Dying* (New York: Macmillan, 1981), and a book she edited, *Death: The Final Stage of Growth* (New York: Simon & Schuster, 1986, copyright 1975).

12. For another voice on grief work, see Stephen Levine — for example, his *Healing into Life and Death,* mentioned above.

13. My wife, Gregg Winn Sullivan, often teaches that to awaken and become a sensitive adult is to learn to live with a broken heart.

14. See John Stevens, trans., *One Robe, One Bowl: The Poetry of Ryokan* (New York: Weatherhill, 1977), p. 75.

15. A Zen Master, like a gestalt therapist, can stand face to face with emotional conflict until the tension has nowhere to go — until the knot tightens and the dead point is reached. Then perhaps, a breakthrough occurs. On gestalt therapy, see Frederick S. Perls, *Gestalt Therapy* (New York: Dell, 1965) and *Gestalt Therapy Verbatim,* ed. John O. Stevens (Lafayette, CA: Real People Press, 1969). For Zen as therapy, see David Brazier, *Zen Therapy* (London: Constable and Company, Ltd., 1995).

CHAPTER TWELVE

Practices of Winter Energy —
Deep Listening and
Learning in Unknowing

Deep in the waters —
a place of unknowing,
where wisdom resides
and remains ever flowing.

Here is the end of a story:

Now, nearly all those I loved and did not understand when
I was young are dead, but I still reach out to them....

Eventually, all things merge into one, and a river runs
through it. The river was cut by the world's great flood and
runs over rocks from the basement of time. On some of the
rocks are timeless raindrops. Under the rocks are the
words, and some of the words are theirs.

I am haunted by waters.[1]

Let all of the rivers run to the seas. Think of oceans in winter
— cold, vast, dark, unknown. Something of winter invites us
downward and inward — into the deep waters, into paradox
where things are and are not as they seem.

A short poem by the Sufi mystic, Rumi, captures this descent:

> *Late, by myself, in the boat of myself,*
> *no light and no land anywhere,*
> *cloud cover thick, I try to stay*
> *just above the surface, yet I'm already under*
> *and living within the ocean.*[2]

At first we experience some fear — trying to stay just above the surface, afraid of going under. Then the poem suggests a turning point, a recognition that part of us is "already under and living within the ocean."

INTRODUCING WINTER PRACTICES

The season of Winter, in the Chinese healing arts, is associated with water and the emotion of fear. It lies on the bottom of the arc of descent. Life slows and moves deeply into hidden places. The landscape or snowscape is silent and still. No wonder that our ancestors often feared this deep, unknown and mysterious point — a descent into death, into the underworld, into the place of darkness and danger. Here, where sight deserts us, we are led by hearing. The yin-yang wholeness appears in listening and speaking, but especially in deep listening.

Here, in the depth of water, in unknowing, there is another ministry for the whole. As an archetype, call it *Minister of Resources* or *Minister of Deep Waters* or simply *Minister of Listening/Learning.*

From this basic power for life, we are invited to perform two key functions:

1. To practice deep listening in unknowing in order truly to understand,

2. To practice creative inquiry, like a Wise Fool, moving beyond what is already known,

   for the sake of the partnership and all it serves.

To *listen deeply,* below the words, beneath the labels; *to remain in unknowing,* even when unpleasant; *to engage in genuine inquiry* for the sake of partnership — these are some of the ways we can learn from this season and archetype.

WINTER, WATER, AND UNKNOWING

The great oceans represent the hidden treasures — the resources on which the community depends, a storehouse of primal realities. Resources can be physical, environmental, monetary, and human. Among all these, *human resources* hold a special place, for good or ill. Humans can learn, can accumulate learning, can revise beliefs and improve situations and produce great goodness. And humans can go into cultural trances and create unparalleled horror.

At the core of the human, as whole and healthy, are traditions of wisdom. No wonder then that some cultures honor their craftspeople, artists, and thinkers as living treasures. No wonder then that recovering a deep wisdom — an ecological wisdom — is central to our times.

Think of midnight moonlight reflected on the deep waters. To enter deep waters is to enter into unknowing. Present consciousness is small and circumscribed. Far vaster is what lies beneath or beyond present consciousness.

We have *in us* both a knowing and an unknowing. The sovereign-in-us cares for the community in terms of the known, the conscious, what is in the light of the summer sun. Yet if we think in a mythic way, we realize that the King and Queen within us are companioned by the Wise Fool, who is at home in what is not seen, in what is overlooked or cannot be voiced. Without the service of the Wise Fool, we can self-inflate, ignore the obvious, turn the other person into our own image, accept old solutions for new problems and on and on.

The Summer Sovereign partners the Winter Minister of Deep Waters. What is conscious and clear faces what is not yet conscious but taking form. We have both capacities. Apprenticing to the Summer Sovereign, we affirm, according to our best judgment, what is good for the whole and fair to the parts. Apprenticing to the Winter Minister, we suspend our cultural certitudes, descend into the waters of creativity and await new possibilities from the deep.

[187]

In the autumn of 1914, the Jewish philosopher Martin Buber was in an other-worldly, mystic phase of his life. One day, after a morning of "religious enthusiasm," Buber was visited by a young man. Perhaps the young man interrupted Buber's meditative prayer. Although Buber was friendly and attentive, he was not present in spirit. Later, he learned that the young man had come to him for a life decision. The elder man had answered the questions the younger man asked, but not the ones he did not ask. For Buber, this was a turning point.

As a result of this event, Buber turned from a spirituality of the other-worldly to a spirituality of the everyday. Commenting on this experience later, Buber wrote, "I possess nothing but the every day... I know no fullness but each mortal hour's fullness of claim and responsibility."[3]

We have all shared such experiences. Persons come to us. They start talking. We know that the issues they are presenting, the questions they are asking, are not what brought them to us.

> How do we listen to what is said and what is unsaid —
>   to the words and to the emotions beneath the words?
> How do we listen beyond our own filters, our own
>   judgments, our own defensiveness?
> How do we know when to speak and when to
>   remain silent?
> How do we learn what to say and how to speak it —
>   with what tone, with what tentativeness?

Listening and speaking are intertwined. The way of partnership is dialogic — to listen and be listened to, to speak and be spoken to, to understand and be understood, to love and be loved.

The simplest guidelines for good listening that I know come from Russ Vernon-Jones. He calls them ground rules for "support listening":

> 1. *People take turns,* equal time for each person.
> 2. *When listening, listen.* Only questions that draw out the talker are allowed (no interruptions, no comments, no giving of advice, no judgments).

3. *If personal matters are mentioned, confidentiality is meticulously respected.* No sharing with others without permission from your partner.

4. *No criticism before, during, or after by either one.*

5. *When feelings are expressed, welcome them warmly.*[4]

The *first rule* stresses reciprocity. We learn to listen through the gift of another who skillfully listens so as to understand us. In a partnership, such reciprocity is crucial. In functional leadership, each person leads and follows in turn, listens and speaks in turn, etc.[5]

The *second rule* alerts us to some of the impediments to listening (of these obstacles, more later).

The *third rule* reminds us that descent into the depth of unknowing requires a corresponding depth of trust.

The *fourth rule* reinforces those conditions of trust.

The *fifth rule* reminds us that such deep listening goes beyond words alone to the sphere of the heart — to the sphere where there is a love for images and drawings, archetypes and metaphors, songs and poetry, memories, feelings, attractions, serendipitous happenings, etc.

The partners in supportive listening need to accept these ground rules in advance and call them to mind as needed.

SETTING THE TONE FOR DEEP LISTENING

The Winter Minister's first function is to conduct a conversation for deep understanding. Beneath the waters, in a place almost timeless, there is no rush to action. We stay in the waters simply to understand deeply. This in itself is healing and freeing for both partners in a relationship.

My college students like to think of themselves as "doers," as "problem solvers." They are very quick to offer suggestions, solutions, advice. This often causes a "rush to early ripening," to use an acupuncture phrase. And it does something else. This quickness to find solutions encourages students to listen deeply only when they perceive a problem! "I could not practice listening this week," one of them said, "because I was not in conflict with anyone."

Conflict is hardly the best context to foster deep listening. Indeed, impulses to "fix problems" result in too much "fixing" and lead us to see "problems" as the only time for listening. My wife often says to those she counsels, "You are not broken. You don't need fixing. Remember who you are." The Minister of Deep Waters might say:

> In this spirit, let us speak and listen in turn — beyond
> labels and old stories.
> In this spirit of interconnection and trust, let us speak and
> listen in turn so that new insights occur —
> *For the sake of the partnership and all it serves.*

SOME OBSTACLES TO DEEP LISTENING

Return for a moment to the Analogy of the Lake.[6] When we are in our surface mode of understanding and responding, we love to take the stage, to be in the spotlight, to show off our skills — human traits, and they get in the way. Three examples illustrate how this can be:

A first obstacle to deep listening is *playing tapes.* Earlier, I mentioned that like a jukebox, we have tapes — prerecorded opinions — on a host of topics: politics, movies, morals, youth, parents, schools, sports, race relations, religion, corporations, money, sex, violence, and on and on. Often our conversations, far from being true dialogues, are dual monologues. I play my tapes and you play yours. Neither of us is present to what the other is saying. Playing tapes requires minimal attention. And neither of us may still believe what is on our tapes! No real listening, no real learning.

A second obstacle is *checklist listening.* An airline pilot, preparing for a flight, has a checklist for her aircraft. Such a list is useful for checking that all is in order. However, "checklist listening" — listening with a "checklist" in hand — is far less useful. Checklist listening goes like this:

"Yes, I agree with this — how sensible, how true!"

"No, I don't agree with that — how strange, how false!"

In such listening, we filter everything through our preexisting beliefs. What we come away with is a checklist of how the other person agrees or does not agree with us! Again, hardly a recipe for deep listening and real learning.

A third obstacle is *being oppositional.* Obstacles to being in large mind are also obstacles to deep listening. Thus, I mentioned JUD A.B.C. as shorthand to remember barriers to dwelling in large mind — JUD A.B.C. standing for Justifying, Defending, Attacking, Blaming and Complaining.

Clearly, the obstacles to listening are legion. We uncover them gradually and ongoingly as we move to large mind-and-heart, and see our own and the other's lens more clearly.

CULTIVATING DEEP LISTENING

Attentive listening attends to the words and their meaning; *empathetic listening* seeks to see and feel from within the other's frame of reference — it is open to words and feelings, the said and the unsaid, verbal and body language.[7] *Deep listening* does this and more. Deep listening plunges us into unknowing, puts us and our certainties into question, opens us to change in small and larger ways.

Deep listening requires that the listener drop into a zone of unknowing, thinking:

> I do not know, in advance, how you experience and label and language this event. I do not know what emotional responses arise in you. I do not know how you see the partnership and your place in it. I truly am seeking to be for you and with you, to understand things as you see and feel them — to hear you in the context of your world of meaning and value. We are in life together. I trust that the bowl of our partnership is solid and in place. Let us see what possibilities emerge as we enter unknowing together.

In deep listening, we move to companion the other, to see as the other sees, to understand words as the other uses them, to feel the emotional charge that the other feels. We partner the other in seeking the sense and significance of what is going on.

INQUIRING IN UNKNOWING

A white man and a native American Indian were walking along the shore together. The white man reached down, picked up a stick, and drew a small circle enclosed by a larger circle. Pointing to the small circle, he said, "This is what the red man knows." Pointing to the larger circle surrounding the smaller one, the white man said, "This is what the white man knows." The native American paused for moment and then, taking the stick, drew an immense ring around both circles. "And this," he said slowly, "is what neither the white man nor the red man knows!"[8]

When we apprentice to the ministry of listening/learning, we are encouraged to go beyond what we already know, into a realm of unknowing.

In deep listening and learning, we are attentive to the words, facial expressions, tone of voice, presence or absence of emotional texture, quality of silence. Such inquiry aims at what is not yet manifest; it is wary of existing words and categories, prefers images and metaphors. In creative inquiry, we hold open even what the "issue" is. For the "issue" may shift as we engage in inquiry together. Thus, early formulations are taken more as symptoms than as the root. The inquiry is conducted under the rubric "maybe."

> Once upon a time, a Taoist farmer had a herd of horses. One night, the horses broke out and ran away. "Oh, what misfortune," the neighbors said. Yet the Taoist farmer simply replied, "Maybe."
>
> Several days later the horses returned, bringing with them many wild horses. "What good fortune," the neighbors said. Yet the Taoist farmer simply replied, "Maybe."
>
> The farmer's eldest son set out to tame the wild horses. In the process, he was thrown from a horse and broke his leg. "What a terrible happening," the neighbors lamented. Yet the Taoist farmer simply replied, "Maybe."
>
> Within a week, the army came by, conscripting young men for military service in a war that had just begun. The farmer's son had a broken leg, so the army passed him by. When the neighbors heard the news, they rushed to congratulate the farmer on such good fortune. Yet the Taoist farmer simply replied, "Maybe."

When we inquire in unknowing, we stay with the phenomena and resist drawing quick conclusions. We are attuned as much to hints and images, symbols and analogies, as to precise language and ordinary logic.

Such learning can occur in the midst of life. Once, in discussing my daughter with a friend, I remarked that my daughter could be "stubborn" and gave an example — the time when she would not tell me or her mother that she had been accepted to a summer program at Governor's School. She feared (rightly) that we would have made her go! She wanted to play traditional music with her band. My friend smiled and said, "Isn't it wonderful how our children are creating their own lives!"

In this instance, I learned that what I called "stubborn" could also be called "creating one's own life." What I was labeling a problem and minor "vice," my friend was seeing as opportunity and significant virtue.

Such insights come as we transform deep listening into joint inquiry — even if only for a few moments.

Enter the Fool

We are simply asked to make gentle our bruised world. To tame its savageness, to be compassionate of all, including oneself. Then in the time left over from these ministries of justice and care, to repeat the ancient tales and go the way of God's foolish ones.[9]

We cannot enter into certain levels of inquiry without embracing our capacity to be a fool. The fool-in-us allows us to see beyond conventional certainties and to puncture pomposity. The fool-in-us can note the obvious, say the unsayable, and celebrate all aspects of the human tragicomedy.

We need courage to play the fool, to own up to the underside of life, to laugh at our own pretensions, to welcome that in us which has been shamed.

In the Sufi tradition, Mulla Nasrudin teaches by being a fool.[10]

The Mulla Nasrudin had never seen a falcon. One day a falcon flew down and perched on Nasrudin's windowsill.

Strange to tell, the falcon allowed Nasrudin to capture it. Holding the falcon in his hands, he said, "My, you are a peculiar looking pigeon. Here, I'll fix you." So he cut the falcon's beak and trimmed the falcon's wings, and pared down the falcon's talons. "Now," he said, "You are a proper pigeon."

How often do we pare down a magnificent new idea to fit current categories? The falcon becomes a "proper pigeon" — and it takes the fool-in-us to notice.

The fool-in-us loves to speak in *metaphors.* (Nothing is exactly this; it is both like AND unlike this.)

The fool-in-us is comfortable with *paradoxical reversals.* (By our wounds we are healed; let the poison be the antidote.)

The fool-in-us can reclaim our *shadow sides* (individual and collective).

Once upon a time, in the dead of winter, a Zen master and his disciples were traveling through a wild region of Japan. Suddenly, they came upon a rude shelter, which turned out to be a forest shrine with dozens of wooden Buddhas. The Zen master took the Buddhas and used them as fuel for a fire. The disciples were scandalized. How could the master do such a sacrilegious act!

In the morning, when the disciples awoke, they found the Zen master deep in meditative prayer, prostrate before the ashes of the Buddhas he had burned.

Here is an example of the reverence and irreverence of the Wise Fool. In Buddhism there is the saying, "If you meet the Buddha on the road, kill him!" And it is good advice: Take back projections; the core of wakefulness is in you. Doubtless, a teaching from the Fool.[11]

In the deep waters, we learn with both sides of our brains, calling into service both prose and poetry, the precise and the evocative, paradox and parable. In the deep waters, we find a place of imagining and re-imagining, of forming and transforming and reforming continually. We are attuned to our creative unconscious and open to nourishing hints in the form of images and metaphors, traces of songs and poetry, memories, feelings, archetypes and

[194]

attractions, serendipitous events, etc. As we apprentice to the Winter Minister, we begin to see all of life as messages from the whole to our best self. As Rumi would have it, we are a Guest House:

> *This being human is a guest house.*
> *Every morning a new arrival.*
>
> *A joy, a depression, a meanness,*
> *some momentary awareness comes*
> *as an unexpected visitor.*
>
> *Welcome and entertain them all!*
> *Even if they're a crowd of sorrows,*
> *who violently sweep your house*
> *empty of its furniture*
> *still, treat each guest honorably.*
> *He may be clearing you out*
> *for some new delight.*
>
> *The dark thought, the shame, the malice,*
> *meet them at the door laughing,*
> *and invite them in.*
>
> *Be grateful for whoever comes,*
> *because each has been sent*
> *as a guide from beyond.*[12]

A TEACHING STORY

The phrase "deep listening" is a reminder that listening has degrees. All listening need not be on the deepest level. It is still a good gift. For example, it can be a gift when a student working at her computer stops for a few minutes and pays attention to her roommate. We have many opportunities to offer the gift of listening every day. A university student, Stacy, told this story:

> Today, my roommate Jenny and I ventured to the mall to pick up this skirt she wanted to buy. After purchasing the skirt, we decided to go to the food court for a snack. As we were sitting there, I noticed Jenny staring at almost everyone who walked by. Before I could ask what she was doing, she explained that she hadn't felt like herself lately.

She felt judgmental and insecure. I just sat there and listened — I tried my best not to interrupt or comment on what she was saying. I waited to see if she could discover on her own what was going on with her. After a while, she did. Jenny said, "You know what it is? I'm lonely here, and I guess I haven't admitted it to myself until now." After that, she asked me to say something. That's when I knew I really had practiced deep listening — in the mall, in a food court!

FOR ONGOING PRACTICE

The Minister of Deep Waters puts us in touch with imagination. Shakespeare writes, "The lunatic, the lover, and the poet are of imagination all compact."[13]

How shall we practice the functions of this ministry day-by-day? First, recall that the ministries are an ensemble, their functions are cumulative:

• Drawing on the Minister of Earth's Abundance, we continue to practice coming from abundance, living in gratefulness and giving simple gifts — for the sake of the partnership and all it serves.

• Drawing on the Minister of Heart's Direction, we continue to practice coming from prior connection, calling each other to large, partnership mind, naming our union, seeing its nature, ennobling its types and tasks — for the sake of the partnership and all it serves.

• Drawing on the Autumn Diplomat, we continue to practice acknowledging and letting go — for the sake of the partnership and all it serves.

Second, optimally, both partners are apprenticing to the ministries and are in practice together — for the sake of the partnership and those within it and all that the partnership serves.

Now, we can add the gifts of the Winter Minister of Resources:

1. **Practice deep listening together** — listening in unknowing, listening in order to understand deeply, beyond what we think we already know.

2. **Practice inquiring together in unknowing** — opening space for new insights, new possibilities to arise.

[196]

3. **Encourage an atmosphere in which both partners can "play the wise fool"** — with good heart.

For the sake of our partnerships and all they serve.

The emblem of the Minister of Deep Waters is indeed the moon on winter waters. To plunge into those unknown waters is to undertake "a night sea journey."[14] To plunge into those fearful waters costs "not less than everything."[15] To emerge from those waters is to become something of the lunatic, the lover and the fool — seeing the mystery of things in the ebb and flow, listening and speaking, reviving and renewing, living and learning — as if by moonlight.

References

1. Closing lines in Norman Maclean's story, "A River Runs Through It," from *A River Runs Through It and Other Stories* (Chicago: University of Chicago Press, 1976), p. 104.

2. See *Open Secret: Versions of Rumi,* trans. by John Moyne and Coleman Barks (Putney, VT: Threshold Books, 1984), quatrain #12.

3. See Maurice S. Friedman, *Martin Buber: The Life of Dialogue* (New York: Harper and Row, 1960), p. 50.

4. See the small (19 pages, unpaginated) pamphlet by Russ Vernon-Jones called *Support Listening* (Amherst, MA: Network for Learning, 1994). Available from Network for Learning, c/o Russ Vernon-Jones, 17 Gaylord Street, Amherst, MA. 01002. This work was brought to my attention by Dr. Diedrick Snoek. If the pamphlet were paginated, the ground rules quoted would be on pp. 3-4. In re-situating these rules in the context of the Winter Minister, I realize that I am bringing in more of the creative unconscious than is in the original.

5. Aristotle long ago defined democracy as "ruling and being ruled in turn."

6. For the Analogy of the Lake, see chapter 3.

7. Stephen Covey speaks of stages: "*ignoring* [not listening at all], *pretending* [to listen], *selective listening, attentive listening,* and *empathetic listening.*" See his *Seven Habits of Highly Effective People* (New York: Simon & Schuster, 1989), pp. 240-241.

8. I retell a story told by Carl Sandburg. See Carl Sandburg, *The People, Yes* (New York: Harcourt, Brace and Co., 1936), section 32, pp. 63-64. Also in Carl Sandburg, *Complete Poems* (New York: Harcourt, Brace and Co., 1950), p. 476.

9. This saying lives in our house on a piece of cross-stitching. I do not know the author.

10. For other stories of Nasrudin, see Idries Shah, *The Pleasantries of the Incredible Mulla Nasrudin* (New York: E. P. Dutton and Co., 1968, 1971). In the Arabic world, this comic character is also called Djuha (also Djawha, Djahan, Giufa). See Inea Bushnaq, trans. and ed., *Arab Folktales* (New York: Pantheon Books, 1986), pp. 249 ff.

11. Actor Peter Falk's television character, Inspector Columbo, is a modern example of playing the wise fool.

12. See *The Essential Rumi,* translations by Coleman Barks with John Moyne (San Francisco: HarperSanFrancisco, 1995), p. 109.

13. *A Midsummer Night's Dream,* act 5, scene 1.

14. I take this phrase from Carl Jung.

15. T. S. Eliot, end of the *Four Quartets.* See T. S. Eliot, *The Complete Poems and Plays: 1909-1950* (New York: Harcourt, Brace and Co., 1952), p. 145.

CHAPTER THIRTEEN

Practices of Spring Energy — Opening Options and Taking Skillful Steps

Bearing danger and gifts
each event comes in view.
Take what is given and
find a way through.

A story from Aikido master Terry Dobson:

The train clanked and rattled through the suburbs of Tokyo on a drowsy spring afternoon. Our car was comparatively empty — a few housewives with their kids in tow, some old folks going shopping. I gazed absently at the drab houses and dusty hedgerows.

At one station the doors opened, and suddenly the afternoon quiet was shattered by a man bellowing violent, incomprehensible curses. The man staggered into our car. He wore laborer's clothing, and he was big, drunk, and dirty. Screaming, he swung at a woman holding a baby. The blow sent her spinning into the laps of an elderly couple. It was a miracle that the baby was unharmed.

Terrified, the couple jumped up and scrambled toward the

other end of the car. The laborer aimed a kick at the retreating back of the old woman but missed as she scuttled to safety. This so enraged the drunk that he grabbed the metal pole out of its stanchion. I could see that one of his hands was cut and bleeding. The train lurched ahead, the passengers frozen with fear. I stood up.

I was young then, some twenty years ago, and in pretty good shape. I'd been putting in a solid eight hours of Aikido training nearly every day for the past three years. I liked to throw and grapple. I thought I was tough. The trouble was my martial skill was untested in actual combat. As students of Aikido, we were not allowed to fight.

"Aikido," my teacher had said again and again, "is the art of reconciliation. Whoever has a mind to fight has broken his connection with the universe. If you try to dominate people, you are already defeated. We study how to resolve conflict, not how to start it."

I listened to his words. I tried hard. I even went so far as to cross the street to avoid the *chimpira,* the pinball punks who lounged around the train stations. My forbearance exalted me. I felt both tough and holy. In my heart, however, I wanted an absolutely legitimate opportunity whereby I might save the innocent by destroying the guilty.

"This is it!" I said to myself as I got to my feet. "People are in danger. If I don't do something fast, somebody will probably get hurt."

Seeing me stand up, the drunk recognized a chance to focus his rage. "Aha!" he roared. "A foreigner! You need a lesson in Japanese manners!"

I held on lightly to the commuter strap overhead and gave him a slow look of disgust and dismissal. I planned to take this turkey apart, but he had to make the first move. I wanted to make him mad, so I pursed my lips and blew him a kiss. "All right!" he hollered. "You're gonna get a lesson." He gathered himself for a rush at me.

A fraction of a second before he could move, someone shouted "Hey!" It was earsplitting. I remember the strangely joyous, lilting quality of it — as though you and a friend had been searching diligently for something, and he had suddenly stumbled upon it. "Hey!"

I wheeled to my left; the drunk spun to his right. We both

stared down at a little, old Japanese man. He must have been well into his seventies, this tiny gentleman, sitting there immaculate in his kimono. He took no notice of me, but beamed delightedly at the laborer, as though he had a most important, most welcome secret to share.

"C'mere," the old man said in an easy vernacular, beckoning to the drunk. "C'mere and talk with me." He waved his hand lightly.

The big man followed, as if on a string. He planted his feet belligerently in front of the old gentleman, and roared above the clacking wheels, "Why the hell should I talk to you?" The drunk now had his back to me. If his elbow moved so much as a millimeter, I'd drop him in his socks.

The old man continued to beam at the laborer. "What'cha been drinkin'?" he asked, his eyes sparkling with interest. "I been drinkin' sake," the laborer bellowed back, "and it's none of your business!" Flecks of spittle spattered the old man.

"Oh, that's wonderful," the old man said, "absolutely wonderful! You see, I love sake too. Every night, me and my wife (she's seventy-six, you know), we warm up a little bottle of sake and take it out into the garden, and we sit on an old wooden bench. We watch the sun go down, and we look to see how our persimmon tree is doing. My great-grandfather planted that tree, and we worry about whether it will recover from those ice storms we had last winter. Our tree has done better than I expected, though, especially when you consider the poor quality of the soil. It is gratifying to watch when we take our sake and go out to enjoy the evening — even when it rains!" He looked up at the laborer, eyes twinkling.

As he struggled to follow the old man's conversation, the drunk's face began to soften. His fists slowly unclenched. "Yeah," he said. "I love persimmons, too..." His voice trailed off.

"Yes," said the old man smiling, "and I'm sure you have a wonderful wife."

"No," replied the laborer. "My wife died." Very gently, swaying with the motion of the train, the big man began to sob. "I don't got no *wife*, I don't got no *home*, I don't got no *job*. I'm so *ashamed* of myself." Tears rolled down his cheeks; a spasm of despair rippled through his body.

Now it was my turn. Standing there in my well-scrubbed

youthful innocence, my make-this-world-safe-for-democracy righteousness, I suddenly felt dirtier than he was.

Then the train arrived at my stop. As the doors opened, I heard the old man cluck sympathetically. "My, my," he said, "that is a difficult predicament, indeed. Sit down here and tell me about it."

I turned my head for one last look. The laborer was sprawled on the seat, his head in the old man's lap. The old man was softly stroking the filthy, matted hair.

As the train pulled away, I sat down on a bench. What I had wanted to do with muscle had been accomplished with kind words. I had just seen Aikido tried in combat, and the essence of it was love. I would have to practice the art with an entirely different spirit. It would be a long time before I could speak about the resolution of conflict.[1]

Are we to imagine the old gentleman himself as an Aikido master? Perhaps. Ai-ki-do is the way (do) of the balancing (ai) of the life energy (ki). Balancing the energy achieves reconciliation, a harmony of forces. The highest mastery of the art of defense is never having to strike a blow.

The story highlights many aspects of spring energy — assertiveness, movement, frustration and anger, and the vision of a way through. Imagine that the winter has passed and everywhere signs of new life appear: the greening of the world; sap rising; upward movement — growth that will not be denied. The outdoors is beckoning; humans join the dance.

Here, in the season of greenery and growth, there arises another archetypal figure, another function for life — the high-energy Spring Minister who excels through skillful strategy and quick response. This fast-moving energy has some of the marks of a warrior, a general, a strategist, a Minister of Defense. Yet this must be understood in the highest and deepest way — as a type of skillful strategy exemplified by the old Japanese gentleman on the train.[2] The yin-yang here has to do first with coming to core stillness (yin) and then acting in timely fashion (yang) — whether by advancing or retreating strategically.

From this basic power for life, we are invited to perform two key functions:

1. To open options for effective action, seeing each event as danger/opportunity,

2. To take skillful steps in timely fashion,

for the sake of the partnership and all it serves.

PRACTICING SPRING ENERGY: SEVERAL IMAGES

The primary archetype of this Spring Minister is that of the *General–Warrior–Strategist*. This archetype can aid us to think in a wider way about strategy and tactics.[3] "The best strategy," as every seasoned general knows, is "not to have to fight at all." The Aikido teacher of the young man in our story would say again and again, "Aikido is the art of reconciliation. Whoever has the mind to fight has broken his connection with the universe. If you try to dominate people, you are already defeated. We study how to resolve conflict, not how to start it."[4]

The Spring Minister as skillful strategist embodies aspects of a *coach* in sports. The best "game coaches" are unpredictable, taking risks, ever ready to adjust to new configurations, to spot a flaw in the opponent, to capitalize on a strength of one's own. The coach of a basketball team in my region once spotted a flaw in an opposing team. The opposition was poor in shooting from the perimeter. So the home team was told to give their opponents opportunity after opportunity to shoot from the perimeter while effectively sealing off the team's excellent inside game. When the opposing team discovered what was happening, it was too late.

Skillful strategy. Teamwork. Effective action. What is taught is put to the test on the field of play. And there is a paradox here, as well. Coaches tutor their players again and again in the basics of the game. Disciplined practice is key. Yet, in a game situation, good coaches also open space for spontaneous play. In diving, the diver practices, practices, practices, and then, in competition, goes out and simply dives.

The skillful strategist also has characteristics of a *navigator*. Here again, skill and spontaneity are partners. Think of a canoeist reading the river, or a tactician in an America's Cup race, or the ancient navigators of Polynesia who could read the wind and waves and stars to sail over vast distances and return. As Edward Gibbons remarked, "The wind and the waves favor the skilled navigator." Like a navigator, this minister reads the current — moment by moment — and adjusts accordingly.

So the Spring Minister of Defense serves as *general, coach, navigator* — all valued skills for life in rapidly changing times.

My emblem for the Spring Minister of Defense is the Chinese ideogram for crisis or transition. This ideogram is composed of two sub-characters. One means "Danger, beware!" The other means "Opportunity." Thus the motto of the Spring Minister is *Transition as Danger/Opportunity*.

The spring strategist sees each moment as crisis, as transition, as danger-and-opportunity. Fast moving like a mountain stream, the Spring Minister loves action and excels at adaptability. A skillful investor operates successfully when the stock market is going up and when the stock market is going down. A skillful strategist takes advantage of each change in events, bringing together the opportunity of this day with the needs of the longer term.

OPENING OPTIONS FOR EFFECTIVE ACTION

The options we seek from the place of the Spring Minister are action options. Here we orient to concrete, practical outcomes. What will we do? How will we do it? What is the sequence of steps? What is the timetable? When will we begin? Often, "now would be a good time."[5]

Action is for the sake of the partnership and all it serves. The Spring Minister takes direction from the Heart as Sovereign concerning what kind of partnership we are in, its type and tasks, values and virtues. The Spring Minister acts in support of that partnership. As a master of change and movement, this minister plans and adapts, taking what each moment brings and finding a way through — so that the partnership is protected and preserved, kept healthy and whole.

Under the emblem of "Danger/Opportunity," the strategist is always opening options. How is this done?

Roger Fisher, William Ury, and Bruce Patton of the Harvard Negotiation Project have offered a useful model, called "Getting to Yes."[6] Their method has four principles:

1. Separate the people from the problem.
2. Focus on interests, not positions.
3. Invent options for mutual gain.
4. Insist on using objective criteria.

In my partnership model, step one follows quite naturally from orienting to the partnership as a collaboration having a common mission or task. Step three may be recast to include triple satisfaction — care for the relationship and care for the two parties within it. However, for present purposes, I wish to focus on step two's useful distinction between interests and positions.[7]

A *position* is a proposed solution. Our *interests* are what lead us to take that position. For any set of interests there is usually more than one solution. So focusing on interests helps us broaden options. Furthermore, beneath opposed positions lie "shared and compatible interests, as well as conflicting ones." The interests we have as human beings and members of the web of life are examples of shared interests.

Both the Spring Minister of Defense and the Autumn Diplomat dislike "either-or" positions. The Autumn Diplomat seeks to "slip through the hypen"; the Defense Minister often "stretches out the hyphen," noticing so many intermediate options that the either-or is again foiled.

To open options is to see every situation as in movement — to give up labeling situations as either good or bad, to see each situation as BOTH danger AND opportunity. More generally, this minister teaches us to

1. notice our own and other's Either-Or thinking;
2. shift to Both-And thinking; and then
3. go beyond Both-And to seek a solution on a totally different level — a Creative, Triple-Satisfaction Alternative.

TAKING SMALL STEPS IN A TIMELY MANNER

My colleagues stress the importance of shifting language from *It is difficult — I can't do it,* to *I am a beginner at this — I can take steps to learn.* This is a gentle mode of speaking. In many things, we are beginners. In some things, we have basic competence. In one or two things, we may display some sense of mastery. To say "I am a beginner" reminds me of "beginner's mind." To say "I am a beginner" reminds me that I can seek assistance, get coaching, and take small steps.

Taking a small step — doing something visible in the world — is therapeutic. If you cannot do everything, do something. If, for example, you lack courage or skill, or think it best not to intervene directly, then intervene indirectly and symbolically. Light a candle, say a prayer out loud for the person you are in conflict with, move a stone from one side of your bureau to another. Take an action in the world.

A Teaching Story

A man in a workshop had a wonderful invention that, if successful, would greatly benefit third world countries. To test it, he needed funds. He was oriented to a very large "for the sake of." He could acknowledge his stuckness and let go of some obstacles. He could enter unknowing in order to learn more. Yet he feared taking any steps to test his plans in the wider world. In the course of the group work, he requested and gained assistance in writing and mailing a letter to a funding source to underwrite the needed testing. To take even such a small step in the world can break a log jam.

Action in the World — Practice and Feedback

Here is a Sufi story:

Three travelers on a long, exhausting journey had become companions, sharing their joys and sorrows, pooling their resources. After many days, they discovered that all they had left was a piece of bread and a mouthful of water. They fell to quarreling over who should have the food. They tried to divide the bread and water, but the quarrel continued.

As dusk was falling, one man suggested that they sleep, and that when they awoke, the one who had the most remarkable dream would decide what to do. They agreed.

The next morning, all three travelers arose with the sun.

"This was my dream," said the first. "I was carried away to a wondrous place where a wise man said to me, 'You deserve the food, for your past and future life is worthy, and you have much to teach.'"

"How strange," said the second man. "In my dream, I saw all my past and all my future. And a person in my future — a person of all-knowledge — said to me, 'You deserve the bread more than your friends. You must be well nurtured, for you are destined to lead the people.'"

The third traveler said, "In my dream I saw nothing, heard nothing, said nothing. However, I felt a compelling presence that forced me to get up, find the bread and water — and consume them then and there. And this is what I did."[8]

The Sufi tradition stresses ongoing practice and timely action. All is talk and dreams unless we eat the bread of the teaching and drink the water of practice. As Rumi puts it: "The door is wide and open. Don't go back to sleep." The Spring Minister would nod in agreement.

Effective action demands that there be a feedback loop. I may go into a classroom and teach my heart out. For me, the class was great. I was understanding the material with new clarity, seeing new distinctions, offering fresh examples, and speaking elegantly. For me, it was superb teaching! However, I may fail to check, "Was any learning going on?"[9]

What is learned must show up on the field of play. Feedback from the field guides further practice.

For Ongoing Practice

Out of the deep power of winter, spring bursts forth in greenery, sap rises in the trees — movement upward and outward. Action, adventure, youthful exuberance. Irrepressible energy that will not be stopped, moving through barriers, 'round obstacles, full of initiative, full of creative strategy. Spring will find a way.

The Spring Minister of Defense takes action — now defensive, now offensive; now intervening with "preventive medicine," now leading through bold initiative. All is for the sake of the continued well-being of the realm and all it serves. The *mission* (tied to the nature of the partnership and its health) is the *measure* by which the Spring Minister advances and retreats, establishing a presence here, releasing an interest there.

How shall we practice the functions of the Spring Minister?

1. **See each situation as both danger and opportunity.**

    Bearing danger and gifts
    each event comes in view.
    Take what is given and
    find a way through.

2. **Open options beyond either-or.**

    Distinguish positions and interests.

    Recall the advice quoted earlier:
    If you have one choice, you have no choice.
    If you have two choices, you are often on the horns
        of a dilemma.
    Only with more than two options do you begin
        to be free.

3. **Take steps, moving into effective action.**

    Even if the step is small, let it be an action in the world.

    Prize constructive feedback as an aid to effective action.

    For the sake of our partnerships and all they serve.

In the end, we return to the scene on the train, to the little Japanese gentleman cradling the head of the drunken workman in his lap. With the young man who sits on the bench in the station, we watch as the train pulls away. We think with him:

> *What I had wanted to do with muscle had been*
> *accomplished with kind words. I had just seen*
> *Aikido tried in combat, and the essence of it was*
> *love. I would have to practice the art with an entirely*
> *different spirit. It would be a long time before I could*
> *speak about the resolution of conflict.*

References

1. See Ram Dass and Paul Gorman, *How Can I Help? Stories and Reflections on Service* (New York: Alfred A. Knopf, 1986), pp. 167-171.

2. At the lowest level, the warrior is one who is a bully, mercenary, lover of violence — operating out of brute strength or cold, cruel cunning. In this mode of consciousness, "winning" takes place at the expense of others. *Single satisfaction* is the rule.
   At a middle level, the notion of warrior shifts to emphasize thoughtful strategy, openness to cooperation, seeking mutual gain — a win-win situation. In this mode of consciousness, the strategist thinks in more subtle terms, opens options beyond "either-or," seeks to preserve the peace. *Double satisfaction* is at the fore.
   At the highest level, where *triple satisfaction* is the goal, the notion of warrior deepens to that of strategist in service of partnership. In this awareness, the skillful strategist understands the deep roots of oneness and the possibilities for true collaboration. Such a warrior is ready to go on offense or defense for the sake of the shared mission, for the sake of caring for "what joins us together" and the genuine needs of the parties.

3. On the warrior way, see Chögyam Trungpa, *Shambhala: The Sacred Path of the Warrior* (Boston: Shambhala, 1983); Sun Tzu, ed. James Clavel, *The Art of War* (New York: Dell Publishing, 1983); Miyamoto Musashi, trans. Victor Harris, *A Book of Five Rings* (Woodstock, NY: Overlook Press, 1974); Arthur Braverman, ed. and trans., *Warrior of Zen: The Diamond-hard Wisdom Mind of Suzuki Shosan* (New York: Kodansha America, Inc., 1994). For a critique of the darker side of the Japanese Zen warrior tradition, see David Loy, *Lack and Transcendence: The Problem of Death and Life in Psychology, Existentialism and Buddhism* (Atlantic Highlands, NJ: Humanities Press, 1996).

4. See Ram Dass and Paul Gorman, *How Can I Help?*, p. 168.

5. A friend, Sam Magill, shared with me that the phrase "now would be a good time" was a favorite of Peter Block, one of his teachers.

6. See their book: Roger Fisher, William Ury, Bruce Patton, 2nd edition, *Getting to Yes: Negotiating Agreement Without Giving In* (New York: Penguin Books, 1991).

7. See ibid., chapter three, pp. 40-55.

8. I am retelling a story from Indries Shah, *Tales of the Dervishes* (New York: E. P. Dutton, 1970), p. 111. The tale is attributed to Shah Mohammed Gwath Shattari, who died in 1563.

9. The theme of actions needing to be effective is sounded again and again by the Sufi teacher Indries Shah in his book, *The Commanding Self* (London: Octagon Press, 1994).

PART FOUR

Living Large
as a Way

Sustaining the
Spiral Path

CHAPTER FOURTEEN

Living Large as a Way —
Walking the Spiral Path

For everything (turn, turn)
there is a season
and a time for every purpose under heaven:
a time to be born, a time to die
a time to plant and a time to uproot
a time to slay and a time to heal
a time to tear down and a time to build.[1]

In the last section, our tasks were:

- to practice the seasonal gifts and archetypal functions
  with regard to one-to-one relationships.
- to see "two" but think "three" — to think of the
  relational field and the parties within it, to consider
  each relationship as a potential partnership.
  "Think partnership first and then you and me."
- to bring the partnership to life more fully for its own
  sake and for the sake of all it serves.

As beginners, we experienced the seasons and apprenticed
to the ministries one by one. Now is the time to see the seasons

and ministries as an ensemble. The archetypes are an ensemble, like a jazz quintet. We apprentice to each. We learn to realize that each role is essential for harmony. We learn to "play a variety of instruments" so as to take on any role when needed.

The arrangement resembles a mandala: four directions, four seasons, with the center as a fifth direction — a fifth season.[2] Each contains a function for living large; each gives rise to an archetype of service.

In walking the path, I suggest that we start and end in the center. From the center, move to the Summer Minister of Heart's Direction. Then visit the seasons Autumn to Winter to Spring. Then back to the center. Think of the center as extending upward like a vertical pole or an elevator. When we return from one cycle, we move upward and begin again.

When we thought of a partnership as a bowl or boat, we placed the Earth/Harvest Ministry beneath the partnership. This is a fitting reminder that we come from interconnection and that we have — in ourselves and others — all we need to live a life of quality. Gratefulness is an appropriate spirit in which to begin and end.

Pick a partnership in which you dwell. Where possible, walk the spiral with your partner. If the partnership is not all it could be, walk the spiral path for the sake of deepening the partnership and all it serves.

Walking the path as a couple is excellent. However, when that is not possible, one person can walk the spiral *for the sake of* the partnership and both parties within it.[3]

Walking the spiral is a way to visit each season and each minister. In this fashion, we become a practitioner to the partnership — giving gifts to the partnership from each ministry, giving a "treatment" to the partnership from each ministry.

Walking the spiral allows us to look at a partnership from five different perspectives. We also grow and deepen as we practice the five functions to bring the partnership to life more fully.

As prologue, begin in the center, in the harvest energy of late summer with the **Minister of Earth's Abundance**. Think of this minister's emblem as a cornucopia such as graces many tables at Thanksgiving.

In this place of earth's abundance, we open our hearts in gratefulness — great-fullness. We come from a sense of prior interconnection and recall the Great Mystery that awakens wonder. We are alive. We are together. In ourselves and others, we have all we need to live a life of quality. Gratefulness wells up. We know life as abundance. We respond with thoughtfulness and by giving simple gifts — *for the sake of the partnership and all it serves.*

On the rim of the circle, we go first to the **Summer Minister of Heart's Direction** whose emblem is the sun. From this place, we call ourselves to large, joyful, partnership mind-and-heart. We name the type and task of the unique partnership before us. What kind of partnership are we in? What are we about when we are together, when we are at our best?

Taking on the role of Minister of Awakened Heart, we define the partnership and invite all the other ministers to aid it to flourish. I repeat: This process is especially crucial where two people are together in several partnerships. For example, a couple may be husband and wife. They may also be parents to children. They may also be colleagues in a common work. So naming the partnership, and calling to mind its nature and task and mission — all this is needed at the outset — *for the sake of the partnership and all it serves.*

Move next from summer into the energy of autumn. Embody the energy of the **Autumn Diplomat** whose emblem is bowing. Bow to the partnership, to the other and to oneself. A triple bow. Acknowledge the partnership exactly as it is — in its deep beauty and value, and in the desires and fears that play around the surface. Acknowledge each partner in the same way.

Ask: What old patterns, old stories, old emotions do we need to release so that the partnership and those within it can have more freedom? Is there grief work to be done? In this autumn spirit, bring acknowledgment and letting go to the partnership — *for the sake of the partnership and all it serves.*

Continue downward and inward into the deep water of winter. Feel the winter energy — bracing and cold, the power of entering into unknowing. Take on the power of this **Minister of Deep Waters** whose emblem is moonlight on the waters and the night sea journey. In the deep waters is space for listening and learning. Be attentive to the quality of listening. Give the gift of deep listening. What dreams are forming? What images arise? What poetry draws us? What teaching stories open our hearts? What new learning might we undertake — *for the sake of the partnership and all it serves?*

When the time is ripe, move upward and outward to the **Spring Minister of Skillful Strategy**. Notice the life situations before us. Think creatively, seeing every situation as both danger and opportunity. Open new options for effective action. Choose to take one or two steps. Decide when and how to realize them. Ask for support needed to take these actions. Do all this *for the sake of the partnership and all it serves.*

Finally, return to the center, to the **Harvest Minister** in a renewed spirit of gratefulness. What new insights prompt new appreciation for the partnership and each partner? What simple gifts are already being exchanged? How will we make sure to notice the gifts of this partnership? What tending will we give and receive — *for the sake of the partnership and all it serves?*

This is one walk around the cycle, one turn on the spiral path. Appendix xiv gives a chart with two functions for each minister.

Appendix xv gives a list of sample "prompt" questions from each of the seasons and ministries.

With each turn on the spiral path, we return to the central axis and move upward and outward. Always we start with gratefulness. Always we invoke the Sovereign of Awakened Heart to declare the partnership — its nature, point, and purpose. Then, with the partnership named and its mission celebrated, we can ask the

Prologue: Beginning at the center

Minister of Earth's Abundance

Receive in abundance
and give generously.
Think partnership first,
and then you and me.

* *

Summer Minister of Heart's Direction

Held by the Oneness
as deep as the sea,
Think partnership first,
then you and me.

Naming our union,
its nature we see.
Think partnership first,
then you and me.

Spring Minister of Defense

Slip through the hyphen —
take action and see.
Think partnership first,
then you and me.

Autumn Minister of Diplomacy

Three times we bow
letting go, letting be.
Think partnership first,
then you and me.

Winter Minister of Deep Waters

Listening and learning
and finding the key,
Think partnership first,
then you and me.

* *

Epilogue: Return to the center

Minister of Earth's Abundance

Receive in abundance
and give generously.
Think partnership first,
then you and me.

assistance of the other ministries. We end each round by returning to the center, consolidating the learning and finding the nourishment we need to continue.

The Ministries as Meditations

I wrote an earlier version of the following short verses as a memory device for each of the ministries. In this spirit I offered them to participants in one of my workshops. Later, I was humbled to learn that they were of real assistance to a woman in the group. She used them as reminders as she went through a very serious illness.[4] Recalling this, I overcame a bit of reluctance. And so I present them on the previous page both as a memory device and as mini-meditations.

Acting as a Practitioner to Life

Each of the seasons and each of the ministries has gifts to give:

Gratefulness — receiving and giving — giving thanks, nourishing all.

Presencing the Awakened Heart —

Following and leading in new ways.
Knowing and being known.
Loving and being loved.
In everything, a path with a heart.

Acknowledging and letting go — the dynamics of the bow.

Listening and speaking — inquiring together in unknowing.

Being and doing — opening options and taking steps.

Returning to the oneness, to gratefulness, to new beginnings.

If we live these practices, if we give and receive these gifts, how much less surplus suffering and how many more creative possibilities manifest in all the partnerships of our lives?

Each relationship arises out of oneness; each is a potential partnership. Some partnerships are very brief — a chance encounter, an exchange with a clerk in a store. Some partnerships last a lifetime. Living life as partnership opens new possibilities for living in a larger way — larger conversations; more space for choosing life, for bringing all our relationships to life more fully. When people share a framework and engage in practice together — what a gift it is.

To embody these powers for partnership, I suggest a daily ritual — a ritual that shifts and changes and stays fresh. The call to daily practice resonates with the great religions of the West and the great "ways" of the East. These wisdom traditions have ample material to open the heart. For those chary of "spirituality," we have the poetry of the seasons, the beauty of nature, and all the arts to enlighten and enkindle the heart.

A daily ritual might devote four minutes in the morning to remembering who we are together; perhaps two minutes at midday to renew our commitment in gratefulness; at the day's end, perhaps four minutes to make a journal entry or read a poem or say a prayer. Appendix ii offers further detail concerning a ritual of daily practice.

THE LIFE AND DEATH OF PARTNERSHIPS

Partnerships have their births and deaths, their beginnings and endings. They are not immune from the ebb and flow of time.

Let us think of friendships, family relations, relationships in organizations ...

Sometimes they *change their outward form* without changing their nature or kind. I think of my relationship with my mother. She is always my mother and I am always her son; yet the outward form shifts as I become an adult and my mother becomes an elder.[5]

Sometimes partnerships *dissolve*. My father has died. This partnership of father and son no longer appears in this world.

Sometimes partnerships *change kind*. A husband and wife may divorce. The man is no longer husband to the wife, or the woman wife to the husband. Are they still in a partnership? Yes, they are at least fellow humans who can wish each other well. They may succeed in remaining friends or colleagues. They may continue to be co-parents of children. Here the weaving continues, yet a new pattern replaces the old.

So it is with larger units, as well. Colleagues may cease to collaborate in shared work. Perhaps the work was completed. Perhaps the work continued but the workers changed. Colleges and universities rise and fall. Corporations are built, merge, downsize, and cease to be. Organizations meet needs and dissolve when the needs change or the impetus diminishes. Nations arise and change and die. "For everything there is a season, and a time for every purpose under heaven."

And yet what was always is. What was woven together with its gifts and wounds remains a part of the world's unfolding. China's great poet, Li Po, offers this verse:

> *The birds have vanished into the sky*
> *and now the last clouds fade away.*
> *We sit together, the mountain and I,*
> *until only the mountain remains.*[6]

The Great Pattern remains and the Mystery that surrounds it — smaller than the small and larger than the large. Yet the Pattern is also *us,* because all that has been done *from the heart* — in the spirit of service — remains always, like the threads in a quilt, like the veins in the rock face of a mountain, like the sound of events echoing still.

Sometimes we are asked to let go of a partnership, to grieve for the loss and, in time, to see the opportunity on the other side of sadness. More often, we are invited to let go of a certain way of relating to a partnership. I am father to my daughter, Heather. What does it mean for me to be her father now, at this later stage in our lives? For Heather, what does it mean to be daughter to me now, at this later age and later stage of life? What needs to die in our partnership, and what needs to be born?

Knowing the seasons and apprenticing to the ministers does not give us a recipe for denying or avoiding death. Still we can attend to whatever is dying and being born with various degrees of skill — with more or less insight, with more or less compassion, with more or less love. We can understand and respond to these changes with a fuller heart. We can lessen surplus suffering and promote creative possibility. What is to be released, we can learn to release. What must be borne, we can bear together.

In this spirit, growth occurs — sometimes in bursts of insights, sometimes in hidden ways. Recall again the poem "Oceans" by Juan Ramón Jiménez:

> *I have a feeling that my boat*
> *has stuck, down there in the depths,*
> *against a great thing.*
> > *And nothing*
> *happens! Nothing... Silence... Waves...*

> *— Nothing happens? Or has everything happened,*
> *and are we standing now, quietly, in the new life?*[7]

References

1. Ecclesiastes 3:1-3, with the "turn, turn" echoing the popular musical setting.

2. In my teaching, I use circles of different colors. In accord with the model of Chinese medicine, summer is red; autumn is white; winter is blue; spring is green; and the fifth season, correlated with earth, is yellow.

3. In workshops, I often use yarn to mark on the floor the oval of the partnership. I then put down five circles representing the ministries, placing the earth ministry in the center. The previous note gives the colors of the circles. A small necklace of yarn (or any other object) can be useful as a reminder that the person is not walking the spiral for himself or herself alone.

4. See the article, "SOPHIA Teaching and Radiation Therapy," by Deborah Derrick in the journal *Meridians,* Spring 1998, pp. 32-33. The mini-poems I then used were these: For summer: "The sun is without and the sun is within, for the sake of the kingdoms that join all our kin." For autumn: "Three times I bow, letting go, letting be. I honor the core and I set myself free." For winter: "Deep in the waters — a place of unknowing where wisdom resides and remains ever flowing." For spring: "Bearing danger and gifts each event comes in view. Take what is given and find a way through." For earth's harvest/late summer: "From earth's good harvest, receiving and giving, we share simple gifts that make life worth living."

5. The Confucian tradition was correct to speak not of "parent-child" but of mother-daughter, mother-son, father-daughter, father-son. These relationships are more flexible; and at certain points in life, they stop us from thinking that roles have reversed — that I now am the parent of my mother, and she, my child. This is both untrue and demeaning.

6. See Stephen Mitchell, ed., *The Enlightened Heart* (New York: Harper and Row, 1989), p. 32. This poem translation is by Sam Hamill. I insert "I" instead of Hamill's "me" in the third line.

7. See Robert Bly, ed., *The Soul Is Here for Its Own Joy: Sacred Poems from Many Cultures* (Hopewell, NJ: Ecco Press, 1995), p. 246.

Chapter Fifteen

Transformation as Ongoing Work

We shall not cease from exploration
And the end of all our exploring
Will be to arrive where we started
And know the place for the first time.

. . . .

Quick now, here, now, always —
A condition of complete simplicity
(Costing not less than everything)
And all shall be well and
All manner of thing shall be well
When the tongues of flame are in-folded
Into the crowned knot of fire
And the fire and the rose are one.[1]

—T. S. Eliot

Transformative work exists between ethics and spirituality, between attention to time and attention to the timeless source. This is true in any age. Yet, suppose we stand in a special time — at an intersection between two worldviews. The modern worldview of the past 500 years has, in a number of ways, served us well. This collective way of thinking has provided us — as individuals, corporations, and nations — with a way to understand and value ourselves and our world. Furthermore, we have acted upon this modern vision and its values. Now, we see clearly that this mode of thinking, valuing, and acting has a destructive side. Given current population and technology, following this path is undermining the very conditions for life on the planet.

Clearly we must change the way we act. Just as clearly, we must change the way we think. Fortunately, there is hope. The shift from the *modern worldview* to the *emerging ecological worldview* was proposed in the introduction. Now, it is time to revisit it.

GAINING PERSPECTIVE — STANDING AT THE THRESHOLD BETWEEN TWO WORLDVIEWS

I begin by diagnosing the modern worldview in terms of its partial and pernicious features. As a memory device, I think of the modern worldview in terms of what I call the six seductive S's: *substances* — seen as *separate* and under conditions of *scarcity,* with the *seen only* and the *short-term* prized, and with *superiority over* (control over, power over) as the way to think of leadership. The following chart uses the six seductive S's to contrast the modern worldview with the emerging ecological worldview.[2]

Modern Worldview moving to c. 1500 to mid-20th century (*parts* are primary)	**Emerging Ecological Worldview** mid-20th century on (*wholes* are primary)
defined in terms of the 6 seductive S's	defined in terms of nested wholes, i.e.
Substances viewed as	**Relationship fields** supported by
Separate in a context of	**Interconnection** and
Scarcity and the	**Sufficiency** where
"Seen only" and the	**Seen & unseen are valued** where
Short-term	**Shorter & longer time frames** are recognized
where action takes the form of **Superiority over**	where action takes the form of **Complementarity/ Connectedness with**
Power over	*Partnership with*

Of course, there is a larger story to be told. Consider a simplified story in three acts — pre-modern (ancient to medieval) worldviews; the modern worldview; and the trans-modern, emerging ecological worldview.

In Act One, think of pre-modern worldviews from the ancient to the medieval worlds. Here, we have *the whole over the part*. Good for stable relationships, not very good for change. Virtues such as submission, obedience, and loyalty are cultivated and thrive. Yet some people are too easily subordinated to others. Hierarchies of dominance gain ground.

In Act Two, think of the modern worldview outlined above. Here we have *the part over the whole*. Good for freedom of thought and action, not very good for relationships and a sense of a large whole. Virtues such as self-reliance, competitive excellence, and risk-taking are cultivated and thrive. Yet a sense of the common good fades. All is reduced to separate substances — individuals alone are perceived to be "real."

For Act Three, think of the emerging ecological worldview outlined above — a trans-modern perspective. Here we seek a *larger sense of interconnection and interdependence* — a worldview that can honor relational fields (wholes) and the potential partners within them (parts). Notice that for this third way to be an advance, we cannot go back; we must go forward. We must recognize the gifts and correct the errors of the ancient worldview. We must recognize the gifts and correct the errors of the modern worldview. The new sense of community and communion must be more than a return to old collectivisms. It must be a view large enough for science and art and spirituality to flourish. (For more on these three acts, see appendix xvii.)

The formula is simple enough: Shift worldviews. Yet thinking in a new way, living in a new way — these are no easy tasks. As we recognize the modern framework as partial and pernicious, we seek an alternative that is wider. The ecological paradigm, as I am sketching it, is wide enough to have a place for the ancient and modern, honoring their gifts and healing their wounds.

To extinguish the unwholesome seeds in the modern worldview and to water the wholesome seeds of the emerging view, we must intentionally shift our thinking in each domain:

- from *separateness*   to   *relational fields* with a new sense of parts (as focuses in fields);

- from *scarcity*   to   *sufficiency;*

- from *"seen only"*   to   *"seen and unseen"* (ordinary and more subtle dimensions);

- from *"short-term only"* to   *longer-term,* generational time;

- from leadership as   to   leadership as
        "superiority over"   *"collaboration with."*

This book is an invitation to embody and practice such a trans-modern shift in all contexts or domains. We are invited:

1. in the large cosmos or macrocosm — the Great Family of Planet Earth (living within even larger horizons) — *to live life as eco-spiritual co-creation;*

2. in what we might call the middle cosmos or mesocosm — the world of institutions — *to live life as collaboration;* and

3. in the smallest cosmos or microcosm — the world of one-to-one relationships — *to live life as partnership.*

For more on these nested contexts and on the deep dynamism that move them to wholeness, see appendix XVI. As we shift to the emerging ecological perspective in any domain, the totality of all domains is subtly changed. We offer coherent practices to aid us in making this shift, beginning with the macrocosm — the web of all life.

THE NEW WORLDVIEW, THE FIVE MINISTERS, AND THE PLANETARY DOMAIN

Suppose we invoke the power of the seasons and ministers to serve the planetary domain, and we do that from a trans-modern perspective. Imagine walking the circle of the seasons and ministers for the sake of the planet as a dynamic organism, as a self-organizing, self-sustaining reality. Imagine the five archetypes surrounding and undergirding the planet as seen from space. Actually, the five functions are not external to the earth as organism; they are within the earth — part of its self-organization, its "energy system" for balancing and adapting. Thus, in apprenticing to the ministers we are, in a deep way, learning from the earth in its cycles and in its evolutionary adaptations.

Consider "walking the circle" on behalf of the earth and our participation in the life of the earth.

Imagine standing in the place of the *Minister of Earth's Abundance*. Let us begin in gratefulness with a sense of abundance — appreciating how well our good earth has served us, how it is in us and we are in it. *Here we move from scarcity to sufficiency.*

Imagine standing in the place of the *Sovereign of Awakened Heart* and learning from the wisdom of nature how to live in a sustainable way, and then how to live in a regenerative way. Such a mission to achieve sustainable planetary life would lead us to welcome resources from science, art, and spirituality.[3] Such a mission would be humble, ready to learn anew from nature and native peoples how to sustain the conditions for our species and all the other species that share our home. *Here we move from separateness to deep interconnection.*

Imagine apprenticing to the *Autumn Minister* to see what needs to be acknowledged and what needs to be let go in our relationships to the wider natural world. Suppose we learned to let go of separateness and to prize interbeing, to let go of false scarcity and reaffirm sufficiency. Suppose we learned to let go of prizing only the seen, the material, the quantifiable in favor of fuller values. Suppose we let go of short-term thinking in favor of standing again in generational time, honoring the ancestors and serving the children. Suppose we let go of human superiority in favor of dwelling respectfully with all members of the biotic community, deeply committed to collaboration rather than dominance. *Here we move from "seen only" to seen and unseen values.*

Imagine apprenticing to the *Winter Minister* to see what resources need cultivating, what deep listening and new learning are required.[4] Suppose we seek new ways of listening to the earth and learn more deeply how to sustain the conditions of life for future generations. *Here we move from "short-term only" to intergenerational time.*

Imagine apprenticing to the *Spring Minister* to open options and take steps in the spirit of skillful strategy, acting offensively and defensively to protect the health and wholeness of the planet — actions we take in harmony with all forms of life. *Here we move from superiority over (power over) to collaboration with (partnership with).*

Imagine returning to the *Minister of Earth's Abundance* with renewed gratefulness and renewed commitment to nourish all the forces for sustainable living, and then "walking the circle" at the next level and doing this again and again.

These five functions can become practices that will aid us to find what is good for the whole and fair to all participant-parts in the planetary context. These five functions, set in a trans-modern worldview, can aid us to learn anew how we can become dedicated to a sustainable future.

THE NEW WORLDVIEW, THE FIVE MINISTERS, AND THE INSTITUTIONAL DOMAIN

At present in the institutional domain, economic institutions (especially multinational corporations) dominate. Here the modern worldview teaches a focus on the *seen only* as quantity, where all values are translated into money and where short-term profits overwhelm all other considerations.[5] This logic of "short-term profits to shareholders alone" leaves little place for a wider view of institutions as concerned with the three P's: profits, people, and planet.[6] Yet, in light of the pain and unsustainability of our way of understanding and organizing institutions, we can shift our approach to living in larger and healthier ways.

When we bring awareness to our situation, we realize that we are living between worldviews — one foot (perhaps even one half of ourselves) in the modern paradigm, and the other foot (the other half of ourselves) in the trans-modern paradigm. Suppose we practice shifting our language and our values and our actions so that we stand more consistently in the ecological frame. As we do, we also notice how easily we fall back "into the box" of the old worldview. For example, suppose that we are thinking of shifting from scarcity to sufficiency. Without awareness, we will interpret "sufficiency" in terms of the modern worldview. Hence we will think of sufficiency in terms of the endlessly changing, never-to-be-fulfilled images that advertising places before us. As a colleague recently remarked, "A sense of limit is very different from a sense of scarcity."[7] We could add, "A sense of limit is, in fact, integral to a new sense of sufficiency." How easily we pour the new wine into old wineskins!

Perhaps we need more preventive medicine. Perhaps we need to coin new terms that, at the very least, will remind us that we are attempting to stand together — already interconnected — in the emerging worldview. In what follows, I present the five shifts with new language, and in the order in which we have been "walking the circle" of the five ministers. In what follows, I accent the relational dimension of the new worldview by restating each ideal with the prefix "inter," pointing to the fact that we already live in relational fields "between" and "among" others. In this voicing and order, we are asked to move:

- from   *scarcity*   to   *intersufficiency;*

- from   *separateness*   to   *interbeing*
                                          (interconnection, interdependence)

- from   *"seen only"*   to   *interweaving of seen and subtle dimensions;*

- from   *"short-term only"* to   *intergenerational time;*

- from   *"superiority over"* to   *interdoing*
                                          (intercollaboration, intersynergy)[8]

Now, let us walk the circle of the seasons and ministers for the sake of an institution. Imagine doing this from the position of standing in the new, trans-modern worldview.

For *intersufficiency,* stand in the place of the *Minister of Earth's Abundance.* Begin in gratefulness with a sense of abundance — appreciating how well our institutions have served us.

For *interbeing,* move to the place of the *Sovereign of Awakened Heart* and call each institution to its deeper function and nature. See our economic institutions and call them to their purpose of providing goods and services for a worthy life. See our educational institutions and call them to pass on the conditions for ongoing learning, thereby aiding people to make a contribution to the common life and to deepen their humanity and global responsibility.[9] See our governmental institutions and call them to "order conduct and adjust relationships" in ways to create "a society fit for human beings."[10] See our religious institutions and call them to cultivate in all of us a deep spirit of oneness, and a response combining stillness and service to all beings dwelling in the great mystery. See our families and call them to understand and practice discerning love where relationships are always held in light of the greater whole.

For *interweaving the seen and subtle,* apprentice to the Autumn Minister to see what needs to be acknowledged and what needs to be let go. Acknowledge the price we pay for dwelling in certain corporate conversations — corporate conversations that stress separateness and scarcity; corporate conversations focusing on the seen only and reducing all to quantity measured by money; corporate conversations favoring "power over" in preference to "partnership with." Move, in a trans-modern spirit, to a deeper sense of whole and parts, coming from sufficiency, honoring seen and unseen, and instilling collaboration in its best sense.

For *intergenerational time,* apprentice to the Winter Minister to see what resources need cultivating, what deep listening and new learning are required.[11] Let the learning consider conditions for sustainability, namely, how we can "meet the needs of the present without compromising the ability of future generations to meet their own needs."[12]

For *interdoing,* apprentice to the Spring Minister to open options and take steps in the spirit of skillful strategy — acting offensively and defensively to protect the health and wholeness of the institution. Let us see the whole organization as learning together and acting in ways that enhance synergy.[13]

Imagine returning to the Minister of Earth's Abundance with renewed gratefulness and renewed commitment to nourish all the forces for sustainable institutions — and then to "walk the circle" at the next level and to do this again and again.

Remember that the five functions are part of our institutions. We invoke them to remind us of a new context. We invoke them to aid us to shift into the emerging ecological paradigm — one that leads us to seek what is good for the whole and fair to the participant parts at every level. We invoke the five ministers to renew our institutions in ways that point to sustainability and even regeneration.

The reigning worldview structures our self-understanding on every level. The emerging ecological worldview likewise structures our self-understanding on every level. Even in our smallest one-to-one relational fields, we can notice how we stand with a foot in the modern paradigm and a foot in the emerging paradigm.

Return to my Lake Analogy. At the surface, we find *small-minded thinking done by our small-minded self* — that part of us that is partial, asleep, enslaved, reactive. The small-mindedness is colored by the six seductive S's. We have come to think of ourselves as "separate, alone, and in danger." When in this frame, individuals are seen as real and the relationship as less real — more like a legal contract than a relational field. Emphasis is on individual self-interest. Hence when times are stormy, we forget what joins us, reaffirm our separateness, and treat the relationship as if it were insubstantial fog — quick to dissolve.

However, at the mid-level of the lake, we discover *large-mind thinking done by our large-minded self* — that part of us that is whole, awake, free, response-able = able to choose our response. What I call the large-minded self can also be called the Observing Self or the Core Self.[14] Tutored by the emerging worldview, the large-minded self thinks "partnership first and then you and me." Thus, in this work I encouraged us to break out of strong individualism and take the one-to-one relationship as primary.[15] I encouraged us to begin with what deeply joined us (the whole) and then honor the participant parts. For the sake of practice, I introduced the five archetypes as surrounding and undergirding each particular relationship, and invited us to apprentice to each. At the risk of repetition, let us walk the circle of the ministers one more time for the sake of a one-to-one relationship.

Apprenticing to the Harvest Minister of Earth Abundance, we find an antidote to scarcity-thinking. We begin from sufficiency, from abundance, from great fullness. The mantra is: *Receive in abundance and give generously. Think partnership first, and then you and me.*

Apprenticing to the Summer Minister of Awakened Heart, we find new ways to affirm interconnectedness and to name and ennoble the whole. Here, the mantra is: *Held by the Oneness as vast as the sea, think partnership first and then you and me.* Another mantra: *Naming our union, its nature we see. Think partnership first, and then you and me.*

Apprenticing to the Autumn Minister of Diplomacy, we acknowledge the partnership exactly as it is, in its surface struggles and its deep beauty; and we acknowledge the partners in the same surface and depth way. We bow to the partnership and to the parties within it. And we are enabled to let go of what no longer serves. The mantra: *Three times we bow, letting go, letting be. Think partnership first, and then you and me.*

Apprenticing to the Minister of Deep Waters, we wait and listen and learn. We learn to honor both knowing and being in unknowing; we learn to respond to the seen and unseen, the manifest and the subtle, what is manifest and what is still coming to light. We learn to listen and learn in a context of intergenerational time, honoring ancestors, collaborating with contemporaries, and serving the children yet to be. The mantra: *Listening and learning and finding the key. Think partnership first, and then you and me.*

Apprenticing to the Spring Minister of Defense, we again exchange "power over" for "partnership with" — this time in strategic actions to protect the whole. Here we move beyond either-or, opening options and taking small steps. The mantra: *Slip through the hyphen — take action and see. Think partnership first, and then you and me.*

Finally, we return to the Minister of Earth's Abundance with renewed gratefulness and renewed commitment to nourish all the forces for sustainable relationships — and then "walk the circle" at the next level, doing this again and again.

THE DOMAINS ARE NESTED

The domains — planetary, institutional and interpersonal — are nested, like Russian dolls where each smaller doll is within a larger doll. We gain another image of this feature if we hearken back to chapter three and think of domains as conversations — conversations about what is meaningful and valuable, about what defines our shared sense of reality. Then we see that our widest conversation (modern or emerging ecological) influences our corporate conversations and our interpersonal conversations. And we see how, for sustainability, coming to large mind means coming to emerging ecological mind, aiding the shift at each level. We also begin to see that because our domains as conversations and relational fields are nested, a shift at any level affects all levels. I am reminded of words of Rabbi Nahman of Bratslav:

> In truth the entire universe is a spinning top, which is called a *dreidel.*
> Everything moves in a circle.... All things in the world are part of this circular motion, reborn and transformed into one another. That which was above is lowered and that which was below is raised up. For in their root all of them are one.[16]

The Great Pattern, seen anew in ecological thinking, is above. Institutions and partnership are below. With this correspondence, living in partnership aids us to live in institutional collaboration and cosmic co-creation. The Great Pattern reminds us that we start from prior connection. In Rabbi Nahman's words: "That which was above is lowered and that which was below is raised up. For in their root all of them are one."

At the depth of the lake, we glimpse unitive consciousness — the resting place of the mystics. Thinking partnership first, we begin with the oneness that unifies a relationship. Thinking collaboration first, we begin with the oneness that unifies an institution. Thinking co-creation first, we begin with the oneness as expressed in the great web of life, in the planet as a self-organizing and self-regulating organism.

Walking the spiral path is a form of spirituality — whether done in the interpersonal or institutional or planetary domains. The seasons echo nature, and the ministries remind us of life among others. The symbols and archetypes evoke the wisdom traditions.

Walking the spiral path is a form of ethical development. The ethical dimension emerges as we commit to coming to life more fully, to acting more wisely and effectively to reduce unnecessary suffering and to promote creative possibility for our common life.

In summary, this book is an invitation to a larger world and a deeper work. It takes the notion of living large as central, and opens a space to integrate the inward movement of stillness and the outward movement of service. Life as spiritual deepening and life as ethical acting dance together at the intersection of spirituality and ethics.

Spirituality brings a very large context — the mystery and the cosmos and, nested within it, our home planet, its institutions, and its one-to-one partnerships. Ethics likewise moves in ever-widening spheres — from ego to relationship, to institutions, and to a more global picture. An ethics of aspiration and a spirituality of deep presence complement each other. The poetry and teaching stories of spiritual practice companion the attention that a solid ethics brings to the good of the whole and fairness to participant-parts.

ONE OR TWO HONEST WORDS

This chapter began with the words of T. S. Eliot:

> *We shall not cease from exploration*
> *And the end of all our exploring*
> *Will be to arrive where we started*
> *And know the place for the first time....*

To live life consciously as co-creators of the Great Pattern, to live life as partnership whatever the size of the relational field — what do we learn when we do this? We learn, perhaps, that maturity and leadership and spiritual deepening are all of a piece and their essence is love.

Union. Communion. Love. "In the twilight of life," St. John of the Cross reminds us, "God will not judge us on our earthly possessions and human success, but rather on how much we have loved."

Could it, after all, be so simple? And is the path of partnership the door? Are interconnection and harmony the theme throughout?

The philosopher-poet Antonio Machado writes:

It's possible that, while sleeping, the hand
that sows the seeds of stars
started the ancient music going again
— like a note from a great harp —
and the frail wave came to our lips
as one or two honest words.[17]

One or two honest words. And the ancient music from the great harp.

When I do workshops, I love to close with one of the Dances of Universal Peace. We are in pairs facing each other — one member of the pair in an inner circle, facing out. The other member, in an outer circle, facing in. The outer circle will revolve.

The dance begins with partners facing, hands out, palms up.

The first line: "From you I receive." — Both raise their arms, crossing them at the chest, receiving and taking into the heart.

Second line: "To you I give." — The hands come down, palms up.

Third line: "Together we share." — The partners join hands.

Fourth line: "In this we live." — Each person holds hands high in the air. Each person turns in place.

Then the outer circle moves by one, bringing a new partner into view. The dance continues.

Turning and turning. Life as partnership.
A few honest words:

From you, I receive.
To you, I give.
Together, we share.
In this, we live.

References

1. The closing lines of "Little Gidding," the fourth of T. S. Eliot's *Four Quartets.* See T. S. Eliot, *The Complete Poems and Plays: 1909-1950* (New York: Harcourt, Brace & Co., 1952), p. 145.

2. This overview owes much to many sources. In particular, I wish to mention Denise Breton and Christopher Largent, *The Paradigm Conspiracy: Why Our Social Systems Violate Human Potential — And How We Can Change Them* (Center City, MN: Hazelden, 1996), and their *Love, Soul and Freedom: Dancing with Rumi on the Mystic Path* (Center City, MN: Hazelden, 1998); Brian Swimme and Thomas Berry, *The Universe Story* (San Francisco: HarperSanFrancisco, 1992); Joanna Macy, *World as Lover, World as Self* (Berkeley, CA: Parallax Press, 1991); Joanna Macy and Molly Young Brown, *Coming Back to Life: Practices to Reconnect Our Lives, Our World* (Gabriola Island, BC, Canada: New Society Publishers, 1998); Rosamund Stone Zander and Benjamin Zander, *The Art of Possibility* (Boston: Harvard Business School Press, 2000); and Ken Wilber's view of "all levels, all quadrants" — see, for example, Ken Wilber, *A Brief History of Everything* (Boston: Shambhala, 1996). I published an earlier version of the domains in my book, *To Come to Life More Fully.*

3. For science, see Karl-Henrik Robèrt, *The Natural Step Story: Seeding a Quiet Revolution* (Gabriola Island, BC, Canada: New Society Publishers, 2002). For something from the spiritual side, see Joanna Macy and Molly Young Brown, *Coming Back to Life: Practices to Reconnect Our Lives, Our World* (Gabriola Island, BC, Canada: New Society Publishers, 1998), and Thom Hartmann, *The Last Hours of Ancient Sunlight: Waking Up to Personal and Global Transformation* (New York: Harmony Books, 1998). See also Lester W. Milbrath, *Envisioning a Sustainable Society* (Albany, NY: State University of New York Press, 1989), and David Suzuki and Holly Dressel, *Good News for a Change: How Everyday People Are Helping the Planet* (Vancouver, BC, Canada: Greystone Books, Douglas & McIntyre Publishing Group, 2003).

4. See, for example, Janine M. Benyus, *Biomimicry: Innovation Inspired by Nature* (New York: HarperCollins Perennial Series, 2002). This was first published by William Morrow in 1997.

5. For a chilling view of the new economic colonialism, see David C. Korten, *When Corporations Rule the World* (San Francisco: Berrett-Koehler, 1995).

6. This is a variant of the "Triple Bottom Line" (3BL), also voiced as society, economy, and environment. The term was first coined in the mid-1990s by the British think-tank AccountAbility, and gained currency with John Elkington's *Cannibals with Forks: The Triple Line of 21st Century Business* (Gabriola Island, BC, Canada: New Society Publishers, 2002).

7. I credit Melora Payne Scanlon with this insight.

8. The term "interbeing" is a creation of Thich Nhat Hanh, as mentioned earlier. The other neologisms follow that lead.

9. For a striking assessment of education in a trans-modern frame, see David W. Orr, *Earth in Mind: On Education, Environment, and the Human Prospect* (Washington, DC: Island Press, 1994), and his earlier *Ecological Literacy: Education and the Transition to a Postmodern World* (Albany, NY: State University of New York Press, 1992).

10. This view of government (as an institution called to adjust social relations and order conduct) I take from jurist Roscoe Pound. The phrase "A Society Fit for Human Beings" is the title of a book by my mentor, E. Maynard Adams. The book was published by State University of New York Press in 1997.

11. On the need for institutions to be learning organizations, see Peter M. Senge, *The Fifth Discipline: The Art and Practice of the Learning Organization* (New York: Doubleday, 1990). For the beginning of a conversation on deep learning and spiritual practices, See Peter Senge, C. Otto Scharmer, Joseph Jaworski, and Betty Sue Flowers, *Presence: Human Purpose and the Field of the Future* (Cambridge, MA: the Society for Organizational Learning, 2004).

12. The phrase is taken from the 1987 United Nations Commission on Environment and Development (the Bruntland Commission). They call for "a form of sustainable development which meets the needs of the present without compromising the ability of future generations to meet their own needs."

13 For this shift to deeper learning and truer collaborative acting, see Linda Ellinor and Glenna Gerard, *Dialogue: Rediscovering the Transforming Power of Conversation* (New York: John Wiley & Sons, 1998) and Williams Isaacs, *Dialogue and the Art of Thinking Together* (New York: John Wiley & Doubleday, 1999). See also Harrison Owen, *Expanding Our Now: The Story of Open Space Technology* (San Francisco: Berrett-Koehler, 1997) and Arnold Mindell, *The Leader as Martial Artist* (Portland, Oregon: Lao Tse Press, 1992).

14. See Rosamund Stone Zander and Benjamin Zander, *The Art of Possibility*, especially pp. 79-97 for a similar distinction. They speak of the *calculating self* (survival thinking, scarcity thinking, dwelling in a world of measurement) and the *central self* (where one lives as a contribution in a universe of possibility).

15. Although our approaches are distinctive, I find resonances with the work of John Welwood. See his *Toward a Psychology of Awakening* (Boston: Shambhala Publications, 2000) and his earlier works, *Love and Awakening* (New York: Harper Perennial, 1997) and *Journey of the Heart: The Path of Conscious Love* (New York: Harper Perennial, 1991). In another sense, I am starting where Zander and Zander end — with the practice of "telling the WE story." See Rosamund Stone Zander and Benjamin Zander, *The Art of Possibility*, Practice 12, pp. 181-196.

16. Rabbi Nahman of Bratslav, quoted by Arthur Green in *Tormented Master* (Tuscaloosa, AL: University of Alabama Press, 1979), p. 310. See also *Nahman of Bratslav: The Tales,* trans. Arnold J. Band (New York: Paulist Press, 1978). A dreidel is a children's top. The body of the top is square, and each of the sides is inscribed with a Hebrew letter. The four letters allude to the miracle of Hanukkah. They spell out: New (N-miracle),

Gadol (G-great), Haya (H-happened), and Sham (S-there, meaning "in Israel"). Legend has it that following the Maccabean victory there was only oil enough to light the temple menorah for one day; yet the oil sufficed for eight days, bringing light to darkness.

17. The translation is by Robert Bly. See *Times Alone: Selected Poems of Antonio Machado,* chosen and translated by Robert Bly (Middletown, CT: Wesleyan University Press, 1983), p. 71.

Acknowledgments

What they undertook to do
They brought to pass;
All things hung like a drop of dew
Upon a blade of grass.
−W. B. YEATS

"GRATITUDE TO THE UNKNOWN INSTRUCTORS"

In her rendering of the Buddhist precepts, Stephanie Kaza of Green Gulch Farm begins each directive with the words, "Knowing how deeply our lives intertwine." Allow me to borrow these words in order to make a series of acknowledgments to people in my life.

Knowing how deeply our lives intertwine, I thank my wife, Gregg. Her presence enriches my work and my life. With her I learn again and again the wonder of a dance where we are "not one, not two" — we are more ourselves through being together.

Knowing how deeply our lives intertwine, I thank my family, extending over generations. On my side, I express gratitude to my grandparents, my father and mother, my sister and my daughter; on Gregg's side, to her grandparents, her father and mother, her brother, her children and their spouses — and the grandchildren as well.

Knowing how deeply our lives intertwine, I thank my friends and colleagues connected with the Tai Sophia Institute in Laurel,

[241]

Maryland. More specifically, I want to thank those who, in 1987, cofounded with me the SOPHIA project (the School of Philosophy and Healing in Action) — Dianne Connelly, Robert Duggan, Julia Measures, and Mary Ellen Zorbaugh. We have been in a teaching and learning partnership ever since. In addition to the administrative staff, I thank those who are faculty in the new Master of Arts in Applied Healing Arts program. In particular, I am grateful to Tom Balles, Dianne Connelly, Robert and Susan Duggan, Barry Fudim, Gail Geller, Mary Alice Hearn, Bridget and Brandon Hughes, Allyson Jones, Diane Kane, Stacey MacFarlane, Helen Buss Mitchell, Melora Payne Scanlon, Cheryl Walker, Amy Wheeler, and Robert Weisbord. With these teacher-mentors stand all those who have participated in these programs over the years. They are true partners in the work of this book.

Knowing how deeply our lives intertwine, I thank my friends and colleagues at Elon University in the administration, faculty, and staff. I especially thank the members of the Elon Philosophy Department: Nim Batchelor, Ann Cahill, Martin Fowler, Elsebet Jegstrup, Yoram Lubling, and Anthony Weston. Philosophy literally means "love of wisdom." These cherished colleagues ensure that our work serves our common life and the world in its unfolding. In addition, I thank my students, those who have taken philosophy courses, and especially those who, since 1992, have participated in the Quest for Wholeness yearlong mentorships that I colead with my wife, Gregg.

Knowing how deeply our lives intertwine, I thank my teachers — in particular, Giovanni Abbo, Maynard Adams, Frederick and Claske Franck.

Knowing how deeply our lives intertwine, I thank all who have helped bring this book to life — especially my gracious editors Mary Ellen Zorbaugh and Guy Hollyday. Their good eyes and kind hearts have made this a better and more accessible book. In addition, I thank John Wilson whose care with design and the final stages of printing brought added creativity to the task.

Knowing how deeply our lives intertwine, I thank all those — known and unknown, named and unnamed — whose loving kindness, compassion, sympathetic joy, and stillness of spirit have touched me deeply.

Appendices

APPENDIX I

How Our
Ways of Understanding & Responding
Can Be Too Small

W ············· U ············· R ············· T

Way of **Understanding** & **Responding** **To**

LABELS & LANGUAGE
Can be too small because of...

a) High interpretive language
   (e.g., He "snubbed" me)

b) Oppositional language
   ("US" vs. "THEM")

c) "Hook" language*

EMOTIONAL CHARGE
Can be too small because of...

a) Over-attraction (liking to greed)

b) Over-aversion (disliking to hate)

c) Hasty identification (a kind of
   ignorance)

All of the above can be recognized and reversed.

*Here are some instances of "hook" language and ways to recognize and reverse such language:

"I have to."	"Duty" conversations	I choose to / I have made a commitment and choose to keep it.
"They make me."	"Victim/injustice" conversations	In the presence of _____, this comes up for me; AND I can learn to shift my response.
"It's difficult — I can't."	"Disempowerment" conversations	I am a beginner at this.
"If only..."	"Language of lack" conversations	I have all I need in myself and others to live a life of quality, AND I can learn to bring other qualities into my life.
"That's just the way I am."	"Determinism" (grandparent/parent/ peer conversations)	I have certain tendencies, AND I can choose to rewrite my script. Or, "That is an old story; I'm older and wiser now." Or, "Let me distinguish phenomena and conclusions."

The lower part of this chart is indebted to Stephen Covey's distinction between Reactive Language and Proactive Language, and his proposals for shifting language. See Stephen Covey, *The Seven Habits of Highly Effective People* (New York: Simon & Schuster Fireside Book, 1990), p. 78. I have expanded and modified this root work. How to deal with the emotional charge — the "R" in the WURT — is discussed in chapter eleven in connection with the Autumn Minister, and in appendix XII, "Exercises for Letting Go."

APPENDIX II

Aids for Daily Practice

1. Think of your practices NOT as burdens, but as "tools for ease" — opportunities to bring more peace, joy, and purpose into life.

2. Take TEN MINUTES A DAY to make an investment in your life and all you will serve.

   In the morning: Take FOUR MINUTES to greet the day with a reading and declaration.

   > *Begin with a short reading* from an inspirational book of your choice.

   > *Choose a particular habit to practice that day.*
   > For example, choose to come from abundance and practice gratitude, or to practice deep listening, or to practice letting go of old stories, etc.

   > *Make a declaration.*
   > For example, "May my thoughts, words, and deeds honor the ancestors, serve my contemporaries, and benefit the children." Or, "In my presence today, may there be less surplus suffering and more possibility for all."

   > [Shift reading and ritual as needed to keep your practice alive.]

   At noon: Take TWO MINUTES to give thanks and reaffirm your practice.

   At night: Take FOUR MINUTES to sum up the day and make a practice log entry: Give one instance where you applied the chosen practice this day. What did you shift — e.g., your language, listening, etc.? What was the result? What did you learn? What difference did your practice make?

3. In working with students, I often suggest a practice log. A small notebook is easy to carry around, is useful and unthreatening. Here is a formula for a "practice log" entry:

   a) *Observing the initial phenomena.* In the presence of (this or that event — a WHAT), I noticed a certain way of labeling and loving/hating arise in me (a Way of Understanding and Responding).

   b) *Assessment.* Is this conversation in which I am living producing unnecessary suffering and reduced possibility? If so, shift it.

   c) *Making a shift.* Can I, in the moment, shift from small mind to large mind?

   d) *Observing the results of practice.*
   What happens when I dwell in and act from small mind-and-heart?
   What happens when I dwell in and act from larger mind-and-heart?

APPENDIX III

WURT — WORD — WORLD

The phrase "way of relating" can be expanded to a Way of Understanding and Responding To [situations] — abbreviated WURT.

Understanding = *making meaning* (through language)
Responding = *generating values* (based on our interpretations)

Remember my interpretation of the locked classroom building; remember Harriet's interpretation of her mother's behavior. On the basis of the story I told, I generated dislike, anger, negative judgments. On the basis of the story Harriet told, she generated dislike, resentment, and disapproval. First the meaning, then the valuing. Put it this way:

In understanding things, we discover/declare their *meaning.*

In responding to things (on the basis of that understanding), we bestow *value* — we approve or disapprove and generate an "emotional charge."

Our way of relating is expressed in words and generates a WORLD, i.e., what is *meaningful and valuable* for us. A "world" is a *meaning and value system.* Put this together and we see that

Individual ways of making meaning and ascribing value generate individual worlds (i.e., what an individual finds meaningful and valuable).

Shared ways of making meaning and ascribing value generate shared worlds (i.e., what a group finds meaningful and valuable).

A culture or worldview — a collective way of making meaning and ascribing value — is like a large conversation. Strong cultural changes occur when what was once meaningful and valuable becomes meaningless and valueless.

Remember: **a WURT — expressed through WORDS — generates a WORLD.**

Small-minded WURT → small WORLD of meaning and value — more suffering, less possibility

Larger-minded WURT → larger WORLD of meaning and value — less suffering, more possibility.

Ways of meaning-making and value-shaping — generate worlds of what is meaningful and valuable.

We live in language, in stories; and these stories can be smaller or larger.

APPENDIX IV

A Diagram of the Eightfold Path

The chart that follows is to be read in clockwise fashion, beginning at the bottom with the "Knowing/Loving" phase. Since we are meant to repeat the eight steps over and over, we can profitably view the Eightfold Path as a Spiral Path.

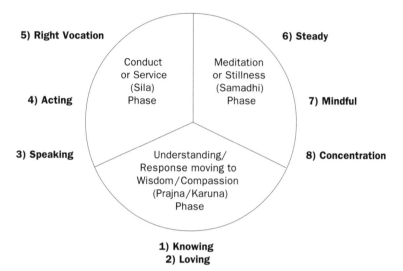

5) Right Vocation   **6) Steady**

4) Acting   **7) Mindful**

3) Speaking   **8) Concentration**

Conduct or Service (Sila) Phase

Meditation or Stillness (Samadhi) Phase

Understanding/Response moving to Wisdom/Compassion (Prajna/Karuna) Phase

1) Knowing
2) Loving

The first phase — **Understanding/Resolve or *prajna/karuna*** — has two steps: **Knowing. Loving.**

At the beginning, the *insight* or *understanding* is simply that we are sick, that we are causing ourselves and others unnecessary suffering. What follows is our *response* or *resolve* to eliminate the suffering. With each turn of the spiral, our insight increases; we become wiser. And because we are following a path with a heart, our wisdom is a wisdom of the heart that issues naturally in compassion. As our wisdom deepens, so does our compassion — our heartfelt concern for all beings. At the highest level, this first phase can be called insight/compassion or *prajna/karuna* — the great understanding (*prajna*) which leads to the great compassion (*karuna*).

The second phase — **Conduct or *Sila*** — has three steps: **Speaking. Acting. Right Vocation.**

The third phase — **Meditation or *Samadhi*** — also has three steps: **Steady. Mindful. Concentration.**

We begin with a certain level of understanding and resolve — a certain level of knowing and loving. The conduct (doing or service) phase sets the context for the meditation (being or stillness) phase. The meditation leads to deeper insight and unfolding compassion. Such wise and compassionate awareness is carried forward into the next round of right speaking, right acting, and right vocation. As we move round and round — becoming aware and acting and meditating — we gain ever greater insight, and our hearts are ever more deeply tutored in compassionate response.

The Eightfold Path is a mode of training that enables us to live more consciously and intensely in large mind — moment by moment.

APPENDIX V

The Twelve Steps

Here are the steps we took, which are suggested as a program of recovery:

1. We admitted we were powerless over alcohol, that our lives had become unmanageable.

2. Came to believe that a Power greater than ourselves could restore us to sanity.

3. Made a decision to turn our will and our lives over to the care of God as we understood Him.

****

4. Made a searching and fearless moral inventory of ourselves.

   A kind of Confession.

5. Admitted to God, to ourselves, and to another human being the exact nature of our wrongs.

****

6. Were entirely ready to have God remove all these defects of character.

   A kind of Contrition. Mindful of what we have done, we sincerely wish to change.

7. Humbly asked Him to remove our shortcomings.

****

8. Made a list of all persons we had harmed, and became willing to make amends to them all.

   A kind of Satisfaction or Making Amends.

9. Made direct amends to such people wherever possible, except when to do so would injure them or others.

****

10. Continued to take personal inventory, and when we were wrong promptly admitted it.

11. Sought through prayer and meditation to improve our conscious contact with God as we understood Him, praying only for knowledge of His will for us and the power to carry that out.

12. Having had a spiritual awakening as the result of these steps, we try to carry this message to alcoholics, and to practice these principles in all our affairs. — The Twelve Steps*

Notes

• The twelve-step program invokes God or a Higher Power as we understand that power. However, the process need not be only for theists. If you are a nonbeliever, what remains central is that you must admit you cannot, on your own, get out of the addictive box in which you currently find yourself. You need help; you need a wider horizon to operate in; you need to draw upon sources of strength beyond what you are accustomed to using.

• I suggest we see the twelve steps in the classic initiation triad: a **Leaving Phase** (leaving the old way of thinking and living); a **Discovery/Change Phase** (tapping into who you are as an addict and what you as an addict have done); and a **Return** to community **Phase.**

• The middle spacing (steps 4 through 9) echoes the phases of Confession, Contrition, and Satisfaction as found in the medieval tradition, e.g., in Dante's *Purgatorio.*

* Information about the twelve steps is widely available in books and on the internet, including www.alcoholics-anonymous.org.

APPENDIX VI

The Institutional Domain

The Big Four institutions are (1) political, (2) economic, (3) educational (including media), (4) religious. As examples, think of a branch of government, a corporation, a college, an organized religious body. Of course, there are many other institutions — think of the numerous voluntary organizations. Lastly, the family itself is a mini-institution; yet it is, perhaps, best thought of in a separate category.

The General Nature of Institutions — Three Paths to Understanding:

A. Institutions may be thought of as *Solutions to a Certain Type of Task.*

Institutions can be viewed as a response to human needs that (1) *recur;* and (2) *affect all or many people;* and (3) *require, or benefit from, cooperative actions.* Since the needs are recurring needs — such as ordering life and settling disputes, providing goods and services, educating the young, etc. — the institution must be relatively stable over time. Since these needs affect all or many, there is a benefit to meeting those needs by division and coordination of labor. Hence, we understand institutions as organized cooperative structures, existing over time, formed to satisfy recurring needs.

B. *Roles, Rules, and Routines* in service of the Task:

Sociologists Berger and Luckman remind us that institutions are formed by people; time passes; and people are formed by institutions.[1] Roles, rules, and routines give a permanence to institutions. In large part, the key institutions are present before we are born and will go on after we die.

The institutions are organized to fulfill tasks: government regulates conduct and settles disputes; economic institutions provide goods and services; educational institutions teach the young; religious institutions provide ways to worship in common, etc. Remembering that institutions fulfill tasks allows us to hold two factors in mind: *Some form of basic institution is necessary* (because the problem will remain), while at the same time, *any particular form of institution is somewhat arbitrary* (being only one possible solution to the problem).

C. Policies, Procedures, and Practices (channeling power) in service of the Task:

Because the institutional domain is the domain of power (through policies and procedures), it is also the preeminent domain for justice to enter in. "Justice," in one striking formulation, "is sorting out what belongs to whom and giving it back."[2]

****

Some problems cannot be properly understood unless you understand the institutional domain. Racism, sexism, and ageism are three such issues. So is speciesism.[3]

CONTINUED

Racism	Sexism	Ageism
is a	is a	is a
SYSTEM	SYSTEM	SYSTEM
of	of	of
racial	sexual	age-related
inequity & discrimination	**inequity & discrimination**	**inequity & discrimination**
which has its roots in	which has its roots in	which has its root in
a generalized feeling of	a generalized feeling of	a generalized feeling of
white superiority	**male superiority**	**youth superiority**
and which is	and which is	and which is
sustained and reinforced by	**sustained and reinforced** by	**sustained and reinforced** by
institutions of the culture.	**institutions** of the culture.	**institutions** of the culture.

Speciesism is a SYSTEM of **species-related inequity and discrimination** which has its roots in a generalized feeling of **human superiority** and which is sustained and reinforced by the **institutions** of the culture.

Notes

1. See Peter L. Berger and Thomas Luckman, *The Social Construction of Reality* (Garden City, NY: Anchor Books, 1966).

2. I heard the quote in this form in a speech given by William Sloane Coffin. Coffin's words are a variant of Walter Brueggermann's definition: "Justice is sorting out what belongs to whom and returning it to them." See Walter Brueggermann, Sharon Parks, and Thomas H. Groome, *To Act Justly, Love Tenderly, Walk Humbly* (Mahwah, NH: Paulist Press, 1986), p. 5.

3. I learned the definition of racism (noted in the chart) from Hal Sieber, former editor and chief of *The Carolina Peacemaker,* the African American Newspaper in Greensboro, NC, while working with Hal and others in facilitating interracial workshops in Greensboro in the early 1970s. The other definitions are my variations on that structure.

APPENDIX VII

On Manipulation, Paternalism, Cooperation, and Collaboration

****

COMING FROM SEPARATION

MANIPULATION   ━━━━━━━━▶   **SINGLE SATISFACTION**

Paternalism — A Halfway House

COOPERATION   ━━━━━━━━▶   **DOUBLE SATISFACTION**
(mutual gain; win-win)

Coming from separation, the best we can achieve is cooperation.

> **"Cooperation," as I am using the term, is a process whereby several people join together to achieve a shared task or goal *for the sake of their individual self-interests.***

> (The key unit is still the individual self.)

****

COMING FROM INTERCONNECTION

COLLABORATION   ━━━━━━━━▶   **TRIPLE SATISFACTION**
(partnership in strong sense)

Coming from interconnection allows a new possibility to emerge: collaboration.

> **"Collaboration," as I am using the term, is a process whereby several people join together to achieve a shared task or goal *for the sake of a unit larger than the parties, yet including the parties within it.***

In the realm of one-to-one relationships, I speak of this orientation as issuing in a true partnership.

> (The orientation is toward a true "we," not simply reducible to several self-interests.)

The mantra is **"Think partnership first, then you and me."** Thus, the partnership is tended and the partners within it — triple satisfaction.

From a model of interconnection, we tend the partnership for itself and for the partners and for the sake of all the partnership serves.

As an individual may turn inward and think of self alone, so a partnership can turn inward and forget that it is part of a larger Pattern. Partnerships as holons see themselves as contributing to larger wholes.

Manipulative Persuasion, Paternalism, Non-Manipulative Persuasion

I manipulate another person
  when I persuade the other to do what I want
  - **against** the other's **Will**, and against the other's **Best Interest**, using techniques of
  - **Deception/Fraud** and/or **Coercion/Force**.

Manipulation carries its own underlying view of the person:
  The manipulator sees the other
  AS IF **a thing to be used** (having no worth in his or her own right),
  AS IF **without intellect** (since the manipulator is willing to deceive),
  AS IF **without free will** (since the manipulator is willing to coerce, to override free consent).

When you understand what manipulation means, you understand that it is **nonreversible.** You cannot reasonably agree to be manipulated in this technical sense, for that would mean agreeing to be treated not as a person but as a thing without value in its own right, without intellect and without freedom to consent.

Manipulators come in a variety of forms. Psychologist Frederick "Fritz" Perls distinguished **Top Dog** and **Underdog manipulators**.

> Top Dog manipulators use coercion or threat of coercion. They typically use an aggressive, bullying style. (My way "or else"!)

> Underdog manipulators are equally powerful, but they use deception (e.g., hidden agenda). They typically play on sympathy or guilt, for example, "Poor me, I can't... Rescue me!"

See Fritz Perls, *Gestalt Therapy Verbatim* (New York: Bantam, 1959/1971). Perls's student, Everett L. Shostrum, gives four types of Top Dog and four types of Underdog manipulators. See his *Man the Manipulator* (New York: Bantam, 1968).

****

Paternalism is a halfway house, similar to manipulation in all but one small respect.

Paternalism is a form of persuasion that occurs when I persuade another to do what I want
  - against the other's will, using
  - deception and/or coercion,
    but with the contention that the course of action is intended to be and can reasonably be said to be
  - **in the other's best interest.**

Thus paternalism is like manipulation in everything except that it is allegedly done in the other's best interest. Suppose your son or daughter is riding a tricycle in the street. You come home and take the child out of harm's way and seek to rationally persuade the child how dangerous it is to ride in the road. But the child is unpersuaded. So you either coerce the child to stay out of the road, or you deceive the child (e.g., by telling the child that there is a monster in a tree that eats children who ride in the road). Here, reasonable coercion seems preferable! The test is delayed reversibility. When the child is grown, if asked, "Remember when you were three and playing in the road, and I forced you to stay out of the road? Do you now agree it was a reasonable thing to do?" the person agrees. Or, if you force a drunk not to drive home, will the drunk, when sober and reasonable, agree that you did in fact act in his or her best interest?

Non-Manipulative Persuasion occurs when manipulation is totally reversible.

You seek to persuade the other by deeply respecting who the other person is, by appealing to the other's intellect, giving solid information and argument, and by offering the other person the full freedom to accept or reject your advice (with no manifest or hidden disapproval or abandonment).

Thus, you are treating the other as a center of worth in his or her own right, with a mind and a free will. In the philosopher Kant's phrase, you are treating the other as "equal, rational, and free."

Such a mode of relating is **fully reversible**. You could agree to be treated in this way whether you are on the side of the persuader or the one persuaded.

****

STEPHEN COVEY'S APPROACH TO WIN-WIN INTERACTIONS*

High

C O N S i D E R A T i O N	LOSE / WIN I will lose in order for you to win.	WIN - WIN Mutual Gain
	LOSE / LOSE	WIN / LOSE I will win even at your expense

Low   High

COURAGE

Note: **High** Consideration + **Low** Courage = **L-W** (I will lose in order for you to win.)

Low Consideration + **Low** Courage = **L-L** (Both parties lose through ineptness.)

Low Consideration + **High** Courage = **W-L** (I will win even at your expense.)

High Consideration + **High** Courage = **W-W** (Mutual Gain: We seek a creative 3rd — like the apex of a triangle — a solution that allows both to gain.)

****

Coming from separation, the best we can achieve is cooperation. The model of win-win or mutual gain is no small accomplishment. Nonetheless, more is possible.

When we reverse assumptions and come from interconnection, we can see the relationship as a new reality in its own right, having its own conditions for health and wholeness. This leads to the possibility of triple satisfaction. Recall:

"Collaboration," as I am using the term, is a process whereby several people join together to achieve a shared task or goal for the sake of a unit larger than the parties, yet including the parties within it.

(The orientation is toward a true "we," not simply reducible to several self-interests.)

****

* The chart presented here is a variant of the chart in Stephen Covey, *The Seven Habits of Highly Effective People* (New York: Simon & Schuster, 1989), p. 218.

APPENDIX VIII

Six-Step Model for Ethical Policy Decision Making

This model is most at home where, from an administrative standpoint, one seeks ethical guidelines suitable for public policy. Putting one's option in standard form has the following advantages:

- It gives one distance on the problem.
- It allows one to construct qualified positions that go beyond "always" and "never" positions.
- It allows one to run certain tests concerning fairness and consequences.

Step 1. **LIST POSSIBLE OPTIONS.**

Step 2. **FILTER OUT** those options that are (a) not really practical (do-able) and/or (b) are so extreme that they raise additional ethical problems (e.g., killing the teacher to avoid cheating on a test).

Step 3. **CHOOSE ONE OPTION and put it in STANDARD (XYZ) FORM:**
In ANY CIRCUMSTANCES X (or in circumstances having features $x_1, x_2, \ldots x_n$),
ANY ETHICAL AGENT(s) Y (or with features $y_1, y_2, \ldots y_n$),
OUGHT/OUGHT NOT DO ACTION Z (or an action having features $z_1, z_2, \ldots z_n$).

Step 4. **Apply the Kantian TEST FOR FAIRNESS.**

These Fairness Tests are indebted to Immanuel Kant and stress that "Persons are not things." Persons are centers of worth having intellects and the ability to choose. They are, as Kant would say, "equal, rational, and free."

A. Reversibility Test
If Z is right to do, then Z is right to do whether I am on the "doer" or "receiver" side.

B. Equal Case Test
If it is right *for me* to do Z, then it is right for *anyone relevantly similar to me.* You must treat equal cases equally, or show that in spite of looking similar, the two cases are relevantly different and can be treated differently.

C. Universalizability Test — generalizes from "equal cases" test. Suppose it is right for A to do Z. If B is *relevantly similar to* A (abbreviated B "rst" A), then it is right for B to do Z. If C is "rst" B, then it is right for C to do Z. If D is "rst" C, then OK for D, and on and on until we must consider *what would occur if everyone (or almost everyone) did Z.* "What if everyone did Z?" is the universalized question.

Steps 5 & 6 are SOCIAL UTILITY (good of the whole) CONSEQUENCES TESTS. (Bentham & Mill: "Actions have Consequences.")

Step 5. **LIST THE CONSEQUENCES** (to you, to others, to what joins you together) if everyone were to follow your rule (i.e., if this rule were to become a PRACTICE).

Step 6. **ASK YOURSELF: Could I truly accept a world in which acting on this rule were a way of life?**

If the principle so stated does not pass the Fairness and Consequences Tests, go back to step 3 and reformulate the principle or policy.

Notice: A principle or policy may be quite complex and may itself contain step-by-step procedures.

APPENDIX IX

Ethics and the Tradition

In my Traffic Light Model, I use the colors red, gold, and green — in a minimal ethics sense and in an aspirational ethics sense. But the notion of thinking of ethics as having three parts is older. One philosopher christened this threefold approach the "Moralberry Pie."

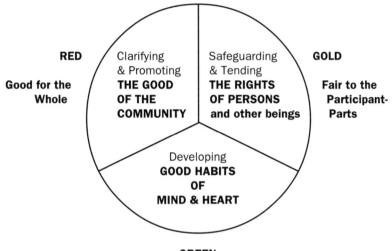

RED

Good for the Whole

Clarifying & Promoting **THE GOOD OF THE COMMUNITY**

Safeguarding & Tending **THE RIGHTS OF PERSONS** and other beings

GOLD

Fair to the Participant-Parts

Developing **GOOD HABITS OF MIND & HEART**

GREEN
Responsibility / Virtues / Good Practice

Suppose we think of the upper segments as the outer side of ethics. Here we see the two fundamental poles of ethics: *Community and Persons*. The upper segments remind us that **actions have consequences** and **persons have rights.**

From this model, we can extend the RED of consequences to utilitarian ethical theories. The most famous of these are the utilitarianism of Jeremy Bentham and John Stuart Mill. In modern times, such theories tend to be rule-based.

From this model, we can extend the GOLD of respect for persons to the work of Immanuel Kant. In fact, Kant's view of persons as equal, rational, and free can be derived from the material in appendix VII on manipulative persuasion and non-manipulative persuasion. In manipulative persuasion, the underlying image of person is as a thing to be used for my gain and treated as if having no mind or will. In respectful persuasion, the underlying image of person is as *one of worth in his or her own right, having mind and having will* (therefore deserving to give "informed consent") — in Kant's terms, as "equal, rational, and free." While Kant spoke of fundamental duties, those following him have tended to speak of fundamental rights.

From this model, we can extend the GREEN to virtue ethics. Aristotle is the usual example of virtue ethics, although most ethical theories in the ancient world — both East and West — tend to start with the development of good habits of attitude and action, i.e., they tend to focus on virtues. In modern times, for example, this approach can be seen in the moral development work of Lawrence Kohlberg and his friend and longtime in-house critic, Carol Gilligan.

Most contemporary moral theories have a place both for consequences to the whole and for rights of the parts. I think of John Rawls's elegant *A Theory of Justice,* which has utilitarian and Kantian strands, and even material on moral development. The "Six-Step Model for Ethical Policy Decision Making" in appendix VIII likewise combines rights and consequences. For a concise introduction to these moral theories, see James Rachels, *The Elements of Moral Philosophy,* 4th edition (New York: McGraw-Hill, 2003).

APPENDIX X

A Word about Archetypes

The seasons, the energies, and the functions for life associated with them can be thought of as archetypes.

When we speak of seasons as archetypes, we are thinking especially of cycles of time and the gifts each season brings.

When we speak of archetypal persons or ministers in a kingdom or commonwealth, we are moving toward a political analogy. We are thinking more of structures such as relationships, institutions, nations, the web of life. Here the ancients personify certain energies for health as ministers or ministries with responsibility for certain tasks or services. Thus, in the United States we have a president and various cabinet ministers — Secretary of State, Secretary of Defense, Secretary of the Treasury, Secretary of Agriculture, etc. In England, there is a king or queen, a prime minister, and the other ministers. With archetypes of minister and ministry, instead of noticing one season flowing into the next, we think especially of what is needed for our life with others to flourish. A division of labor appears. We see different archetypes with different tasks or functions serving the whole and its participants.

To me, an archetype is a notion that carries a superabundance of meaning. Mother or Father as archetype carries all the associations and resonances of particular mothers or particular fathers — and all the added resonances of all mothers and fathers in song and story, poetry and prose. The archetype is *super-enriched* — so rich that no one image will capture all aspects of the reality. Conversely, I think of a stereotype as *super-impoverished* — so poor that it carries only one aspect. A stereotype reduces the rich range of meaning to one dimension only, producing a dangerous caricature of the reality.

To utilize archetypes has several benefits:

1. As any archetype is richer than this or that image, it keeps the functions open to mystery.

2. We have the seeds of these capacities within us. We can cultivate the habits of mind-and-heart associated with each season and function, each minister and ministry. The powers are powers-in-us.

3. In this approach, there is room for freedom, creativity, and discovery. Each of us is free to embody these powers in our own style. Each of us is able to discover more and more about these creative possibilities. The archetypes are larger than any present understanding of them.

In the acupuncture tradition, these personifications of the energy systems are often called "officials." I prefer the terms "minister" and "ministry." For more, see my earlier book, *To Come to Life More Fully* (Columbia, MD: Traditional Acupuncture Institute, Inc., 1990), chapter 6, pp. 75-87. For still further detail, see Professor J. R. Worsley, *Classical Five-Element Acupuncture, Vol. III: The Five Elements and the Officials* (privately printed by J. R. and J. B. Worsley, The Worsley Institute, 1998).

Preparing an Emblem/Banner/Shield for a Partnership

Native Americans of the plains would construct an emblem (symbolic shield) that they would place outside their teepee. This served to identify each unit.

****

Take a sheet of paper and draw the outline of a circle as indicated below. (Omit the numbers.)

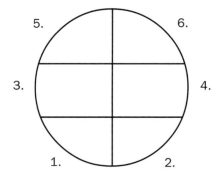

Draw a circle that covers the entire sheet of paper from top to bottom. (Numbers are included here only to refer to instructions below.)

****

Preliminary Work

Think of the Great Pattern in its widest contexts: all humankind, the web of life, the Great Mystery. Think of the smallest unit — potential partnerships.

A. What is the **type** and **task** of the partnership you have selected? Examples: friendships, family relationships, work roles. Each has certain "tasks" or functions flowing from its nature when seen at its best.

   What sort of relationship is it, and what sort of goals does such a relationship have?

B. Give two admirable qualities for each partner — at his or her best.

   For Person A: For Person B:

****

In light of these preliminary reflections, construct a shield representing the partnership.

1. In field 1, write some of the finest gifts that this partnership (at its best) provides the two partners within it.

2. In field 2, write some of the contributions this partnership (at its best) provides to people beyond itself.

3. In field 3, draw or describe the type of natural setting that symbolizes this partnership (e.g., ocean or river or lake or mountains or grasslands, etc.). Consider these questions: How do you see this natural setting going through a cycle of seasons? What season would you pick to symbolize the special power of this relationship? Now draw or describe the natural setting as it might appear in this season.

4. Draw, in field 4, a flag to symbolize this partnership.

5. In field 5, write a mission statement in one to two sentences that declares how this partnership will show up in life — how those within the partnership and those it serves will come to life more fully because of the partnership.

6. The Native American shaman tradition speaks of animals as guides. What animal would you invite to be a spirit companion to this partnership? Consider why you would choose this animal. Draw this animal in field 6.

Exercises for Letting Go

I learned these two exercises from my teaching colleague, Julia Measures. They arise from work she had done with the Sedona Institute in Sedona, Arizona. The exercises described below have, no doubt, evolved from the original; they may or may not resemble the form and purpose they served in their initial versions.

****

1. The **"Could you? Would you? When?"** Exercise

This exercise moves toward a release via three questions and three affirmations:

Could you? Yes.
Would you? Yes.
When? *Now.*

Two people work together. Person A has an issue — some wobble, some squawk. Person B is the facilitator. The facilitator asks, "Could you let go of this squawk?" Or alternatively, "Could you let go of the way you are labeling and emotionally caught up in this issue? Could you? Is it at least *possible* for you to do this?"

If there is resistance to giving a genuine "yes," the facilitator might try "chunking down" the issue: in space (extent) — *Could you let go of a part or aspect of the issue?* Or in time (duration) — *Could you let go for a few minutes or an hour?* Again, the facilitator might try to create a larger "for the sake of": *Could you let go for the sake of all that your partnership has been and can be? Could you let go for the sake of the ancestors and the children?*

Then move to the next question: ***Would** you let it go?* ***When?***

(Or, *Would you let go of your attachment or resistance?* ***When?***)

The work is to gain a genuine "Yes. Yes. *Now.*" — however small the aspect, however short the time. The beauty of this exercise is that it bypasses "story." The facilitator need not know what the issue is.

****

2. The **"I Allow"** Exercise

This is an indirect approach, a "skillful stratagem" to defuse the emotional charge that keeps us going round and round in a fruitless manner. Here are some examples:

- I allow myself to smoke AND I allow myself not to smoke.
- I allow myself to please this person AND I allow myself not to please this person.
- I allow myself to accept this criticism AND I allow myself not to accept this criticism.
- I allow myself to have this resistance AND I allow myself not to have this resistance.

The exercise is best modeled by the group leader working with a group member. Then group members can work in pairs.

The group member willing to model the process is asked to reveal enough "story" about the issue so that a first formulation can be tried: "I allow myself to_____ AND I allow myself NOT to_____." The facilitator invites the group member to shift posture in his or her chair, shifting toward the right when saying, "I allow myself to_____." The facilitator asks the group member to say the first half of the sentence out loud three times, then asks, "In the presence of saying this half of the sentence, what arises? What emotions? What thoughts? What phenomena in your body?" Then the group member shifts posture and says the second half of the sentence out loud three times. Again the facilitator asks, "What arises? What do you notice?" The group member keeps moving back and forth, voicing the affirmative and voicing the negative, observing where resistance or discomfort arises.

Remember that the person with the issue is in partnership with the facilitator and may suggest to the facilitator ways to question — may even help to "chunk the issue down." The partner/group member may prompt the facilitator to ask questions such as these: "Can you *allow yourself to do* **a part** of what you are struggling with? Can you *allow yourself NOT to do* **a part** of what you are struggling with?" Or ask, " Can you *allow yourself to do* [such and such] **for a few minutes**? Can you *allow yourself NOT to do* [such and such] **for a few minutes**? Can you *allow* (and *not allow*) this **for the sake of something large**?" The facilitator may even suggest that something be "done" in fantasy. For example, "I allow myself to kill my boss (in fantasy), AND I allow myself NOT to kill my boss (in fantasy)." What comes up on the one side? What comes up on the other side? In doing this exercise, participants often find that resistances arise on sides where they did not expect resistances to emerge.

For the facilitator: As things come up, move with them. Do not assume that you know where the stuck point is. Be in partnership. Be in genuine inquiry, seeking where the issue might lie. When the issue shifts, shift the "I allow" formulation. Be alert to tone of voice and body language. Let the person working on the issue guide you when he/she begins to gain some insight.

When the person working on an issue experiences equilibrium, then (at least for a moment or two) there is no emotional charge on either side. In this moment, the person is *free to do* and *free not to do,* and therefore is not hooked on either horn of the dilemma. The person's own wisdom has a chance to surface. The pain of going back and forth between (typically) "I must" and "I couldn't possibly" dissolves. The way becomes clear, often with a bit of laughter.

APPENDIX XIII

Seeking to Understand and to Be Understood

A modification of Phases 1 and 2 from Tom Rusk's
The Power of Ethical Persuasion.

In **exploring the other's viewpoint:**	In **presenting your own viewpoint:**
1. Establish your immediate goal as understanding, not problem-solving.	1. Ask for a fair hearing in return.
2. Elicit the other person's thoughts, feelings, and desires about the subject.	2. Begin with an explanation of how the other's thoughts and feelings affected you. Avoid attack or self-defense.
3. Ask the other to help you understand.	3. Present your thoughts, desires, and feelings as *your* truth, not *the* truth.
4. Repeat the other's views in your own words to show you understand.	4. Ask for restatement of your views.
5. Ask the other to correct any misunderstanding.	5. Review respective views.

In general,
rephrase content; reflect feelings.

In general,
follow the rules for feedback.

See Tom Rusk, M.D., with D. Patrick Miller, *The Power of Ethical Persuasion* (New York: Penguin, 1993), pp. 67-106.

****

Comments:

When we listen in order *to understand,* the spotlight is on the other, and whatever shifts the spotlight interrupts the other. When we speak in order *to be understood,* the opposite is true.

In the rules of feedback, I am requested to "Speak from the 'I.'" Here is a formula to use: "In the presence of this, I find myself labeling matters in such a way. I notice certain emotions arising in me — anger, resistance, defensiveness, sadness, sorrow, fear or joy. I find myself drawn to you or pushing away from you."

To "speak from the 'I'" means not saying how the other is, not reporting what the other does (always or never), not judging in open or subtle ways — it is simply providing feedback:

> "When that occurs, this is how I understand you. These are the feelings that arise in me. I am not saying you intend this. I am simply observing that when this occurs, I think and feel in such and such a way. Perhaps I am the only one to respond this way. Yet I want you to understand from 'inside' my process."

When we speak in this way, the data are on the table as phenomena (not conclusions). The other can decide if learning another way of speaking or acting will reduce suffering and increase possibility — for the partnership and the persons within it. Or I, on my part, may learn to shift my pattern of understanding and responding — for the sake of reducing suffering and promoting possibility for the partnership and those within it. When the speaking and listening is for the sake of mutual understanding, the partners can express concerns rather than state positions, can explore interests rather than demand "my way or no way."

APPENDIX XIV

The Five Ministries and Their Key Functions

****

SUMMER MINISTRY OF HEART'S DIRECTION

A. **Call to large, joyful, partnership mind-and-heart,**
inviting us to transform relationships into partnerships;

B. **Name, cultivate, and ennoble each partnership,**
evoking the great "for the sake of" —

for the sake of the partnership and all it serves.

SPRING MINISTRY OF DEFENSE

A. **Open options** for effective action, seeing each event as danger/opportunity.

B. **Take small steps** in timely fashion —

for the sake of the partnership and all it serves.

TYPE OF PARTNERSHIP

Bowl
Boat
Garden
Mini-kingdom

AUTUMN MINISTRY OF DIPLOMACY

A. **Acknowledge** the situation exactly as it is, with surface and depth features.

B. **Let go** of what no longer forwards life —

for the sake of the partnership and all it serves.

WINTER MINISTRY OF DEEP WATERS, OF HIDDEN TREASURES

A. **Practice deep listening** in unknowing in order truly to understand.

B. **Practice creative inquiry,** like a Wise Fool, moving beyond what is already known —

for the sake of the partnership and all it serves.

****

A fifth ministry appears in the center,
beneath the partnership:
LATE SUMMER MINISTRY OF EARTH'S ABUNDANCE

A. **Show gratefulness** for life, living from a sense of abundance.

B. **Nourish all** by thoughtful tending and with simple gifts —

for the sake of the partnership and all it serves.

APPENDIX XV

Walking the Circle:
Sample Questions from Each of the Seasons/Ministers

I envision a coach asking these questions of one person who is walking the spiral of the ministries for the sake of a partnership.

If a person is walking by herself or himself, or if a couple is walking the spiral for the sake of a partnership they share, then the questions need to be reframed — from "you" to "I" or "we."

****

Sample Questions from the Harvest Minister of Earth's
Abundance-in-Us

- Are you dwelling in conversations of scarcity or in conversations of abundance?
- Do you realize that (within all your webs of relationships) you *have enough* and *are enough* to live a worthy life?
- Do you realize that, in Gandhi's words, "there is enough for your need, but not for your greed"?
- Are you nourishing and allowing nourishment for (i) your partnership, (ii) your partner, and (iii) yourself?
- Is there nourishment — giving and receiving simple gifts — on all levels, on the bodily, emotional, mental, and spiritual levels?
- Do you regularly remember who you are as partners in this partnership?
- Do you practice gratefulness, expressing thanks for the partnership you have co-created and continue to co-create?
- Do you express appreciation for each other — in the midst of everyday life?
- Do you and your partner need a touch, a hug, a cup of tea, a helping hand, a presence, ears to be heard, and eyes to be seen?
- Will you request what shows up as missing? Will you do this from a sense that what is needed is already present in the abundance that surrounds you in the life you share with others?
- Will you give and receive thoughtful tending — beyond keeping score or expectation of return?
- Will you give and receive *empathy,* not pity or sentimentality?

Will you do these things for the sake of
the partnership and all it serves?

****

Sample Questions from the Summer Minister of
Awakened Heart-in-Us

- Are you in large mind, partnership mind, eco-spiritual mind-and-heart?
- What sort of partnership is this?

- What are its root tasks or purposes?
- What does the partnership jointly bring forth when both partners are at their best — when you are both present to the vision, values, and virtues of the partnership itself?
- What is the partnership "for the sake of" — within itself and beyond itself?
- Do you both share this goal or mission?
- Can you move easily from me to WE, seeing the whole, the "for the sake of"?
- Are your hearts open?
- Are you dwelling in a big enough conversation?
- Will you find joy together in bringing your partnership to life more fully?

Will you do these things for the sake of
the partnership and all it serves?

****

Sample Questions from the Autumn Minister of Diplomacy-in-Us

- Are you allowing the partnership to be exactly as it is — with its surface disturbances and its deep potential?
- What labels and emotional likes/dislikes need to be released?
- What in your speaking about the partnership, your partner, and yourself is too small a conversation and needs to be made larger?
- Will you make such a shift in these internal and external conversations for the sake of what you have been and can be?
    If letting go of all is too much, will you let go of a part?
    If letting go for a long time is too great, will you let go
    at least for a short time?
    Will you do this for the sake of something that really matters?
- Will you examine together how the emotionally charged issues affect your partnership?
- Will you both acknowledge clinging or compulsive attachments and let them go?
- Will you both acknowledge resistances, resentments, angers, and jealousies, see the suffering they cause, and — for the sake of a larger vision — release them?
- Will you both acknowledge locking in likes and dislikes, old habits and fixed behaviors with justifications such as "That's just the way I am (or it is)"?
- For the sake of the large, will you let go of the small?
- Is there a grieving to be done before moving on?
- Will you allow yourselves to grieve over losses and changes and, in due season, allow yourselves to move on?

Will you do these things for the sake of
the partnership and all it serves?

****

Sample Questions from the Winter Minister of
Deep Waters-in-Us

- Are you seeking first to understand?
- Are you awake to the traps of language and the "hooks" of liking/ disliking?
- Are you listening past what you already know, past deep assumptions and fixed ideas?
- What fears do you notice arising as you listen and inquire together?
- Are you willing to play the fool — not to have the easy answer, but to be in inquiry, asking for the other's help?
- Will you follow the inquiry wherever it leads, facing shadows, ugliness, and evil — facing all fears and desires?
- Will you explore images, metaphors, dreams — the nonverbal as well as the verbal?
- Will you rely on the deep trust that at depth all is sound and whole?
- Will you contact the unconscious, the wild part, the spontaneous and sexual?
- Will you allow yourself, the other, and the partnership *new possibilities*?
- Will you admit when you are a beginner?
- What new learnings are needed to bring this kingdom to life more fully?
- What coaching will you request?
- Do you have the resources for your task?
- Are you willing to assemble them?
- Will you ask for support in gaining the power needed?

Will you do these things for the sake of
the partnership and all it serves?

****

Sample Questions from the Spring Minister of
Defense-in-Us

- Are you seeing each event as *both danger and opportunity*?
- Are you moving beyond *either-or* to *both-and*?
- Are you seeing interests beneath positions?
- Are you seeking a creative third?
- Are you ready to take a small step? If you cannot do everything, will you do something — if not publicly, then privately?
- Are you turning anger and frustration into excitement and movement?
- Are you planning skillfully — with discipline and flexibility?
- Are you managing your time well?
- Will you notice when your actions are effective and when they need revision?
- Will you design feedback loops so that good ideas are tried and assessed?

Will you do these things for the sake of
the partnership and all it serves?

****

Return again to the
Harvest Minister of Earth's Abundance-in-Us.

Reestablish interconnection. Experience gratefulness anew. See what simple gifts are needed to nourish the partnership and the parties in it, now that you have completed one turn of the spiral.

The Three Domains and Shifting Worldviews — Revisited

A. Exploring a Change in Worldview:

The shift in worldview can be seen in this fashion:[1]

Modern Worldview c. 1500 to mid-20th century (*parts* are primary)	moving to	Emerging Ecological Worldview mid-20th century on (*wholes* are primary)
defined in terms of the 6 seductive S's		defined in terms of nested wholes, i.e.
Substances viewed as		**Relationship fields** supported by
Separate in a context of		**Interconnection** and
Scarcity and the		**Sufficiency** where
"Seen only" and the		**Seen & unseen are valued** where
Short-term		**Shorter & longer time frames** are recognized
where action takes the form of **Superiority over**		where action takes the form of **Complementarity/ Connectedness with**
Power over		*Partnership with*

In addition, we might add these characterizations:

Industrial Growth Society extractive & self-destructive	moving to	**Life-sustaining Society**[2]
	(in Sigmund Kwaloy's terms)	

Finite Game Model e.g., The purpose is to win	moving to	**Infinite Game Model**[3] The purpose is to improve the game.
	(Charles Hampden-Turner, using Carse's distinction)	

****

At the "surface" of time and history, there is the movement from one epoch to another, from one cultural worldview to another. In oversimplified form, think of

Shared Worldview 1 (pre-modern) → Shared Worldview 2 (modern) →
Shared Worldview 3 (trans-modern, ecological) → ...

At the depth, we can imagine a deeper current — call it the *Wholeness Principle*[4] or the *Holomovement.*[5] It appears in humans as the unrestricted desire to love, to care for the whole.[6] In religious language, the movement is from God and of God and toward God. In philosophical language, it is from and of and toward the True, the Good, and the Beautiful. To align with the Holomovement — to be at one with the Tao — to be in harmony with the "Force" (Star Wars) — is a very large-minded way of being in the world in its unfolding. It reminds people of participating in the earth's and universe's calling.

In the emerging worldview, we are *relational beings* through and through. We are both *particles and waves* (having a place all our own in the web, and deeply interconnected with everything). We are *individuals and embedduals.* We are *holons — wholes unto ourselves and parts of larger units.*

Perhaps most important, in the emerging worldview we come from a deep sense of interconnection, interdependence. Wholes and parts co-arise, and parts are not able to be specified in their fullness outside of the wholes in which they participate.

Thich Nhat Hanh coined the term "interbeing" to highlight this radically relational approach. In chapter 15, I take the concept further by suggesting a common feature in all of the transitions, namely, they all must be seen not individualistically but in the "between" of relatedness. Thus, our practice will take us:

- from   *scarcity*   to   *intersufficiency;*

- from   *separateness*   to   *interbeing* (interconnection, interdependence)

- from   *"seen only"*   to   *interweaving of seen and subtle dimensions;*

- from   *"short-term only"*   to   *intergenerational time;*

- from   *"superiority over"*   to   *interdoing* (intercollaboration, intersynergy)

The units (holons) are nested — like three concentric circles, like smaller to wider contexts.

B. Three Domains and Three Aspects within Each Domain:

In an earlier book,[7] I distinguished six domains surrounded by the sphere of mystery.[8] My six domains are the personal, interpersonal, familial, institutional, cultural, and planetary. In this work, I simplify to three key domains: the planetary carrying an epochal worldview,[9] the institutional, and the interpersonal. I also note that for each of these domains there are three aspects:

1. a Cultural aspect (culture as "shared conversation concerning basic meaning-value-purpose")

2. a Physical Organization aspect

3. a Wholeness aspect

In the spirit of chapter 3, I think of culture in terms of shared "conversations" — pervasive, meaning-value-purpose conversations. More specifically, I am concerned with the deep structure of our basic worldview, how we think and speak about what is most meaningful and valuable to us, what defines our shared sense of reality. The philosopher Heidegger says, "We dwell in language." I would say that we dwell in conversations. Our fundamental or paradigm conversations are those that teach us what is meaningful and valuable to our group. At any level we can distinguish the conversations that are too small to live in and conversations large enough to live in. At this time, we are questioning seriously the modern conversation that has structured our thinking for 500 years, a conversation that has become globally present and persists at every level. We are beginning to see that it is too small a conversation to allow sustainability, too small a conversation to shape our lives in the twenty-first century. This modern mode of self-understanding is being acted out in massive ways with massive ecological consequences. To be large-minded in our time, I argue, is to dwell more and more in the emerging ecological worldview.

PLANETARY DOMAIN

1. Epochal Culture/Conversation aspect: The *Big Epochal Worldview* [10] becomes the shared conversation concerning meanings, values, purposes that define the predominant worldview — a people's shared sense of reality.

   In our time, as above, we see:
   the **Modern Worldview** moving to the **Emerging Ecological Worldview**.

2. Physical Organization aspect: The planet can be seen as a self-organizing structure/process — earth-sphere, water-sphere, atmosphere, biosphere.

3. Wholeness Principle aspect (phrase from Anna Lemkow): The wholeness principle operates here to assess and revise paradigms. This movement toward wholeness appears in humans as an unrestricted desire to understand and to care for our home, to understand when ways of thinking and acting are too small, and to revise them. In this way, we seek *what is good for the whole and fair to the participant-parts (humans and other species and systems)*.

INSTITUTIONAL DOMAIN

(This domain is composed of organizations, especially the Big Four — governmental, economic, educational, and religious — plus other voluntary organizations, and, as a special case, family.)

1. Corporate Culture/Conversation aspect: The corporate culture reflects the big epochal worldview, and also reflects the culture of each type of institution — its vision and values, mission, etc.

2. Physical Organization aspect: Organizations are structured in terms of

roles, rules, routines, policies, procedures, practices.

3. Wholeness Principle aspect: The wholeness principle operates here to assess and revise the Meaning-Value-Purpose component, and roles, routines, policies, procedures and practices. In other words, the wholeness principle calls us to assess and revise organizational structures and processes *in light of fundamental aims* and in the context of *what is good for the whole and fair to the participant-parts.*

At the surface, corporate bodies have *surface physical organization* and a *surface cultural conversation* (or call it a Meaning-Value-Purpose conversation). Both can shift positively or negatively. Some structures and some self-understandings are small-minded and others are large-minded.

At their depth, institutions reveal another manifestation of the wholeness principle — this time manifesting as their *core purpose (mission/vision)* and *deepest goals and values.* To align with the deep purposes and tasks is to align with the wholeness principle operating at the institutional or systems level — it is to remind people of the calling of each organized way of life. Of course, since the domains are nested, the institutional aims must be in harmony with sustaining the conditions for planetary life. Put differently, institutional enterprises must be seen in light of the emerging ecological worldview.

INTERPERSONAL DOMAIN

1. Culture/Conversation aspect: The predominant stories that define the relationships reflect the big epochal worldview as filtered through institutions and family, and particularized through the type of relational field.

2. Physical Organization aspect: Two people within the relational field, which is structured in various ways according to type (e.g., friendship, mother-father/son-daughter, spouse/spouse, brother/sister, doctor/patient, lawyer/client, teacher/student, etc.)

3. Wholeness Principle aspect: Operating to take the individual-embeddual from smaller habits of mind-and-heart to larger habits of mind-and-heart, seeking *what is good for the whole and fair to the participant-parts.*[11]

At the surface, one-to-one relationships have a *surface physical organization* and a *surface cultural conversation* (or call it a Meaning-Value-Purpose conversation). Both can shift positively or negatively. Some structures and some self-understandings are small-minded and others are large-minded.

At their depth, relationships reveal another manifestation of the wholeness principle — this time manifesting as their *core purpose (mission/vision)* and *deepest goals and values of the friendship, marriage, professional relationships, etc.* To align with the large-minded purposes and tasks is to align with the wholeness principle operating at the interpersonal level. It is to remind people of the calling of each organized way of life. Of course, since the domains are nested, the interpersonal aims must be in harmony with sustainable institutions and a sustainable way for humans to live lightly on the earth. Put differently, interpersonal relationships must be seen in light of the emerging ecological worldview.

Notes

1. This overview owes much to many sources. In particular, I wish to mention Denise Breton and Christopher Largent, *The Paradigm Conspiracy: Why Our Social Systems Violate Human Potential — And How We Can Change Them* (Center City, MN: Hazelden, 1996) and their *Love, Soul and Freedom: Dancing with Rumi on the Mystic Path* (Center City, Minnesota: Hazelden, 1998); Brian Swimme and Thomas Berry, *The Universe Story* (San Francisco: HarperSanFrancisco, 1992); Joanna Macy, *World As Lover, World As Self* (Berkeley, CA: Parallax Press, 1991); Joanna Macy and Molly Young Brown, *Coming Back to Life: Practices to Reconnect Our Lives, Our World* (Gabriola Island, BC, Canada: New Society Publishers, 1998); Rosamund Stone Zander and Benjamin Zander, *The Art of Possibility* (Boston: Harvard Business School Press, 2000); as well as Ken Wilber's view of "all levels, all quadrants." See, for example, Ken Wilber, *A Brief History of Everything* (Boston: Shambhala, 1996).

2. These terms come from Norwegian eco-philosopher Sigmund Kwaloy. See Joanna Macy and Molly Young Brown, *Coming Back to Life,* pp. 15-17.

3. The reference is to James B. Carse, *Finite and Infinite Games* (New York: Ballantine Books, 1986). For a brief summary, see the adaptation in Charles Hampden-Turner and Fons Trompenaars, *Mastering the Infinite Game: How East Asian Values Are Transforming Business Practices* (Oxford, England: Capstone Publishing Limited, 1997), p. 30.

4. For the phrase "the wholeness principle," I am indebted to Anna F. Lemkow. See her *The Wholeness Principle: Dynamics of Unity Within Science, Religion and Society* (Wheaton, Illinois: Quest Books, 1990).

5. The phrase is from physicist David Bohm. See his *Wholeness and the Implicate Order* (London, Routlege, 1980) and his *On Dialogue,* ed. Lee Nichol (London, Routlege, 1996). For more on Bohm, see F. David Peat, *Infinite Potential: The Life and Times of David Bohm* (New York: Addison-Wesley Helix Books, 1997).

6. For this way of putting the matter, I am indebted to the work of theologian-philosopher Bernard Lonergan. See, for example, his *Method in Theology* (New York: Herder and Herder, 1972).

7. John Greenfelder Sullivan, *To Come to Life More Fully* (Columbia, MD: Traditional Acupuncture Institute, 1990), pp. 38-41, with further discussion in Part III, chapters 7-13.

8. In my earlier work, I called the sphere of mystery a domain, yet pointed out that this characterization was not quite accurate. The sphere of mystery is more like the paper on which all the other domains are written.

9. This is similar to Chardin's noosphere. See Pierre Teilhard de Chardin, *The Phenomenon of Man* (New York: Harper and Row, 1965).

10. In seeking to specify the worldview (what many call basic paradigm), I am pointing to something more pervasive than national or tribal cultures. I think of this deep cultural context as epochal. In appendix XVII, I look at pre-modern, modern, and trans-modern epochal cultures or worldviews.

11. See Rosamund Stone Zander and Benjamin Zander, *The Art of Possibility*, especially pp. 79-97, for a similar distinction. They speak of the *calculating self* (survival thinking, scarcity thinking, dwelling in a world of measurement) and the *central self* (where one lives as a contribution in a universe of possibility).

APPENDIX XVII

The Story of Humankind in Three Acts

To expand our context in time, imagine a simplified story of humankind as a drama in three acts.[1]

Act One. The first act of our story opens with the dawn of humanity and extends through the classical and medieval ages. People are deeply embedded in a set of relationships — embedded in family and clan, place and region, village, city or kingdom. Call this period the *pre-modern epoch.* Living at that time, I would be conscious of being a part of a larger unit. I would know my role and place in that unit. Here, the whole is primary; the part, secondary.

Act Two. As time passes, a reversal happens. In the West, place it around 1500 CE, around the time of the voyages of discovery. Call this period of roughly the past 500 years the *modern epoch.* Living in this next context, I would be conscious of being an individual. My individual wants and needs would come to the forefront. The "whole" would be seen as resulting from agreement among individuals like me. The whole would be seen largely as existing to protect individual freedoms. Here the part is primary; the whole, secondary.

Act Three. Sometime in the second half of the twentieth century, a new seeking emerges.[2] The shift is seen most dramatically with the astronauts viewing planet earth from space. There is a new global awareness, a growing realization of interconnection, an expanded ecological perspective. Furthermore, much in the new experience of the world resonates with the wisdom traditions of native peoples or First Peoples. Perhaps we might recover the best of the ancient and the best of the modern in a wider paradigm. Call this emerging period the *trans-modern epoch.* A different sense of whole and part, a different way of walking on the earth.

In Act One, we have the *whole over the part* — good for stable relationships, not very good for change. Virtues such as submission, obedience, and loyalty are cultivated and thrive. Yet some people are too easily subordinated to others. Hierarchies of dominance gain ground.

In Act Two, we have the *part over the whole* — good for freedom of thought and action, not very good for relationships and a sense of a larger whole. Virtues such as self-reliance, competitive excellence, and risk-taking are cultivated and thrive. Yet a sense of the common good fades. All is reduced to separate substances — individuals alone are perceived to be real.

Act Three looks to a *larger sense of interconnection and interdependence* — a worldview that can honor relational fields (wholes) and the potential partners within them (parts). Notice that for this third way to be an advance, we cannot go back, we must go forward. We must recognize the gifts and correct the errors of the ancient worldview. We must recognize the gifts and correct the errors of the modern worldview. The new sense of community and communion must be more than a return to old collectivisms.[3] The Borg on Star Trek are hardly a blueprint for a more expansive future!

Notes

1. Those with philosophical background will recognize echoes of Hegel in the three-part structure moving to more inclusive synthesis.

2. I think of Rachel Carson and Jacques Cousteau, among others, calling attention to the poisoning of the oceans in the 1950s, to issues of population and pesticides in the 1960s, issues of nonrenewable resources and toxic waste in the 1970s; and I think of discussions by such figures as E. F. Schumacher, Arne Naess, Barry Commoner, and the Ehrlichs, which brought ecology and eco-science to a wider public. I think of the UN World Charter for Nature in the 1980s. [For more on these earlier markers, see my book *To Come to Life More Fully,* pp. 109-121.] In 1987, the United Nations Commission on Environment and Development (the Bruntland Commission) drew attention to the fact that economic development often leads to a deterioration, not an improvement in the quality of people's lives. The commission therefore called for *a form of sustainable development that* ***"meets the needs of the present without compromising the ability of future generations to meet their own needs."*** Following up on this initiative, the Earth Charter Commission in early 1997 formed an international drafting committee. In March 2000, after intensive worldwide consultations, the commission approved the final version of the Earth Charter. The charter broadens earlier contexts and points to three crucial dimensions:

   - Relations between human beings and the greater community of life
   - Relations among human beings in society
   - Relations between present and future generations

   For more on this extraordinary work, see http://www.earthcharter.org.

3. I take it as one of the virtues of Ken Wilber's work that he attempts to do just this. See, for example, his *The Marriage of Sense and Soul: Integrating Science and Religion* (New York: Broadway Books/Random House, 1999).